SPANISH PRACTICES
LITERATURE, CINEMA, TELEVISION

LEGENDA

LEGENDA, founded in 1995 by the European Humanities Research Centre of the University of Oxford, is now a joint imprint of the Modern Humanities Research Association and Maney Publishing. Titles range from medieval texts to contemporary cinema and form a widely comparative view of the modern humanities, including works on Arabic, Catalan, English, French, German, Greek, Italian, Portuguese, Russian, Spanish, and Yiddish literature. An Editorial Board of distinguished academic specialists works in collaboration with leading scholarly bodies such as the Society for French Studies and the British Comparative Literature Association.

MHRA

The Modern Humanities Research Association (MHRA) encourages and promotes advanced study and research in the field of the modern humanities, especially modern European languages and literature, including English, and also cinema. It also aims to break down the barriers between scholars working in different disciplines and to maintain the unity of humanistic scholarship in the face of increasing specialization. The Association fulfils this purpose primarily through the publication of journals, bibliographies, monographs and other aids to research.

Maney Publishing is one of the few remaining independent British academic publishers. Founded in 1900 the company has offices both in the UK, in Leeds and London, and in North America, in Boston. Since 1945 Maney Publishing has worked closely with learned societies, their editors, authors, and members, in publishing academic books and journals to the highest traditional standards of materials and production.

MOVING IMAGE

Editorial Committee
Professor Emma Wilson, Corpus Christi College, Cambridge (General Editor)
Professor Robert Gordon, Gonville and Caius College, Cambridge
Professor Annette Kuhn, Queen Mary, University of London
Professor Jo Labanyi, New York University

Legenda/Moving Image publishes cutting-edge work on any aspect of film or screen media from Europe and Latin America. Studies of European-language cinemas from other continents, and diasporic and intercultural cinemas (with some relation to Europe or its languages), are also encompassed. The series seeks to reflect a diversity of theoretical, historical, and interdisciplinary approaches to the moving image, and includes projects comparing screen media with other art forms. Research monographs and collected volumes will be considered, but not studies of a single film. As innovation is a priority for the series, volumes should predominantly consist of previously unpublished material.

Proposals should be sent with one or two sample chapters to the Editor, Professor Emma Wilson, Corpus Christi College, Cambridge CB2 1RH, UK.

Managing Editor
Dr Graham Nelson, 41 Wellington Square, Oxford OX1 2JF, UK
www.legenda.mhra.org.uk

Spanish Practices

Literature, Cinema, Television

PAUL JULIAN SMITH

Moving Image 1
Modern Humanities Research Association and Maney Publishing
2012

Published by the
Modern Humanities Research Association and Maney Publishing
1 Carlton House Terrace
London SW1Y 5AF
United Kingdom

LEGENDA is an imprint of the
Modern Humanities Research Association and Maney Publishing

Maney Publishing is the trading name of W. S. Maney & Son Ltd,
whose registered office is at Suite 1C, Joseph's Well, Hanover Walk, Leeds LS3 1AB

ISBN 978-1-907975-04-2

First published 2012

Printed in Great Britain

Cover: 875 Design

Copy-Editor: Richard Correll

CONTENTS

ACKNOWLEDGEMENTS

I would like to thank Professor Emma Wilson of the University of Cambridge, the editor of this new 'Moving Image' series, for her kindness, encouragement, and efficiency. Dr Graham Nelson, managing editor of Legenda in Oxford, was very helpful. My thanks are also due to the anonymous reader, who rightly suggested that my work be seen in the context of the critical debate on 'intermediality', not a term I had used in the manuscript.

Material from this book was first published as 'Almodóvar's Unpublished Short Stories and the Question of Queer Auteurism', *Screen*, 50.4 (2009), 439–49; 'La distancia cultural de una adaptación entre España y Estados Unidos: *Yo soy Bea* (Telecinco) y *Ugly Betty* (ABC)', in *Mercados globales, historias nacionales*, ed. by Lorenzo Vilches (Barcelona: Gedisa, 2009), pp. 171–84; 'Re-visions of Teresa: historical fiction in television and film', in *Spain on Screen*, ed. by Ann Davies (New York: Palgrave, 2011), pp. 60–78; and 'Cinema and Television in the Transition', in *The Politics and Memory of Democratic Transition*, ed. by Diego Muro and Gregorio Alonso (New York: Routledge, 2011), pp. 199–214. I am grateful for permission to reprint some of that material here. The book as a whole was written within the context of a collective research project devised by Norberto Mínguez of Madrid's Complutense University entitled 'New Trends of the Fiction/Non-Fiction Paradigm in Spanish Audiovisual Discourse, 2000–2010' (reference number CSO2009–07089). This project is financed by the Spanish government's VI Plan Nacional de Investigación Científica, Desarrollo e Innovación Tecnológica 2008–11.

Most of the material in the book was first read as the result of kind invitations from many friends and colleagues in Spain, France, Israel, the US, and the UK to whom I remain extremely grateful. The book was written as I was coming to the end of some twenty-five happy and productive years teaching in two British universities: Queen Mary University of London (1984–91) and Cambridge (1991–2010). It is dedicated to my new students and colleagues in the Hispanic and Luso-Brazilian Program of the Graduate Center, City University of New York.

New York, January 2011

LIST OF ILLUSTRATIONS

INTRODUCTION

Spanish Practices

This book is the first to explore the interaction of three media in contemporary Spain. Focusing on some of the best-known and most important books, feature films, and television series in the country (including texts by novelist Antonio Muñoz Molina and director Pedro Almodóvar and the Spanish version of *telenovela Ugly Betty*), it addresses three pairs of linked issues central to Hispanic studies and beyond: history and memory, authority and society, and genre and transitivity. While much of the material is very recent and thus as yet unstudied, the book also focuses on issues that have long been central to scholars: the representation of gender, sexuality, and transnationalism. Drawing on approaches from both the humanities and social sciences, *Spanish Practices* combines close readings of key texts with the analysis of production processes, media institutions, audiences, and reception.

Historical memory is arguably the most important topic in contemporary Spain, the subject of a Law by the Socialist government in 2007. The first three chapters of the book address this topic by making connections between literature and visual media. Thus the first bloody years of Franco's dictatorship are explored in very different ways by a successful film on the young female martyrs who lost the War and an autobiography by one of Spain's best known women novelists, who grew up amongst the winners. The second chapter treats two versions of the death of the dictator: a fable on the resurrection of Franco written by the most popular comic writer of the 1970s and the special episodes on the same theme by Spain's most popular TV drama, some thirty years after the event. Finally, a third chapter sketches the audiovisual ecology of the Transition to democracy and investigates the role of film and television in a prize-winning novel by the best-known writer of his generation.

The second section of the book explores questions of authority and society as depicted mainly in cinema. It begins by examining unpublished works by Spain's most famous filmmaker, Pedro Almodóvar, short stories that stake a precocious claim to authorship even before his first feature, and relating them to his subsequent cinema. A second chapter contrasts two very different fiction films on the same traumatic topic: a missing child. While one is an accomplished and popular horror movie, the other is an austere art film. Pursuing a further urgent social issue, the final chapter in this section addresses the small and much-studied canon of feature films on the vital social issue of immigration and ethnicity, contrasting it with the less-known (but much larger) corpus of episodes of television series on the same theme.

The final section focuses mainly on television, as yet little researched for Spain and hence the medium that is treated at greatest length in the book. This section addresses the questions of genre and transitivity, or the passage between both formats and nations. The first chapter examines the key figure of Saint Teresa of Avila, a litmus test for the discussion of spirituality and sexuality, as depicted in a studiously respectful TV series and a wilfully scandalous feature film. The second explores the blurring of boundaries in two long-running and innovative series that hybridize situation comedy with soap opera and pseudo-documentary. The final chapter addresses perhaps the most famous of the transnational TV formats that have originated in Latin America, *Ugly Betty*, in its very different Spanish and US versions, which are read as examples of 'bridge-crossings' between genres and continents.

It is my hope that *Spanish Practices* will be of interest to academics and researchers in the fields of both Hispanic studies and general media and cultural studies. If this book has claims to originality, they are that it treats a wide range of new or little-studied material (from popular novels to art movies via national TV series) and that it makes new links between Spanish texts and more general contexts (queer and gender studies, world cinema, TV studies). It aims to shape knowledge by engaging literary scholars with visual culture and vice versa; and the subject areas covered are not only key questions in Spanish studies, but also debates in media and cultural studies and gender and queer studies.

There remains much to be done in making connections between these diverse fields. It is striking that there is still little contact between Peninsularists, who came to film overwhelmingly from a literary background, and specialist media scholars. For example at the Fiftieth Annual Conference of the Society of Cinema and Media Studies, held in Los Angeles on 17–21 March 2010, there was only one panel in over four hundred that treated Spain: 'C12 The Reality/Fiction Paradigm in Contemporary Spanish Film and Television' was proposed by myself and Norberto Mínguez Arranz, and also boasted a paper from Marsha Kinder, one of the very few distinguished media scholars who also has an interest in the Peninsula.

But if it is urgent to continue to make connections between Hispanism and media studies, it is also important to acknowledge that the former remains deeply engaged in literary studies, especially in the United States. I have thus returned to literature myself here in an attempt to investigate the parallels between print and the visual culture that has become my own specialization. In this spirit I make close analyses of three texts in diverse genres: autobiography, popular fiction, and prestigious novel.

In spite of this literary address, the book's methodology draws more on current trends in media studies. Thus I carry out empirical, historicizing accounts of production, distribution, and exhibition, investigating how texts of all kinds are created, circulated, and consumed. This research turns up some surprising results in the first section of the book. For example, *Las 13 rosas* ('The 13 Roses', 2007) was directed by Emilio Martínez Lázaro, a filmmaker better known for contemporary romantic comedies than tragedies of the Civil War; and, unseen abroad, it was exploited in Spain by 'psycho-pedagogues' who sought to reproduce the experience of Francoist terror in the young schoolchildren of the now established democracy. Conversely Fernando Vizcaíno Casas, the best selling and ubiquitous novelist of the Transition (1975–82), is almost forgotten today, although his fantasy cum satire on the resurrection of the Generalísimo is, I argue, comparable to the replaying of the past in Spain's most prestigious and best loved TV series, *Cuéntame cómo pasó* ('Tell Me How It Happened', TVE 2001–). Returning to the same period, we discover curious connections between two works, simultaneous in time, by Víctor Erice, Spain's most prominent and austere film auteur, and Antonio Mercero, the country's most durable and best-loved creator in television. Meanwhile the rapidly changing experience of the media is indelibly incorporated into Antonio Muñoz Molina's epic novel encompassing the Civil War, Dictatorship, Transition, and new democracy, *El jinete polaco* ('The Polish Horseman', 1991).

In the book's second section film studies are put to uncommon uses. Thus I retread the hallowed ground of auteur theory, but in an attempt to account for unknown print texts by Almodóvar, short stories which also go back to the time of the late dictatorship. Addressing vital social themes, I explore how Bourdieu's account of 'the rules of art' (of the twin competing economies of commerce and aesthetics) comes under pressure when a popular and an art house director (J. A. Bayona and Jaime Rosales, respectively) treat the same topic in the same year (2007). My account of the important and recent cinema and television on immigration and ethnicity draws heavily on a Hispanist and humanist cinema scholar (Isabel Santaolalla) and a Spanish TV specialist with a social science background (Charo Lacalle). In general I aim to reconcile such qualitative and quantitative interpretations, asking both 'What kind of meanings do texts take on?' and 'What precise position do these texts occupy in the cultural field?' My intention here is in part to avoid Hispanism's continuing focus on a small body of feature films (such as those on immigration), which are held (erroneously) to embody both social conditions and cultural preferences in Spain.

The final and lengthiest section of *Spanish Practices* begins by confronting a meticulous study of the Hollywood genre of the biopic (by George F. Custen) with two texts on the vital historical and proto-feminist figure of Saint Teresa, contrasting her representation in different periods and different media. More recent changes in the genre formats of both *telecomedia* and *telenovela* (serials aired during daytime in Spain) are related closely to the industrial conditions under which Spain has evolved an impressively professionalized TV fiction sector that is comparable only to the US in the quantity and quality of its series drama. For much invaluable detail on production and reception I rely here on Spanish scholars such as Mario García de Castro (also a practitioner) and the research team in the Universidad de Navarra led by Mercedes Medina.

On the other hand, my emphasis in this final section on 'travelling narratives' (the way foreign formats break down the barriers between genres and nations) and 'indigenization' (the way in which they are adapted to fit local circumstance) draws heavily on Milly Buonanno, the doyenne of European television studies. Buonanno is herself openly indebted to such British sociologists as Zygmunt Bauman and Anthony Giddens (on bridge-crossing and mediated experience, respectively) and to Indian-born Arjun Appadurai (on mediascapes). In a rather similar example of cross-cultural fertilization, Spanish TV itself borrows from and exports to its European neighbours and American rivals (both Northern and Latin). Such empirical and theoretical sources permit me to propose that a soap opera, no less than a critically praised novel or an award winning feature film, can be an exploration of possibilities and imagined alternatives that are not alienating but rather enriching of everyday life.

The *Oxford English Dictionary* tells us that the phrase 'old Spanish custom or practice' (which it characterizes as 'jocular') means 'a long-standing though unauthorized or irregular practice' (s.v. 'Spanish'). I trust readers will forgive me the negative associations of my rather archaic punning title. While some of the textual practices discussed in this book may well be long-standing (the scabrous humour in Spanish sitcoms dates back to the picaresque novel, if not earlier), they are by no means unauthorized or irregular. Rather the literature, cinema, and television analysed and celebrated here offer examples of cultural and industrial sophistication that have few equals elsewhere.

PART I

Literature: History and Memory

CHAPTER 1

Winners and Losers in Cinema and Memoirs

Emilio Martínez Lázaro's *Las 13 rosas* ('The 13 Roses', 2007) and Esther Tusquets' *Habíamos ganado la guerra* ('We Had Won the War', 2007)

Affect and aesthetics

Since the Transition to democracy, Spanish cultural and media producers have compulsively returned to the tragic inheritance of Civil War and Dictatorship. Most recently, with the seventieth anniversary of Franco's victory, they have turned their attention to the earliest and most brutal years of that legacy. In Madrid in the summer of 2009 the Conde Duque arts centre presented 'Presas', a major exhibition documenting Francoist women prisoners and drawing on the rich archives of the Communist Party; and the Reina Sofía art museum rehung its collection, exhibiting new photographic and documentary material to place in context a revised display of Picasso's *Guernica*. Arguably the most consistent and prominent exploration of the so-called 'years of hunger' comes from a less expected source: Televisión Española's daytime serial *Amar en tiempos revueltos* ('Loving in Troubled Times'), whose expert and surprisingly distressing first season premiered in 2005.

This first chapter treats two very different texts on the legacy of the Civil War and the early period of Francoist repression, which both appeared in Spain in 2007, the year that the Law of Historical Memory was passed by the Spanish Congress. Emilio Martínez Lázaro's feature film *Las 13 rosas* is a dramatic reconstruction (based in part on Carlos Fonseca's historical study) of a celebrated case of young women executed in Madrid in 1939 (they also featured in the exhibition 'Presas'). Well received by audiences, if not critics, it still won four Goya awards. Esther Tusquets' *Habíamos ganado la guerra* is a first volume of personal memoirs from a major writer best known for her pioneering novels with a lesbian theme, published some thirty years earlier. This book also begins in 1939, with the Francoist occupation of Barcelona when the author was just three years old.

Las 13 rosas focuses exclusively on the earliest victims of the Regime, offering an extreme case of terror, repression, and violence. The fact that some of the women had left written testimony to their experience (their words used in the film itself) heightens the pathos and immediacy of their predicament, personalizing a grand historical narrative in a unique way that connects with modern viewers. Arguably, however, Martínez Lázaro (a director better known for romantic comedies than historical tragedies) aestheticizes the women's plight through insensitive use of the picturesque mise en scene typical of the costume drama or heritage picture. As we shall see, his film was also used nonetheless in an unprecedented way as a pedagogic tool for Spanish schoolchildren, who were encouraged to engage in educational activities such as the reconstruction of their own family history through discussion with grandparents.

Tusquets' narrative is very different and, indeed, overtly polemical. Claiming that the losers' point of view on the early Francoist period has already attracted great attention in memoirs and fiction, Tusquets sets out to document the perspective of the winners, in this case the privileged Barcelona bourgeoisie into which she was born. Far from being triumphalist, however, the book focuses on the subjective, and indeed eccentric, experience of a child and adolescent and on the perils (but also pleasures) of everyday life, necessarily distant from the grand narrative of the new regime.

Taken together, these texts thus clearly suggest two conflicting ways in which writers and filmmakers of contemporary Spain continue to work through the trauma of the earliest years of the Franco regime. And their evident success belies the impression of 'memory fatigue' that has greeted other recent treatments of the period, such as the recent feature film *Los girasoles ciegos* ('The Blind Sunflowers', an impeccably correct account of a Leftist in hiding after the War), which, against all expectations, received no major prize at the Goya awards of February 2009.

In this chapter, then, I take it for granted that artistic representations of the past are always also a comment on or an intervention in the present, thus risking the instrumentalization of historical tragedy. And it is worth making three more initial propositions and reservations to frame our readings of the two chosen texts: firstly, history and story are not easily separable (although the truth claims of narrative in documentary and fiction are clearly distinct); secondly, cognition and emotion need not be opposed (although the effects of affect remain unruly and unpredictable); and, thirdly, the objective and the subjective often go hand in hand in film and memoirs (although certain points of view are more generalizable than others). We shall return at greater length to this meshing of history and story in Chapter 7.

Clearly such considerations are inseparable from gender, when treating texts on or by women; and we should take care not to reconfirm the continuing subordination of the feminine when vindicating imagination, emotion, and subjectivity, albeit in newly defined terms. In general my position coincides with two major scholars of this area: I agree with Jo Labanyi that the culture of what is still called (and for how much longer?) the post-Franco period results not from a 'pact of forgetting' but rather from a refusal to let the past determine the future (123); and with Joan Ramon Resina in *Disremembering the Dictatorship* that, however postmodern that culture may be, it remains haunted by affect; and by an aesthetic that seeks, however vainly, to reconcile or mediate between the particular and the universal (3, 10).

Text, field, audience

Cultural analysis must also pay close attention to the stylistic forms of distinct media. Indeed it is an irony, but not an entirely unexpected one, that (as Virginia Guarinos has noted in her excellent article on the various versions of the story in many media) Jesús Ferrero's novel *Las 13 rosas* should have praised by critics for its recourse to lyrical inventiveness, while the feature film of the same name should have been attacked for its appeal to the creative imagination. The film's studied use of mise en scene, cinematography, and editing (like the memoir's expert exploitation of description, narration, and syntax) are an essential part of its meaning. And if we are to consider female subjectivity in these works we must address specific audiovisual and textual constructions of point of view and focalization. (I hope to work towards this kind of close formal analysis later in this chapter.) But, beyond close reading, one final preliminary remains: the placing of the texts within the current cultural field of producers and institutions within which they take on meaning and without which they could not exist.

Surprisingly, perhaps, the industrial conditions of cinema and of publishing pertinent to *Las 13 rosas* and *Habíamos ganado la guerra*, respectively, have much in common and, I would argue, contribute to the unusual success of both works in the crowded, even exhausted, market for historical memory in contemporary Spain. A survey carried out by the Ministry of Culture for the year the two works appeared (I have rounded decimals up or down) revealed that 52% of Spaniards had participated in the 'cultural activity' of cinema going in the past twelve months, a proportion surpassed only by the 58% who claim to read books and the 88% who listen to (unspecified) music (Estadística). (Typically, television, which reached 98% of the population in the previous month, is classed separately as an activity that is 'audiovisual' and not cultural.) Cinema going declines rapidly with age, with 87% of 15–19-year-olds attending theatres, while only 6% of over 75-year-olds do so (the middle-aged, who retain memory of the late Francoist era [45–54], come in at a still significant 51%). Film going rises markedly with educational attainment (9% for those who did not finish basic education; a massive 78% for those who completed a university degree); and is also gender specific, albeit to a less extreme extent (men: 54%; women: 50%). Turning to informants' evaluation of Spanish cinema in particular, we find that those who rarely visit theatres (women and older viewers) have a higher opinion of local production than more frequent attendees (men and teenagers), although the highly educated also claim to prefer Spanish features to the Hollywood films that dominate the multiplex.

According to official figures, *Las 13 rosas* (which failed to achieve commercial distribution in foreign territories) was the third-biggest grossing Spanish film in its home market with an audience of 786,000, surpassed only by the expert horror films *El orfanato* and *REC* (Ministerio de Cultura 'Largometrajes'), which I study in Chapter 5 of this book. In a year when Spain produced no fewer than 173 features (compared to just 80 in 1997), this is a clear sign of its exceptional reception from

Spanish audiences; and an initial hypothesis would be that this was a rare title that coincided with those substantial, but minority, demographic segments of filmgoers (women, older people, and the educated) who claim to prefer Spanish film, even though they are rarely tempted into the cinema by the standard offer. Such audiences are infrequently seen as a target by film producers of whatever nationality.

This evidence of overproduction in the film sector (the domestic market cannot support three releases a week throughout the year) is echoed in publishing. As María Ganzabal notes in her report for 2005, Spain boasts low rates of readership, here given as 57% (cf. France on 72%), combined with a high number of titles at almost 70,000 a year (cf. France with 53,000). As elsewhere (and unlike in the case of film), women are more voracious consumers of books than men. Yet, as Christine Henseler notes in her study of contemporary Spanish women's narrative and the publishing industry, such statistics lead editors and critics to 'overrate the privileged position of women writers and the power of female readers' (10), even as they disparage them. (Tusquets herself, as long-time director of publishing house Lumen, was one of the very few women with some real power in the profession.) Henseler notes that in male-dominated literary supplements the adjective 'femenino' tends to be associated with four negative categories: the feminist and opportunist; the intimate and emotional; the commercial; and the particular (rather than the universal) (11). Significantly she locates Tusquets within a precise and precariously balanced segment: the women who are collectively viewed as 'best sellers *cultos*' [*sic*], defined as they are by the three factors of name recognition, perceived quality, and gender (9).

Tusquets's self-created public image as licensed heretic (not dissimilar to that of Juan Goytisolo) seems equally finely balanced: she is a Catalan writer who writes in Castilian and is not a nationalist; a Leftist who, since a youthful dalliance with the Falange, has never been a member of a political party; and a sponsor of women and lesbian writers at her own publishing house who has never made either identification herself although she pioneered the literary treatment of female homosexuality. In spite of such apparent marginality, she (like Goytisolo, again) has some access to the most consecrated channels of the Spanish press. In the year before and after her memoirs were published, she contributed to *El País* characteristic op. ed. and interview pieces defending sybaritic Leftists who take pleasure in such luxuries as yachts and chalets (15 May 2007); attacking the poor quality of the teaching of Spanish in Catalonia (6 December 2007); and denouncing the 'political correctness' which allegedly threatens such freedoms as dog-walking on the beach or smoking in restaurants (27 January 2008). Tusquets' memoirs themselves, excerpted in *El País*, which also ran a positive review, quickly went into a third reprint.

An educated best-seller, Tusquets, I would argue, occupies a location in the cultural field analogous to that of Emilio Martínez Lázaro, a position which can be identified as 'middle-brow' (as Bourdieu defines it: 'the major works in minor genres or the minor works in major genres' [16]). Best known for his massively popular sex comedy *El otro lado de la cama* ('The Other Side of the Bed', 2002; sequel 2005), Martínez Lázaro has had a lengthy and consistent, if not wholly distinguished, career in Spanish film. It was telling that the four Goyas his film received were in technical or minor categories (cinematography, costume design, original score, and supporting actor), thus lending only qualified distinction to the work. He was perhaps perceived by writer-producer Pedro Costa (who is indeed known for historical projects) as a safe and skilled pair of hands for a cultural property that was already widely known. Guarinos lists no fewer than eight previous versions: two novels, two documentary films, a non-fiction book, a poem, a play, and a flamenco dance piece (92). Her valuable table, charting the differences between the same characters in text and film (98–99), also reveals how malleable and virtual these female figures are, however anchored they may originally be in historical documents and oral testimony.

Critical response to the feature film was mixed. Seeking to distance himself from the middlebrow, Carlos Boyero, *El País*'s famously truculent new chief critic, was merciless, pronouncing the film 'as correct [*cierto*] as it is feeble [*endeble*]'. Beginning with an awareness of memory fatigue (the perceived 'obligatory nature' of not forgetting past horrors), the critic pronounces himself still willing to accept a 'Manichean' vision of barbarous torturers and angelic victims. But he remains unconvinced. The 'perfect makeup' of the actresses, the insistence of the (prize-winning) score, and the hectoring tone of the narration do not produce the 'tears' that they are so clearly intended to. The formal elements of cinematic style are thus held to undermine the film's persuasive and emotive effect. Interestingly Jonathan Holland's review in *Variety* (intended for a US industry audience) coincides with many of Boyero's points, finding the film historically and dramatically 'unconvincing', even, or especially, where it is factually accurate, as in a tap-dancing scene that takes place in prison. While praising *Las 13 rosas*' 'superb' visuals, *Variety* also decries the 'neatly made up' and 'uniformly angelic protags' [*sic*], accurately prophesying that 'business beyond the Spanish-speaking territories looks thin'.

Yet this critical consensus could not be further from the response of the film's target female audience. For example a forum at the aptly named Spanish gossip magazine, *Cuore*, attests to deeply felt emotion experienced by viewers, who confess to tears and gooseflesh even as they praise the visuals and exclaim '¡Viva la República!' Here expert mise en scene (the prize-winning wardrobe) actively furthered the transmission of both affect and political message. In the 'making of' documentary included with the Spanish DVD, Martínez Lázaro himself claims to have indulged in 'small betrayals of history' in order to focus not on action but on character and psychology (e.g. the girls' mostly invented romantic back stories which make up the first half of the picture).

I would suggest, then, that the disagreement over *Las 13 rosas* is thus not simply a case of a failure of historicity (the implausibility of perfect lipstick in prison) but rather a more fundamental conflict over affect and aesthetics. As Resina suggested, emotion still haunts the postmodern work, however enfeebled that work may seem to critics; and art (or at least, art design) can still claim to mediate between a particular perspective (here young and female) and the universal sphere (here grand national narrative). The true question is not whether the film is historically convincing or documentarily accurate, but whether it uses affect and aesthetics for the purposes of coercion (telling us what to think about a terrible time) or of cognition (leading us to reflect for ourselves on that time).

FIG. 1. The perfect lipstick of Blanca (Pilar López de Ayala): *Las 13 rosas*

'Las 13 rosas': close reading

Let us look more closely at the film itself, focusing on three moments which I shall also treat in Tusquets: the entrance of the Francoist army into the city; the depiction of the horrors perpetrated by the new regime; and the evocation of a female community that to some extent resists or transcends those horrors, that regime. After credits (pseudo-period still sepia photos starting into movement) set to a stirring symphonic score, the first scene has fiery militants Virtudes and Carmen (the sole survivor) haranguing a sceptical audience of townspeople from an improvised platform: surely peace is worth nothing without freedom and dignity? Next we meet radiant Julia (Verónica Sánchez) and Adelina (Gabriella Pession), serving food to orphans at the Republican soup kitchen. Sympathetic comrade Teo (Fran Perea), also seen here, will later turn informer on the women. A Nationalist air raid drops bread not bombs. A third (unspecified) location is shown in the next scene, a rather handsome café where the immaculate Blanca (Pilar López de Ayala) watches her husband's band perform a French song popular in the period (Fig. 1). Here the air raid is for real, and Blanca, sheltering with her son under a table, meets Julia and Adelina for the first time.

What is striking here is that, breaking with a Spanish tradition of historical cinema such as the *Juana la Loca* which also starred López de Ayala, Martínez Lázaro provides us with no titles or voice over to establish time, place, or historical context (indeed we will not see a title until the final shot of the film and that simply serves to establish the authenticity of the moving letters read at its end). This lack of specificity continues in the next sequence, which depicts the troops' arrival in the capital. Martínez Lázaro pans right, following anonymous but enthusiastic Falangist women and offering a brief glimpse of the huge (but relatively little known) basilica of San Francisco el Grande in La Latina down the Carrera ('avenue') named for the

FIG. 2. Virtudes (Marta Etura, left) and Carmen (Nadia de Santiago)
arrive in La Latina: *Las 13 rosas*

same saint (anachronistic modern buildings are digitally replaced). In the (unidenti-fied) little square of Puerta de los Moros (wooden scaffolding conceals the colourful mural and graffiti that currently decorate the square), Virtudes and Carmen have arrived (from where?) on the back of a mule. They watch (we watch) in horror (Fig. 2) as a single Nationalist soldier forces all to give a fascist salute and brutalizes an (unknown) old man and his wife, culpably unfamiliar with the *Cara al sol* (the fascist anthem).

Although later sequences will show such celebrated monuments as the Cibeles (buried up to her neck in sandbags) and the Ventas bullring, Martínez Lázaro here chooses a location that is likely to go unrecognized and sets in motion a small-scale, even intimate, version of a grand historical event. And this is not for budgetary reasons: in the prison scenes real life extras were digitally duplicated to produce a massive crowd, an effect that could easily have been used to multiply troop numbers here. Subjective shots also focalize the entire scene from the young women's point of view, thus ensuring sympathy and empathy from the audience.

This preference for an intimate affective charge rather than the wide-screen spectacle more typical of historical film as a genre, in Spain as elsewhere, continues with the depiction of torture, which remains discreet (the mass execution itself will not be shown at all). Only one woman (Julia) is shown to be stripped, beaten, and brutalized by the suave torturer, played by Adriano Giannini, one of the three Italian actors in this co-production who are unconvincingly dubbed. It is striking, however, that true horror is projected on to the supporting male characters, one of whom slashes his own throat with a shattered light bulb. While Martínez Lázaro himself admits to 'sweetening' his source material, this aestheticization could perhaps be read not as culpable mendacity but rather as an attempt to engage the sensibility of a target audience less desensitized to graphic violence than young male habitués of the multiplex.

This rare spectator is clearly encouraged to identify with the on-screen female community of the prison through both shooting style (group and point of view shots once more) and narrative focalization (we see nothing from the Nationalists' perspective). Strikingly, Martínez Lázaro shows no conflict whatsoever amongst the uniformly angelic women captives, despite the diverse social backgrounds he has sketched for them in the first half of the film. Indeed the only character gifted with a traditional 'arc' of self-realization is devout Catholic Blanca, arrested for aiding a Communist friend of her husband, who moves from at first protesting her innocence to finally identifying with the radicals whose fate she has come to share. Even Goya Toledo's frigid and smirking lesbian guard sheds a silent tear as the young women are taken from her care to the place of execution. Once more, it is not so much a question of the documentary basis of such female solidarity (as mentioned earlier, even the improvised tap dance is historically attested), but of its effect within the context of the film itself. Intimate relations between women, which (unlike in Jesús Ferrero's novel) dare not include sexual acts, are presented as a haven, however fragile and provisional, from masculinist terror, a moral clearly not lost on contemporary women spectators, however opportunistic it might appear to other, more sceptical viewers.

Two further contexts point to the film's unique reception. *Las 13 rosas* was exploited for unusually explicit educational purposes by the Association of Psycho-pedagogy of the Open University of Catalonia. Based on its belief that mainstream media are actively harmful to children, the Association recommended exercises in solidarity and empathy associated with the viewing of the film (this material was included in slightly different forms in a full-colour printed press book and on a website shared by University and production company). For example, children were encouraged to ask questions of their grandparents to discover their experience in the War (a potentially conflictive activity); or to explore the film's use of contemporary song. Beyond interview and popular culture, however, other activities were physical or embodied: a blindfolded child is instructed to run at full speed towards a wall, trusting his or her fellows to save him from harm; another is confined for five minutes within a restricted space that simulates the experience of prison. In spite of its avowedly empathetic aims, such 'education in values through film', informed as it is by a systemic and constructivist approach to family therapy, seems somewhat coercive in its methods.

A second and less overt context than psychopedagogy is television, which worked silently to establish the audience's intimacy and familiarity with *Las 13 rosas* even before the film was released. Many of the feature's young stars are known from the small screen. Indeed *Las 13 rosas* was something of a reunion for Verónica Sánchez (Julia) and Fran Perea (Teo) who had played stepsiblings cum lovers over four seasons of top-rated contemporary comedy-drama *Los Serrano*, a title especially favoured by young women, as we shall see in Chapter 8. Félix Gómez, who plays a resistance fighter impersonating a Nationalist, and courts the modest tram ticket collector Julia, was familiar to daytime audiences from his more than one hundred episodes as Rodrigo, tragic antihero of *Amar en tiempos revueltos*, where he wore the same Falangist uniform. Moreover the season arc of the series' female protagonist,

Rodrigo's sister Andrea (Ana Turpin), parallels that of Blanca in the film: she is a bourgeois Catholic who through bitter experience comes to identify with working-class Leftist militants. Confident in the familiarity of the young TV stars, the film can afford to use casting to play with their established images: thoroughly modern Verónica Sánchez is in *Las 13 rosas* the modest girl who sews up her blouse buttons before a date; amiable Fran Perea here turns out to be a turncoat, delivering his comrades to the torturers; Félix Gómez, a convinced rightist on television, only feigns fascism in the feature.

Las 13 rosas's favoured shooting location in Madrid, the central but relatively anonymous barrio of La Latina, is also anticipated by the TV series, which often employs its modestly scaled squares and streets; while the film's ensemble cast (albeit focusing on just five of the thirteen girls or on the three who look out, white-faced and red-lipped, from the poster) is reminiscent of television's choral narrative. Although this televisual trace paved the way for the film's unusual box office success in Spain (in 2009 the two commercial hits of Spanish production also used this casting strategy), it clearly could have no efficacy abroad. Furthermore, it also failed to engage Spanish film critics, actively hostile to a medium such as television, which could serve in their eyes only to reconfirm the middle-brow aura that already enveloped *Las 13 rosas* and its director.

'Habíamos ganado la guerra': close reading

If I have suggested that *Habíamos ganado la guerra* can also be called 'middle-brow' it is not because I am sceptical about the quality of the text in itself. An instant 'educated classic', the memoir engages the long standing memories of faithful readers of Tusquets' fiction (frequently quoting the early novels at length) and tends to reconfirm those aspects of writing disparaged as 'femenino' by the male critics of literary supplements: it is moderately feminist (openly lamenting, say, the stunted lives of women in the generation of Tusquets' unfulfilled mother); it is intimate and emotional (focusing above all on the fearful daughter's failed relationship with that fearsome mother); and it stresses the particularity of the child's position, consistently placed as it is against the tide of history. Thus the teenage Tusquets contrives to be unaware of the tram strikes that marked the momentous first organized resistance to Franco in her beloved Barcelona; and she chooses to join the Falange as late as the 1950s, when her Leftist student colleagues were already organizing against the regime. Even the woman at the Sección Femenina with whom she attempts to enlist is puzzled why should do so at such a curious time.

This eccentric position is stressed from the start. With her very title Tusquets polemically reverses the topos of the 'pact of forgetting', arguing that it is not the losers but the winners who have been silent. And in the preface she states explicitly that her recollections are fallible, failing even to coincide with those of her brother and faithful only to 'her' own truth, which need not be 'the truth of all' (7). And Tusquets at times marshals her formidable command of literary style and syntax to call attention to the particularity of her perspective. The first of the book's twenty-eight short sections evokes in one immensely long and modulated sentence the horrors of wartime Barcelona: where all (except her) were dying of hunger; where all (except her) were terrified; where her father, a deserter from the Republican front, dared not raise his voice or look out of the window; and where her mother suffered interminable tedium (17). Then comes the coup de grace: 'Yo fui extraordinariamente feliz' ['I was extraordinarily happy'] (18).

This accomplished aesthetic serves intermittently at least (as in *Las 13 rosas*) to reconcile or mediate between the particular and the universal. Certainly, by focusing so intently on the author's limited point of view the memoir renders identification with other perspectives difficult indeed. And Tusquets' disconcerting fusion of memoir, fiction, and history (she also incorporates a lengthy citation from Paul Preston's essay on her anti-Semitic uncle priest) lays claim in its defiant heterogeneity to being postmodern.

Tusquets thus incorporates into her already hybrid testimony strategies of description, narration, and syntax that are distinctively novelistic. Reality effects are produced by well-chosen details: the precious tin of condensed milk, saved for the daughter, that her mother devoured herself when the Civil War was safely concluded; the discoloured mark left on the wall of the child's school when a portrait of Hitler was, finally, taken down; her uncle's mini-Nazi museum, with its yellowing news clippings and toy soldiers. And Tusquets, faithful to her own truth once more, risks reaffirming her status as licensed heretic. The fascist uncles are presented as more sympathetic than a lone anti-Francoist aunt, determined to destroy all chance of happiness for herself and those around her. The Communist maids with whom heedless parents left their small children stuff them with emblematic *ensaladilla rusa* ['Russian [egg] salad'] and recklessly shout slogans in the street. Vindicating imagination, emotion, and subjectivity, even as she stresses the tragic limitations placed on the lives of women of all classes, Tusquets risks reconfirming here the subordination of the feminine. The epic and the domestic are wilfully and bathetically juxtaposed as in the typical chapter title: 'the Second World War and various other fears' (49).

Yet, where *Las 13 rosas* is glossily non-specific in its Madrid locations, *Habíamos ganado la guerra* is conscientiously precise in placing its action in the urban geography and distinctive domestic spaces of the Catalan capital. Thus the war sees the family exiled in distant Pedralbes before they return to the strictly limited, but treasured, confines of the Ensanche. A move beyond the Diagonal is a great adventure. While the child's world is bound by a few city blocks, the adult, with wider perspectives, ironizes on urban and class location: the family's avowedly 'terrible situation' in 1939 included a 200-square-metre flat in the Rambla de Barcelona, two live-in maids plus a laundress, a car, a subscription to the opera, a holiday home on the beach, skiing trips, a fee-paying school, a Fräulein for German classes, and a Sunday señorita so the parents were spared the burden of childcare on the one day of the week that the rest of the help took off (26). It is also striking that descriptions of people and places tend to alternate in the text: Nazi uncle Víctor and the German School in Moià street; the beloved and despised Liceu Opera House (whose Hall of Mirrors graces the memoir's cover) and the teenager's first love, her Andalusian teacher señor Jiménez. However eccentric Tusquets' own subjectivity may be, it is always precisely located in time and space.

Let us look now at the equivalents of the three moments we saw in *Las 13 rosas*: the entrance of the Francoist army into the city; the depiction of the horrors perpetrated by the new regime; and the evocation of a female community that to some extent resists or transcends those horrors.

As mentioned earlier, Tusquets' first chapter begins with what she claims as one of her 'first memories': a 'multitude' of soldiers marching along a 'road' or 'avenue', as crowds cheer them on (9). This wide shot is, however, immediately particularized, as the narrator cuts in for close ups. The child herself is held up by her father, who, we are told, had not walked in the street for two years; and her mother is shouting out Franco's name with an 'enthusiasm' the daughter will see on very few occasions in the rest of their lives. A typically lengthy and tangled sentence then fleshes out the family's predicament, calling attention to class conflict: Tusquets' maiden aunts supported the semi-clandestine household by sewing jobs commissioned by Leftist women who would in 'normal circumstances' have been their servants (10). And this primal scene (whether reality, imagination, or memory worked over by fantasy) is concretized in a single, resonant detail: the red and yellow paper flag that a smiling soldier gave her (perhaps gave her) to wave with the rest of the crowd. Historical event, political conflict, and personal circumstance fuse into a rich, but disturbing and inconsistent, narration.

As befits once more the specificity of her own placing (as a wealthy and privileged, but timid and neurotic, female infant), the memoir offers little testimony to the horrors of the new regime. But repression is felt with a special force within this privileged domestic context. For example Tusquets tells us of a child victim of the war, taken in by a more comfortable family, who has forgotten the everyday use of a bed; surely, she asks, the sheets are intended to cover the face of the dead? Another chilling anecdote repeats the precise placing of perspective we saw in the flag episode. Following the rest of their class in drifting away from the sea towards the hills, Tusquets' family move to an ample flat opposite the extravagant Casa de les Punxes, a modernist monument despised by the Barcelona bourgeoisie. To the child's surprise it still boasts a mosaic with lettering in Catalan asking San Jordi to give back Catalonia its freedom (136). But the building is also opposite a police station. As the ten year old looks from her bedroom window, a man is dragged into a police car, 'howling' and 'begging' for help: 'They're going to kill me!' (137). Passers-by look the other way. Tusquets asks herself: what could they have done? What could she have done? And was the man, just perhaps, a dangerous criminal? Still the scene becomes part of her 'nightmares'.

A more typical, and extended, scene takes place at Tusquets' German school, where a relatively progressive and coeducational regime was supplemented for the Spanish kids by Catholic observance. Tusquets cites one of her own novels at some length on May, the month of Mary, the month of flowers. White lilies and roses fill the chapel, the warm sensuality of their cloying scent provoking fainting fits in precocious adolescents (116). The yellow 'penises' of stamens combine with the white 'semen' of tiny flowers that Tusquets has seen only on altars decked for the Virgin. This hushed, sickly space is rent by a 'terrible howl' once more. One of the cloistered nuns has died and has been placed in a white coffin, framed by thick, smoking candles (117). This is the child's 'first contact with death', with a body that was (unlike hers) surely never truly alive in the first place.

While it is tempting to read such a scene as a displacement of the horrors of the regime with which the Church was complicit, it is Tusquets' typical attention to the senses (especially, in this case, smell) that stands out. Judgement (the dawning awareness of religious repression) is thus inseparable from emotion (that harrowing howl), and sensation (budding sexuality and the visceral fear of mortality). In such complex and disturbing passages Tusquets uses affect and aesthetics for cognitive and non-coercive purposes, refusing to tell us what to think, but provoking us to reflect. One striking difference with *Las 13 rosas* is Tusquets' hostility to visuality: while the film was, as we have seen, attacked by critics if not audiences for its too glossy mise en scene, Tusquets refuses to include any photographs in her memoir (even the cover shot of the Liceu was taken at least a decade after her own coming out there); and in the texture of her writing she focuses, as in her fiction, on touch, taste, and smell as much as sight.

It remains unclear, however, to what extent Tusquets has succeeded in rendering her wilfully eccentric position generalizable and (as *El País*'s critic claimed) 'taking on board [*asumir*] her contradictions'. The memoir ends with a definitive resolution: the twenty-year-old now knows that, although she was born amongst the winners and in spite of all her privileges, she truly belongs to the 'band of the losers' (276). But this psychological arc is less convincing even than that of bourgeois Blanca in *Las 13 rosas*: Tusquets left the Falange after a trivial row over an obligatory hike in the sierra that, typically, she refused to attend. History and story (nation and narration) fail to coincide.

Such inconsistencies are not necessarily a criticism of Tusquets' text. As she convincingly shows through her marshalling of point of view and focalization, female subjectivity was necessarily marginal to the regime. And if women's vain attempts at agency are not as harshly punished in *Habíamos ganado la guerra* as they are in *Las 13 rosas*, Tusquets shows herself to be sympathetic even to the well-meaning members of the Sección Femenina and the quixotic female activists who sought, much too late, a Falange of the Left. This sympathy and empathy with a female perspective is not to be dismissed.

However the placing of these two texts set in the past within the current cultural field of producers and institutions also teases out their meaning for the present. *Las 13 rosas* is to be read within a tradition of historical or heritage film that has been continuously built up since the Transition, although it has perhaps only recently become more vulnerable to political instrumentalization. Tusquets' memoir falls within not only the substantial body of work in that genre but also the current novelistic trend baptized as the 'literatura del yo' or 'autoficción' (Vázquez). Her blurring of the boundaries between fact and fiction is thus highly typical of the present, even as it seeks to represent the past. Moreover we might hypothesize that the audience for the two texts coincides to some extent: the substantial, but minority, demographic segments of filmgoers (women, older people, and the educated) who claim to prefer Spanish film may well overlap with the reading public for educated best-sellers. But still we should take care not to overrate the privileged position of women writers and the power of female readers or cinema spectators. After all, if *Las 13 rosas* was a success it was because it was atypical of the offer at the Spanish multiplex.

To conclude: I have argued that my continuing unease with the film derives not simply from the supposed failure of its historicity (that perfect lipstick in prison) but from a more fundamental conflict over affect and aesthetics. Unlike the consistently glossy visuals of *Las 13 rosas* (the stars even posed as part of a fashion spread in *El País*'s Sunday supplement [30 September 2007]), the equally expert literary execution of *Habíamos ganado la guerra*, some of it directly taken from Tusquets' fiction, is intermittent, often interrupted by more prosaic passages or, indeed, text borrowed from other writers. Likewise Tusquets' autobiographical self is only infrequently generalizable and never seeks to embody the nation, whether that nation is taken to be Catalonia or Spain. It thus follows that, unlike *Las 13 rosas*, *Habíamos ganado la guerra* employs affect and aesthetics not for the purposes of coercion (telling us what to think about a terrible time) but for cognition (leading us to reflect for ourselves on that time). While this may not appear to be an adequate response to the tragic past — what could be? — it is clearly an important and telling contribution to the response to that past in the present.

Works cited

BOURDIEU, PIERRE. *Distinction* (Cambridge, MA: Harvard University Press, 1984)

FERNÁNDEZ SANTOS, ELSA. 'Microrrelatos, autoficción y otras fronteras', *El País*, 7 June 2009, p. 50

FERRERO, JESÚS. *Las trece rosas* (Madrid: Siruela, 2003)

FONSECA, CARLOS. *Trece rosas rojas* (Madrid: Temas de Hoy, 2005)

HENSELER, CHRISTINE. *Contemporary Spanish Women's Narrative and the Publishing Industry* (Chicago: University of Illinois Press, 2003)

LABANYI, JO. 'Introduction: The Politics of Memory in Contemporary Spain', special issue of *Journal of Spanish Cultural Studies*, 9.2 (2008), 119–25

RESINA, JOAN RAMON. 'Introduction', *Disremembering the Dictatorship* (Amsterdam: Rodopi, 2000), pp. 1–16

TUSQUETS, ESTHER. *Habíamos ganado la guerra*, 3rd edn (Barcelona: Bruguera, 2007)

Web sources all accessed 26 June 2009:

ASOCIACIÓN DE PSICOPEDAGOGÍA DE LA UOC. 'Los piscopedagogos y la educación en valores a través del cine', <http://www.apuoc.org/node/106>

——'Las 13 rosas: proyecto cine y educación', <http://www.altafilms.com/las13rosas/descargas/Press_LasTreceRosas.pdf>

——'Actividades', <http://www.altafilms.com/las13rosas/descargas/Actividades.pdf>

BOYERO, CARLOS. 'Tan cierto como endeble' [review of *Las 13 rosas*], *El País*, 19 October 2007, <http://www.elpais.com/articulo/cine/cierto/endeble/elpepuculcin/20071019elpe picin_4/Tes>

Cuore. Foros: Cine y DVD Cuore. las trece rosas, 24 October–15 November 2007, <http://www.revistacuore.com/foros/tema.asp?id=139404>

GANZABAL, MARÍA. 'La industria editorial en España: una excesiva producción y corta tirada para bajos índices de lectura', *Sala de Prensa*, 10.4 (January 2009), <http://www.saladeprensa.org/art803.htm>

GUARINOS, VIRGINIA. 'Ramos de rosas rojas. *Las trece rosas*: memoria audiovisual y género', <http://descargas.cervantesvirtual.com/servlet/SirveObras/90259517659025043910457/0 30949.pdf?incr=1>

HOLLAND, JONATHAN. Review of *13 Roses*, *Variety*, 30 October 2007, <http://www.variety. com/review/VE1117935265.html?categoryid=31&cs=1&p=0>

LECH, IURY. 'La Cataluña frenéticamente franquista' [review of *Habíamos ganado la guerra*] *El País*, 29 December 2007, <http://www.elpais.com/articulo/Babelia/Cataluna/frene-ticamente/franquista/elppor/20071229elpbab_2/Tes>

MINISTERIO DE CULTURA. 'Estadística 2008. Anuario de estadísticas culturales', <http://www.calameo.com/read/0000753350dd3c08daaef>

—— 'Largometrajes españoles con mayor recaudación', 1 January–31 December 2007, <http://www.mcu.es/cine/MC/CDC/Anio2007/CinePeliculasEspaniolas.html>

TUSQUETS, ESTHER. 'La falangista Tusquets' [extract of *Habíamos ganado la guerra*], *El País*, 18 November 2007, <http://www.elpais.com/articulo/reportajes/falangista/Tusquets/elpep usocdmg/20071118elpdmgrep_7/Tes>

VÁZQUEZ, JUANA. '¿Literatura del yo? ¿Qué yo?', *El País*, 17 January 2009, <http://www. elpais.com/articulo/cine/cierto/endeble/elpepuculcin/20071019elpepicin_4/Tes>

CHAPTER 2

Resuscitating Franco in Popular Narrative and Television

Vizcaíno Casas's ... *Y al tercer año resucitó* ('And in the Third Year He Rose Again', 1978) and *Cuéntame cómo pasó* ('Tell Me How It Happened', TVE 2001–)

Interest without sympathy

The death of dictator Francisco Franco on 20 November 1975 continues to fascinate Spaniards. For example in 2005 journalist José Oneto, himself a minor actor in the historical events he describes, published a chronicle of *Los 100 días que cambiaron España: de la agonía de Franco a la coronación del Rey* ('The Hundred Days that Changed Spain: From the Death Throes of Franco to the Coronation of the King'); and in 2008 a dramatization of the Caudillo's extended agony (*20N: Los últimos días de Franco* ['November 20th: The Last Days of Franco']) was screened by Antena 3 on the anniversary of his death and named best TV movie by the Spanish Television the following year.

This second chapter treats two different but complementary versions of the disappearance and uncanny resurrection of Franco, produced some thirty years apart. Fernando Vizcaíno Casas's ... *Y al tercer año resucitó* (1978) is an extraordinarily popular novel which went into forty reprints and sold over half a million copies by 1986. It was also adapted into the most successful Spanish feature at the box office for 1980. Based on the slender and bizarre premise that, three years after his death, Franco has risen from his lavish grave at the monumental Valle de los Caídos ('Valley of the Fallen'), this comic novel offers a satirical panorama of the political and cultural scene of the early Transition, whose detail is now difficult to retrieve (I return to the period of the Transition in Chapter 3 of this book). This panorama is crosscut with 'inserts' (a typically cinematic term) in which selected protagonists of that scene (Communist leader Santiago Carrillo, then President Adolfo Suárez, future leader Felipe González) react to the greatly exaggerated rumours of the Generalísimo's return. While Vizcaíno Casas's satire is often as coarse as his prose

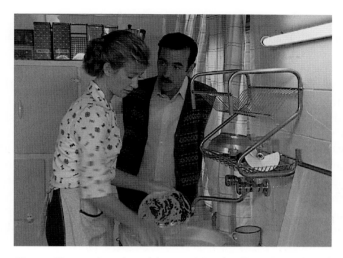

FIG. 3. Domestic micro-history: Merche (Ana Duato) and
Antonio (Imanol Arias) in *Cuéntame cómo pasó*

style and his rightist politics appear to identify him with the 'nostálgicos', yearning
for past certainties in a time of accelerated change, his novel serves, in a manner
similar to much period television drama, as an ephemeral and perplexing, but
nonetheless valuable, testimony to the lived experience of a historical moment.

The ninth season of the most prestigious and durable TV drama in contemporary
Spain, *Cuéntame cómo pasó* ('Tell Me How It Happened') also treated the death of
Franco and its immediate aftermath. I focus on two special episodes screened for
the Christmas holidays of 2007 and set on 20 and 21 November 1975. Although
Cuéntame has sometimes been criticized in general terms for facile nostalgia, which
is especially pernicious when it comes to depicting everyday life under a repressive
regime, at this particular point in its lengthy career (some six years after the first
episode) the series directly confronts an epochal event for its characters, as for its
older viewers. It is an event that also serves as a test case for the avowed aim of
the creators of the series, which is to offer (like Vizcaíno Casas in his much cruder
way) a history of Spain integrating the macro-history of public protagonists with
the micro-history of private individuals (Fig. 3). As we shall see, it is *Cuéntame*'s
focus on the family as a locus for historical change that most closely connects the
period depicted in the programme with the current conditions in which the show
is produced and consumed.

Clearly both fictions, whether they were made three or thirty years after the
events they treat, are contributions to the debate on historical memory whose broad
outlines are well known and to which I referred in the previous chapter. Thus,
on the one hand, historical memory may serve the purposes of group creation
through a perception of shared experience, which legitimizes an existing regime.
Such group myths lead to a social cohesion which is itself reinforced by operational
codes and systems of ethics. On the other hand, historical memories may also be
containers for grievances that give rise to political mobilization against the status

quo or can be instrumentalized for contentious purposes in post-conflict situations. Conversely, once more, the same memories can be made to serve the purpose of reconstruction and the prevention of future conflict (see Smith).

Jo Labanyi's subtle and influential account of the Spanish debate on 'Memory and Modernity' focuses on the trope of 'haunting.' As she does in the later piece I mentioned in Chapter 1, Labanyi contests here the widely held view of a 'pact of oblivion' after the death of the dictator, arguing that actors in the Transition strove not to forget the past but to prevent it from shaping the future (93). She notes here the 'vast output' of historians in the field that has been published since the end of the regime. Suggesting that Spain's post-Franco 'leap into modernity' is best understood in cultural not economic terms (Opus technocrats had already modernized the dictator's impoverished autarchy) (94), she retraces how 'memory boom' (95) became 'memory war' (97), with the exhumation of mass graves competing with Right-wing historical revisionism, and each side staking a greater claim to victimhood.

Labanyi charts the cultural responses, mostly in canonic cinema and prose fiction, to this problematic. 'Haunting' uses suggestion, not statement, in feature films shot before the death of Franco (e.g. Víctor Erice's *El espíritu de la colmena* 'The Spirit of the Beehive', 1973) or as the dictator lay dying (e.g. Carlos Saura's *Cría cuervos*, 1975). Later texts, especially in print, attempted more simply the recovery of facts in accordance with a principle of verisimilitude. This second strategy sometimes produced printed collections of testimonies whose exhaustiveness left 'no space for recollection', forming an 'indistinguishable mass' mixing accounts of victims of both sides (104). The two approaches saw the difficulty of reconstructing the past in two ways: the first focused on the problems inherent in narrativizing history; the second on purely practical obstacles to gathering evidence (105). Likewise they manifested conflicting versions of ethics: the paradoxes characteristic of the 'haunting' mode suggested that no narrative could do justice to the original suffering it (obliquely) depicts, while 'docu-realism' sought to recreate experience directly, exploiting what Labanyi calls the 'bad faith of empathy' (111).

Here, and most originally, Labanyi attempts to separate interest and sympathy. If we adopt as she recommends (after Susan Sontag) 'emotion tempered by reflective distance' (112), then we can perhaps respond appropriately to the suffering of victims whose politics we cannot condone. Taking our lead from the texts of haunting, then, we would understand their postmodernism not as a break with the past but as a redefinition of our relation to it; and 'a belief in the possibility of a better future' in which 'the memory of the past [can still] be honoured' (113).

Such an approach (of interest without sympathy) offers the critic a point of entry into the work of a massively popular author such as Vizcaíno Casas, who has been hitherto ignored by scholars who find his politics repellent. And Labanyi's thesis complements the constructivist account of group creation and social cohesion versus grievance and contention by proposing a new mode of reconstruction or of conflict prevention that is grounded not in the shared social ideas that are held to structure human association but in the detail of cultural texts. Here, then, I hope to extend Labanyi's analysis, beyond the well-known feature films and novels she treats, to embrace little-studied popular fiction and television drama. But first we must address the placing of our chosen texts within the cultural field of their respective times. As we shall see, popular narratives, in print and television, offer similar problems, and opportunities, to the scholar interested in exploring the historiography of everyday life at a time of radical change.

Narrative, history, public

A sometime film critic and television writer under the regime before he achieved success as a novelist, Vizcaíno Casas also practised as a lawyer, specializing in the entertainment industry. In spite of his reactionary reputation (which was no doubt enhanced by his continuing attachment to the moustache that was a prominent and recognizable sign of a reactionary politics), Vizcaíno Casas was well placed to explore the cultural institutions of his time; and, indeed, film and television as media are woven into the fabric of his satirical chronicle. ... *Y al tercer año*, singled out in *El País*'s obituary as his first real success in fiction, was published by Planeta, which had by the 1970s already expanded from its Barcelona base to become a multinational publishing house, and to which Vizcaíno Casas remained faithful throughout his writing career. The novel was placed, however, in Planeta's *Fábula* strand, which was intended for 'unconventional' authors. The maverick status proclaimed by *Fábula* was a broad church: Vizcaíno Casas shared the collection at that time with such strange bedfellows as Antonio Roig, a priest defrocked because of his profession of homosexuality. Vizcaíno Casas was thus at once central (supported by a powerful publisher) and marginal (restricted to its maverick imprint).

El País's obituary (which appeared on 3 November 2003) presented Vizcaíno Casas simply as a best-selling right-wing novelist whose greatest success was in the now distant 1970s and 1980s; and late press coverage confirmed an impression of continuing and partisan political conflict. Thus the paper reported that the Partido Popular had been denounced for retaining Vizcaíno Casas as a legal counsel (11 November 2001), or that the College of Lawyers had been attacked for inviting him as a speaker (18 October 2002). References to Vizcaíno Casas in *El País* in the 1970s prove more nuanced. Thus he is cited as presenting a fellow novelist at the Planeta awards as a 'serious humorist', dedicated to exploring Spanish life in depth through comedy (22 November 1977), a clear description of his own aims at the time; and a review of one of Vizcaíno Casas's novels also in 1977 praises it along similar lines as a 'book of national humour' that traces the '*petite histoire*' of Spain with such accuracy that it deserves to be read for years to come (3 April 1977).

Certainly ... *Y al tercer año*, however date-tied its satire, had some staying power as (in *El País*' words) 'a chronicle of Spanish life' after its initial publication. Not only did the novel continue to sell in the following decade, but the film version, released on 1 March 1980 and directed by Rafael Gil, a veteran filmmaker with a lengthy track record in military and religious pictures who had lately turned to comedy, attracted an audience of 1,343,870 spectators. Although this adaptation is not readily available today, such figures put it well ahead of the audience for feature films in 1980 by then notorious Leftist Eloy de la Iglesia (*Navajeros* ['Thugs'], 801,000), let alone for current releases by the auteurs later favoured by film scholars

(Pilar Miró, *Gary Cooper, que estás en los cielos* ['Gary Cooper who art in Heaven'], 446,000; Almodóvar, *Pepi, Luci, Bom*, 216,000). In a further striking comparison, a feature-length documentary on Franco, also released theatrically in the same year as Vizcaíno Casas's self-scripted film, sold just 13,000 tickets. This suggests that the topic was not in itself attractive to audiences so soon after the dictator's death.

It would thus seem to be the case that, as *El País* had rather generously written in its review (the new newspaper of the democracy was one of the author's favourite targets), Vizcaíno Casas combined extreme particularity with a 'moderate' dose of universality. Certainly his comic formulae seem to have inspired Spaniards to reflect, beyond the immediate moment, on their recent and troubled history. We shall see that *Cuéntame* also is held by its audience to be at once especially characteristic of its time and place, yet not irrelevant to present circumstance.

Vizcaíno Casas's blend of entertainment and sociopolitical commentary might also be read as a kind of continuation of Francoist cultural policy, on which Spanish scholars reflected critically both shortly before and soon after the death of the dictator. I take television here as an extreme case of a medium whose commercialism and manipulation by the regime was already thought by many to make it incompatible with serious art. Thus Jesús García Jiménez, surveying the 'old age' of the regime, cited one Director General of RTVE who claimed in 1973 that television, the most publicly scorned of media, was an 'instrument for the promotion of the culture and politics of the Spanish people', albeit insisting on the supposed 'peculiarities' of that people (566). In the same year *ABC* had argued, with surprising sophistication, for a third mode of culture between the mass entertainment of rural dramedy *Crónicas de un pueblo* ('Chronicles of a Village', widely dismissed in the press) and the minority high art of *Estudio 1* and *Los libros* (venerable strands for the adaptation of classic literary texts) (567). Everything, argued *ABC*, could be cultural, from TV movies, to talk shows, to sport. Vizcaíno Casas's version of 'national humour' is not so different to this belief.

A symposium in 1979 on 'Free Television in the New Democracy' proposed that, with the supposedly imminent arrival of private channels, public service TV would be able to devote itself to 'cultural' programming, in the traditional sense of the word (Aguilera and Vergès 354). But, as Manuel Palacio notes in his study of TVE's 'historical fiction' directed in the Transition by cinematic auteurs such as Juan Antonio Bardem, the reality was to be very different. With the much-delayed launch of private broadcasters Antena 3 and Tele 5 in 1990 came a 'transformation' in the structure of the TV ecology. The conscious cultural and ideological 'pedagogy' of TVE, embodied in 'great' series of the 1980s that were based on literary masterpieces or exemplary biographical figures, was now impossible in a TV ecology marked by fierce competition for market share (150). It is thus not the least of *Cuéntame*'s achievements that it has carried on that televisual exploration of the past that has a distinguished, if little recognized, tradition in Spain in a format more popular than that of the now archaic 'classic serial' and in a much more competitive broadcasting environment. Confirming that popularity is not inconsistent with quality, this family drama thus fulfils *ABC*'s farsighted prescription for a 'third way' of cultural programming on television.

Like Vizcaíno Casas, then, *Cuéntame* resurrects the dictator, or his memory, in the service of a national narrative of the present. And, uniquely in a primetime schedule biased towards contemporary dramas, it (like ... *Y al tercer año* once more) strikes a deep chord with Spanish audiences: the two episodes on the death of Franco reached 4,061,000 and 3,744,000 viewers, respectively. Moreover, unlike in the case of the novel, we have detailed data on the processes of production and consumption which underwrite this televisual chronicle and thus connect it to social life in contemporary Spain.

A meticulous book-length study by a team of researchers under the direction of Mercedes Medina has placed *Cuéntame* (2001–present) in the context of other landmark family dramas on Spanish TV: *Médico de familia* (1995–99) and *Los Serrano* (2003–08) (we shall return to Medina's team and to Los Serrano in Chapter 8). All three titles profited from and contributed to the rise in production standards in Spanish fiction that began in the 1990s (48). This crystallized around the innovative genre of the long-form 'dramedy', whose episodes, uniquely in Spain, approach feature film length, taking up as they do the whole of prime time once a week (51). This new 'professional praxis' (which involved for the first time in Spain team written scripts, skilled ensemble casts, and generous budgets for studio sets and location shoots) was all the more vital to the *Cuéntame* which boasted a unique and explicit aim: to make visible the historical changes experienced by the collective 'Spanish people' as they were experienced by individuals (56). The 'realism' of this aim was enhanced by the series' unique access to TVE's archive (57), fragments of whose newsreel, drama, and commercials are frequently used in the show. Other distinctive features of the series were its use of four plotlines per episode (the others had only three) (63) and a 'less standardized' and a freer mode of production, that brought its creative process closer to feature film than television (it was also the only series whose exterior sequences were shot on celluloid) (64). Such consistent care and expense (the initial budget was 360,000 euros per episode [63]) is rewarded by continuing audience loyalty: in the jargon, 'seriality', properly executed, goes hand in hand with 'fidelization' (80).

This prize-winning quality title also served to enhance the perceived prestige of the embattled public broadcaster TVE, which remained funded in part by government subsidy (Medina's other two titles were aired on private Tele 5) (89). And, while *Cuéntame* attracted a mass audience, the demographic breakdown changed from the first to the second series, as the show became increasingly attractive to women and to older audiences (91, 92), even as it appealed also to children: *Cuéntame* was the choice of 43% of the 4–12 year olds who were still watching TV during the uniquely late Spanish prime time that begins at 10 p.m. (106). Surprisingly perhaps in a period fiction, profitability and verisimilitude were also enhanced by extensive product placement, featuring brands that (by definition) had lasted at least thirty years in Spanish homes. Five out of the top ten (such as Solares mineral water and San Miguel beer) were domestic in origin (114), no doubt contributing to the 'authentic Spanish flavour' cited by scholars (137). Yet while 60% of fan informants view the show as an 'exclusively Spanish story' (146) and 56.5% say it shows a 'traditional family', 38.4% claim that family is also in touch with 'current values' (152).

The emotional investment of such spectators, caught between the represented past and the viewing present, is intense. A woman of 45 says that she hopes the series will 'never end', that she 'sincerely needs' it (153). She cites as reasons for her fidelity the fact that she was the same age as the child protagonist at the time; that she was barely aware of the material privations and lack of freedom of speech back then; and that she took great pleasure in the domestic appliances (refrigerator, washing machine, TV set) which slowly made their first appearance in historical Spanish homes, just as they do in that of the fictional Alcántara family (153). Pre-publicity for the ninth season of the show was equally heterogeneous in its range of references: highlights of 1975 that would be recreated in the fiction were said to be: the death of Franco, the first steps in the emancipation of women, and Atlético Madrid winning the football cup (*El Mundo*, 13 September 2007).

Tellingly, a book published jointly in 2004 by the production company (Grupo Ganga) and the broadcaster (TVE) begins with a similar kind of chaotic enumeration. 'That Spain', we are told, was the Spain of the 600 (a make of car), the Singer washing machine paid on instalments, of liquorice and of Roberto Alcázar comics, of 'La, la, la' (Spain's winning song in Eurovision) and its singer Massiel's miniskirt, of prisons, and of cops attacking students who were growing their hair long (9). Such historical details, many of which are clearly inaccessible to foreigners and young Spaniards alike, risk turning into that 'indistinguishable mass' which, for Labanyi, leaves no space for critical recollection or reflection, even as it seeks to record every detail of the past. And, somewhat hermetically, the book of the series presents TV itself as a model for national historical change: Spain went, we are told, 'from black and white to technicolour' (9). As we shall see, Vizcaíno Casas's ephemeral chronicle of the Transition also raises similar questions of relevance and persistence. Yet, as in *Cuéntame* also, its resuscitation of Franco (at once desired, feared, and disavowed) provides a rare opportunity for redefining Spaniards' relation to the past.

Close reading: '... Y al tercer año'

... *Y al tercer año*, Vizcaíno Casas's episodic and fragmentary fresco of Spain in the early Transition to democracy, consists of a preface, eleven chapters, seven inserts, and three epilogues. Defined as a novel of 'fiction–history' and written over the summer and autumn of 1977, it begins with mock news stories of 1978: two hundred people attack the police and free a thief who had been caught in the act; plaques recording the names of those who 'fell for God and Spain' are removed from public buildings; Fregenal de la Sierra (a tiny town in provincial Extremadura) declares home rule; the International Brigades are honoured in Madrid's Plaza Mayor, with free balloons given out to those present; documents reveal that the defence of the Alcázar in Toledo during the Civil War was carried out with the assistance of a Nazi submarine operating in the River Tagus; and the Dictatorship raised the living standards of 'oppressed' Spanish workers only so they would lose their lives in car crashes on the new motorways (11).

This typically chaotic enumeration, devoted to present fears and past grievances alike, breaks off and the narrative begins. It is 6 a.m. on 20 November 1978 and the sacristan is lighting the candles in the Basilica of the Valle de los Caídos. A mass is to be said for the soul of the dictator on the third anniversary of his death. Suddenly the sacristan stands 'hypnotized' before the tomb of Franco, with its 'immense' granite slab on which visitors would leave flowers as a 'devout souvenir' (12). The tomb is empty. The slab has been displaced. And the sacristan runs shouting through the Basilica, his voice echoing around the vaults, chapels, choir stalls, and richly woven tapestries: '¡Ha resucitado! ¡Ha resucitado!' ('He is risen! He is risen!') (13).

Vizcaíno Casas will return only intermittently to this premise, which, rather weakly, is finally discounted as a fantasy of the 'alcoholic' sacristan (the film version has a more developed causal logic). But the 'inserts' interpolated in the main body of the narrative reveal how political figures of all stripes (recognizable enough to be cited by only their first names) react to the supposed resurrection. Thus 'Santiago' (Carrillo, Chairman of the recently legalized Communist Party) books a ticket to Paris, readies his wig (in which had had famously returned from exile in disguise), and prays before an image of the Virgin, whose cloak, we have been told earlier, is embroidered by 'Dolores' (Ibárruri, 'la Pasionaria') with the hammer and sickle (81–82; 15); 'Adolfo' (Suárez, the current President) resolves more soberly that 'a historical figure as great as the Caudillo never dies' (99); 'Felipe' (González, head of the PSOE, who will not take power until 1982) purses his 'thick and sensual lips' before giving orders in an Andalusian 'lisp' for a private plane to take him to the Germany whose Chancellor 'Willy' (Brandt) is allegedly funding his Spanish Socialists (138–39); and Carlos Arias (Navarro, who famously and tearfully announced Franco's death on television), sinks to his knees, sobbing and giving thanks to God (156).

The main body of the novel refers, however, not to the resurrection of the ghostly Caudillo, but to the then current stakeholders in post-Franco society. Hence the Communists peruse, over caviar, their monthly 'diary of strikes', which includes actors demanding only one performance at weekends (23, 27); and they propose that, just as Franco's birthplace El Ferrol was named 'del Caudillo', so Gijón should henceforth now be known as 'de Carrillo' (26). But the business community is as venal and ineffectual as the Leftist politicians. Swiftly moving their cash to Switzerland (34), Spanish capitalists can turn a profit only on pornography or Molotov cocktails (37). And a Friday meeting to discuss the economic crisis is ill-attended by delegates anxious to get back to the more important tasks of skiing, hunting, and playing golf (38). Meanwhile the 'Organization of Iberian States' (the entity previously known as 'Spain') summons sybaritic local leaders, such as the 'Mandamás' ('Bigshot') of Eastern Andalusia, to Barcelona for a gastronomic encounter with simultaneous translation (even the Basque delegates need this when their Lehendakari chooses to speak in his 'sonorous euskera') (48, 49).

Social changes in gender and sexuality are not neglected. The new Union of Prostitutes issues a labour statute setting up official categories of members (peripatetic, home workers, those who ply their trade in public places) and enforcing additional charges for clients who are marines or Moroccans (68, 69). Meanwhile the Domestic Union of Homosexual Dudes ('Majos') loudly protests that whores have been legalized before gays (74); and feminists, both Trotskyites and Anarchists, complain also, demanding as they do equality in every sphere, except military service and shaving (76). One of their number airs her views in a 'new newspaper' (clearly *El País*), whose contributors are 'wholly independent', just so long as they keep strictly to the daily's ideological line (77).

Beyond party and gender politics, then, culture and the media loom large in Vizcaíno Casas's satirical sights. A hypocritical Socialist proclaims culture under Franco a 'desert' with only a few exceptions such as (respected writers) Cela, Delibes, Buero Vallejo, and a long etcetera (95). The regime is said to have proved incapable of the task of making construction workers read Cervantes or housewives prefer Ortega y Gasset to romantic novels. With the new freedoms, the film industry can now make a cinema that 'explores the nation's soul' and serves as a 'vehicle of culture' and 'faithful mirror of society' (101). In this vein, one producer, who had previously specialized in military and religious pictures, sponsors a long-haired director's opus in which a wife commits adultery with a horse (her husband fights back with a Guinea fowl) and where a slaughterhouse sequence places a photo of Franco amidst the blood and offal (102, 103). (The reference here seems to be to Eloy de la Iglesia, whose *La criatura* ['The Creature/Child', 1977] had treated zoophilia.) Meanwhile a reformed RTVE seeks to impose high culture on the masses by playing a soundtrack of Beethoven and Wagner over football broadcasts (116); while noted Catalan singer-songwriter Joan Manuel Serrat laments that his high-minded anti-Francoist protest songs are no longer newsworthy (125).

In the breadth of its satire (if not its lack of subtlety), then, Vizcaíno Casas seeks to employ recent historical memories to create a conservative national group through the perception of shared experience. His purpose is not, however, to legitimize an existing regime (the UCD government of Suárez) but rather to delegitimize it as chaotic 'desgobierno' ('ungovernment', a frequent word of the time). If Vizcaíno Casas creates a group myth, then, it is one not of social cohesion, but of social breakdown, in which operational codes and systems of ethics no longer apply. For his readers, memories of the War and Dictatorship seem to function as containers for grievances, but they cannot give rise to political mobilization against a status quo that is itself fractured and unstable. It is also hard to see how such memories can be fully instrumentalized in this chaotic situation for the contentious purposes of the extreme Right: Vizcaíno Casas is merciless in his parody of the 'Patriotic Nazi Confessional and Orthodox Front' (branded 'nostálgicos'), who swear blood brotherhood in an exact reproduction of Hitler's bunker (122–23). Vizcaíno Casas thus responds to the problems inherent in narrativizing recent history by simply multiplying the number of his satirical targets.

An equal opportunity offender, in spite of his own transparent nostalgia for the regime, Vizcaíno Casas can even be read as supporting in his own way the purposes of reconstruction and the prevention of future conflict. But for this we need to move from his parodic macro-history to his more sensitive *petite histoire*. Late in the novel we are given parallel lives of two fictional characters, both born (like the author) in 1926. They are clearly intended to be emblematic of the two Spains. Citizen Pérez's father, a self-made man, lost his business to union expropriation in 1936 and lived in fear of the 'Reds' until the end of the War (160–61). In spite of some hardship suffered by his family in the years of hunger, he has qualified as a doctor and worked hard to become prosperous (163–65). Now in 1978 he asks himself what would happen 'If Franco returned…'. Citizen López's father was, conversely, on the losing side of the War and was imprisoned until 1942 (168). Only gradually could this family improve their desperate position, excluded as they were from most opportunities by the new regime. But by the time of the death of Franco, López, now also prosperous, feels a 'strange sensation', neither sad nor happy (170). Although his family have been 'victims of persecution', still he fears for the future. Ironically both Pérez and López argue with their teenage children, exclaiming 'Don't get me started!' when the latter invoke the name of the current President (172–73).

Through these twin biographies, prominently placed in his novel, Vizcaíno Casas thus seeks to salve the 'memory war' already waged by national politicians and to undercut the claim to victimhood by both winners and losers. By mixing accounts from both sides, however, he clearly indulges in what Labanyi calls an 'indistinguishable mass' of recollection which exhibits the bad faith of easy (too easy) empathy. But Vizcaíno Casas's use of the haunting topos, with Franco's ghost stalking the nation's winners and losers alike, offers a chance at least of tempering the crude emotion of his satire with a certain reflective distance, offering readers of the time not a break with the immediate past but a redefinition of their relation to it. Such a redefinition would necessarily include, for many, ambivalent recollections of the dictator.

At the end of the novel, the 'nostálgicos' demonstrate in the Plaza de Oriente and 'a million pairs' of eyes, hoping in vain to see a miracle, stray to the Palace balcony from which Franco had so often addressed the nation. Vizcaíno Casas writes, unexpectedly perhaps, that the 'average citizen' (whether Pérez or López), certain that Francoism had died 'with its founder', now 'looked to the future' (196). While it is hard to read … *Y al tercer año* with much sympathy today (the crudeness of its prejudices rules that out), its 'serious humour' deserves our interest as a popular chronicle of Spanish life that gives some access to the particularities of a historic moment. The fact that much of the detail of Vizcaíno Casas's satire is no longer accessible (that figures once so familiar as to need only first names are now forgotten) can only increase that sense of historicity for a modern readership.

Cuéntame: 'Los pingüinos del invicto Caudillo' ('The Penguins of the Unconquered Caudillo'); 'Españoles, Franco ha muerto' ('Spaniards, Franco is dead.')

The titles of both special episodes of *Cuéntame* on the death of the dictator cite television: the first refers to the nature documentary which, it was rumoured, would be transmitted by TVE when Franco had finally passed away; the second to the words of a tearful Arias Navarro, officially confirming the historic news the following morning. And the opening sequence of the first episode resurrects Franco for the last time in the series. Beginning with a shot of his would-be regal profile on a coin, it reassembles a collage of clips from NoDo newsreel, charting the dictator's career over forty years and ending with him smiling unsteadily in a hospital dressing gown. But the voiceover that plays during these documentary clips, sourced as ever from the omniscient position of the now adult child protagonist, Carlitos, proposes a *petite histoire* perspective for the fictional family with whom audiences were already so familiar: Franco may have been on his death bed, but 'life carried on.'

The scenes that follow show somewhat schematically the differing responses of regular characters situated, as ever, according to their class, gender, and age. Thus father Antonio (Imanol Arias) gloomily shares a drink with his unsympathetic boss Don Pablo (Sancho Gracia), who tucks into prawns: who knows when they will enjoy such luxuries again? On this of all nights, Don Pablo invites Antonio and his wife to a musical review at the theatre (he will ask a showgirl to carry cash for him over the border to France). When Antonio suggests that his wife will surely refuse the invitation at such a tense time, Pablo retorts: 'Who wears the trousers in your house?'

We cut to the workers in mother Merche's hairdressing salon (the prominent 'Spejo's' brand, still familiar today, is a product placement). These women are the first to mention the penguins whose incongruous presence haunts the episode. One suggests in wonder that Franco may well prove immortal: he survived a bullet long ago in Africa. More sophisticated political terminology is placed, ironically and humorously, in the mouths of the children. Over a game of table football, Carlitos and his teenage friends wonder how long it will take for the death of Franco to bring the dictatorship of the proletariat. They meditate on what their 'tactical plan' (another recurring phrase) should be in response to the historic change they are living through. Meanwhile the men in the familiar neighbourhood bar listen glumly to official reports on the radio. Don Pablo turns to Antonio, his employee, expressing unconvincing sympathy for the Dictator: 'Poor man. Do you want a prawn?'

Even here in extremis, political opinion is thus always inflected by character type. The businessman Don Pablo's supposed concern for the Caudillo is clearly undercut by his much greater loyalty to his own interests, both financial and gastronomic; the teenagers' interest in politics is motivated by their hope that the free love that will surely follow the death of Franco will improve their chances with radical girlfriends. When one bar customer criticizes another for 'looking at girls' bums while the Caudillo's dying', it is not because he is a Francoist but because he himself is attracted to the girl in question.

But beyond such individualism, *Cuéntame* (like ... *Y al tercer año* but to very different effect) takes care to place the media at the centre of historical drama. The Alcántaras' eldest child, Toni, and his girlfriend, Juana, are journalists at a radical newspaper, who fear aggression at the hands of the extreme Right. Toni phones his uncle Miguel (distinguished film veteran Juan Echanove) warning him not to visit the flat that both use that night in case of a raid. And as the episode continues, it literally darkens with frequent nighttime exterior sequences. Toni and Juan will cower in their car as the police brutally raid a safe house where they were intending to spend the night; Miguel will be harshly beaten later that night by masked 'Warriors of Christ the King', the deadly real-life equivalents of Vizcaíno Casas's fanciful 'Patriotic Nazi Confessional and Orthodox Front.'

The team of writers (led by creator Eduardo Ladrón de Guevara) use some subtle contrasts and parallelisms here. The murky terrors of the street are crosscut with the technicolour delights of the musical review: don Pablo's showgirl mistress, all feathers and sequins, voices a desultory hope that the Caudillo's 'Calvary' will soon come to an end, even as she accepts her boyfriend's illicit stash of banknotes. Don Pablo's bitter wife, fully aware of her husband's extramarital adventures, tells Merche that when Franco dies and divorce comes in she will 'take [Pablo] to the cleaner's'. Their dead marriage, the image of a patriarchal past, is contrasted with the egalitarian union of the main characters: Antonio hides nothing from Merche, who serves in this series as a clearer harbinger of the Zeitgeist than her husband (owner of her own business, she has just started attending university).

Later, callow Carlitos will seek refuge for a Maoist female school friend at the family home, just as the older Toni will too for his Leftist comrade and colleague Juana. As no fewer than ten characters bed down for the night in the Alcántaras' modest flat, the camera cuts to each in turn in a recapping device familiar from the last moments of countless TV dramas: the grandmother prays there will no war; naive and pretentious Carlitos tells his more seasoned and sceptical brother that Santiago Carrillo is 'just a reformist'; and the young Maoist earnestly tells journalist Juana that from now on there will be 'no marriage, no exploitation.' By the time TVE cuts abruptly to the famous penguins in the early hours of the morning, all are safely asleep.

In the second episode, television is yet more central to the everyday experience of a unique historical event. The opening voiceover stresses the 'tremendous silence' that fell over Spain, caused by a mixture of 'fear, hope, and disbelief', while the first sequences show representative spaces where citizens watch and listen to Arias Navarro's extended speech: the home (Carlitos and grandmother in their flat), the workplace (Antonio's printing press), and the leisure place (the neighbourhood bar). Once more, responses are diverse. One worker warns middle manager Antonio to watch out: things are going to change when 'the tortilla turns over' (another idiom frequent at the time); when Carlitos is told to show respect, he rejoins that Franco showed no respect to those he murdered; some bar regulars weep with Arias Navarro, while others hold their tongues, at least for now. The sheer exceptionalism of the event confuses others: as one hairdresser notes, naively: 'It's the first time a Caudillo's died on me.' Conversely, when the priest offers to say a rosary for the dictator's soul, a customer in the bar remarks sarcastically 'Perhaps he'll rise again on the third day.'

Confirming the *petite histoire* focus on the continuing importance of the everyday even at moments of momentous historical change, the Francoist father of Juana (Toni's journalist girlfriend) has also died that night. And continuing the contrasting parallelisms of the earlier episode, the screenwriters juxtapose two social events of right and left, respectively. Thus progressive Toni attends the wake at Juana's house where he encounters a ruthless police inspector who makes a gesture of reconciliation that the young man rejects (the funeral will see violent conflict between representatives of this more conciliatory rightism and the rejectionist bunker). Meanwhile Merche takes husband Antonio to a lunch of 'progres' (middle-

class political progressives) hosted by Begoña (Blanca Portillo), her university
lecturer. Here conflict is more muted, with Antonio, soberly suited, saying that
liberty will be useless without justice, while Begoña, clad colourfully in period
knitwear, claiming that it is not worth having peace at any price. The habitués of
the Leftist salon compromise with their somewhat uncomfortable guests, toasting
not the death of the dictator, but the return of exiles (the Alcántaras' daughter is
in distant Paris).

   While *Cuéntame*, unlike Vizcaíno Casas's crude satire, thus takes care to encompass
all political positions, it cannot be dismissed as an indiscriminate mass of conflicting
testimonies. The sympathy and empathy of viewers earned by the central characters
Antonio and Merche (not to mention the sensitive and underplayed performances
by Imanol Arias and Ana Duato) privilege their perspectives over those of the wide
but ephemeral supporting cast. The key dialogue here, typically unstressed, but
deeply moving, is between don Pablo and his employee Antonio. When the former
claims Franco was a 'good man', that 'Spaniards [now] live better [than they did]'
since 'we won the War', Antonio replies gently but firmly that he did not win the
War: his father was killed by the Nationalists. Antonio (and the series as a whole)
thus honours the memory of the past, but crucially stakes no claim to victimhood
or resentment, tempering emotion by reflective distance. Hence, although
Cuéntame's raison d'être is the recovery of facts in accordance with the principle of
verisimilitude, it remains focused on the problems inherent in narrativizing history
and most especially on that of perspective: the variable generalizability of different
and competing points of view.

   As so often, this moral is rendered explicit in the final voiceover. All of the
cast, for very different reasons, have queued to see Franco lying in state, an excuse
for some impressive exterior sequences shot at the Oriente Palace and Square,
where the Caudillo had so often appeared in his lifetime. The characters' reactions
(whether making the fascist salute or defiantly displaying a treasured photo of a dead
Republican grandfather) are crosscut with period colour footage of the dictator in
his coffin. But Antonio and Merche choose not to go in, clinging to each other in
the cold outside the Palace. The adult Carlitos says that this is what the Transition
means to him: not famous politicians, but his insignificant parents, who had
spent their whole lives trying not to draw attention to themselves. In the credit
sequence that follows, more period footage of Franco's funeral at the grotesquely
monumental Valle de los Caídos is set to the plangent voice of the emblematic
singer-songwriter of the time, Joan Manuel Serrat. Hence while the series clearly
directs sympathy to the central family, encouraging modern viewers to empathize
with them by recreating their experience of the past, there is no bad faith or easy
sentiment involved. Rather *Cuéntame* proposes a new mode of reconstruction or of
conflict prevention which remains fully conscious of the difficulties of historical
representation.

   One conspicuous sign of this self-consciousness is the fact that the series regularly
schedules special documentary episodes which disrupt the smooth flow of family
fiction. In the case of the death of Franco (and separately to the two episodes I
have examined) the creators offered a programme in which actors from the series
interviewed surviving figures from the period they recreate, such as Santiago

Carrillo, even eliciting what was claimed to be new historical material from such witnesses as Franco's doctors. (Other special documentary episodes focused on less momentous historical trends, such as the *destape* or new sexual explicitness in Spanish media.)

To conclude: I have argued in this chapter that Vizcaíno Casas's resuscitation of Franco in ... *Y al tercer año, resucitó*, which was written so soon after the dictator's death, attempted to serve the purposes of conservative group creation through a perception of shared experience, intended to delegitimize the then existing regime of the Transition. It did so by invoking memories as containers for grievances in a time of apparent social breakdown (or *desgobierno*) when operational codes and systems of ethics were in flux. Separating interest from sympathy, we can nonetheless respond to this example of historical testimony that was massively popular in its historical moment. Partial and ephemeral as it is, the novel remains symptomatic of the spirit of its time.

As one would expect, the haunting topos also employed by *Cuéntame* some thirty years later reworks the death and legacy of the dictator in a very different way. The series recovers facts and mixes accounts from both sides, but also tempers emotion with the reflective distance that is of course much easier to achieve in a fully established democracy. In spite of *Cuéntame*'s will to truth, however, it is also recognizably postmodern in its appeal to a mix of documentary and drama, of past and present, that is sometimes left wilfully unresolved. The series thus offers its longsuffering characters the possibility of a better future, which will be the present of those faithful viewers watching at home, a future (and a present) in which the memory of the past will still be invoked, enjoyed, and honoured.

Works cited

AGUILERA, JOAQUÍN DE, and JOSEP C. VERGÈS (eds.). *La televisión libre en la nueva democracia española. Conferencias y coloquios del simposio internacional de Madrid, 6 y 7 de diciembre de 1979* (Madrid: Sirocco, 1980)

GARCÍA JIMÉNEZ, JESÚS. *Radiotelevisión y política cultural en el Franquismo* (Madrid: CSIC, 1980)

GRUPO GANGA and RTVE. *La España de Cuéntame cómo pasó: el final de los años sesenta* (Madrid: Santillana Ediciones Generales, 2004)

LABANYI, JO. 'Memory and Modernity in Democratic Spain', *Poetics Today*, 28.1 (2007), 89–116

PALACIO, MANUEL, and JUAN CARLOS IBÁÑEZ. 'Biografía y ficción histórica en la obra del Bardem televisivo', in *El cine a codazos: Juan Antonio Bardem*, ed. by José Luis Castro de Paz and Julio Pérez Perucha (Ourense: Festival Internacional de Cine Independiente, 2004), pp. 139–51

VIZCAÍNO CASAS, FERNANDO. ... *Y al tercer año, resucitó*, 40th edn (Barcelona: Planeta, 1986)

Web sources both accessed 30 July 2010:

El País, Archive search for Fernando Vizcaíno Casas, <http://www.elpais.com/todo-sobre/persona/Fernando/Vizcaino/Casas/4814/>

SMITH, MARGARET. 'The Many Functions of Historical Memory', paper presented at the Annual Meeting of the International Studies Association, Montreal, 17 March 2004, <http://www.allacademic.com/meta/p_mla_apa_research_citation/0/7/4/1/9/p74198_index.html>

CHAPTER 3

The Audiovisual Transition

Cinema, Television, and Muñoz Molina's *El jinete polaco* ('The Polish Horseman', 1991)

Paradoxical productions

The most recent (and most extended) study of the cinema of the Transition is included in a volume with a significant title: *Historia(s) del cine español: la nueva memoria* ('History/ies of Spanish Cinema: The New Memory', Castro de Paz, Pérez Perucha, Zunzunegui 178–253). Pablo Pérez Rubio and Javier Hernández Ruiz call attention to the many paradoxes of production in the period they take to be 1973–83. Although the authors claim not to be 'obsessed' with periodization (Pérez Rubio and Hernández Ruiz 242, n. 5), they offer a certain justification for dating the start of the Transition, in the cinematic sector at least, to before the death of Franco in 1975, which we explored in the previous chapter of this book. Thus the 1970s as a whole were characterized by an increasing extension of what could be said on film, giving rise to an unprecedented originality and variety (180). And in the last years of the Dictatorship, a political opposition was already emerging into the public sphere, taking advantage of official 'instability' and internal Francoist conflict between reformists and the *bunker*, to 'make its voice heard' in varied forms of cultural production, albeit barely tolerated by the more reactionary sectors (181).

More specifically in the case of film, Pérez Rubio and Hernández Ruiz propose that, after a time of renewed repression when hardliner Sánchez Bella held responsibility for cinema as Minister of Information and Tourism (1969–73), there came a first period of 'post-Francoism' dating from 1973 to the first democratic elections of June 1977. The ambivalence of this early period is revealed by the Norms of Film Censorship of 19 February 1975. While this document abolished the requirement to submit scripts for censorship in advance of production, it insisted nonetheless that films should exhibit 'shared social values' of the State that were (for Pérez Rubio and Hernández Ruiz) by now 'flagrantly anachronistic'. Still prohibited were such themes as suicide, euthanasia, violence 'as a means of solving social and human problems', prostitution, sexual perversions, adultery, illicit sexual relations, abortion and anything harmful to the institution of marriage and the family, drug addiction, and alcoholism (182). Individual or social 'defects' were admitted only so long as they did not undermine 'the principles of natural order and the common good' and were subject to a 'properly made critique'.

This slow but inexorable liberalization was famously characterized by a new permissiveness with regard to nudity on screen, but also gave rise to genuine controversies such as the banning of Ricardo Franco's *Pascual Duarte* (1976), with its graphic final scene of garrotting. The process reached a turning point in 1977, which the authors take to mark the beginning of a new period within the wider development of the Transition, a period they call the 'Full Democratic Transition' for film (182). The cinematic counterpart of that year's political milestones (the legalization of the Spanish Communist Party, amnesty for political prisoners, and first free General Elections) was the Law of 11 November 1977, which marked the official disappearance of censorship and a new freedom in film production (182).

Unlike other times of profound social change and in spite of the sheer volume of the corpus produced (Pérez Rubio and Hernández Ruiz give an estimate of one thousand features between the two end dates of 1973 and 1983) the Transition did not produce radically new modes of filmmaking analogous to Soviet montage or Italian neorealism. Suggesting that both sociological and auteurist approaches have failed to account for the cinema of the period, the authors attempt an analysis of the symbiosis between film practices and ideological discourses (179). They stress, however, the sheer variety of films made, often in marginal genres, a plurality that, ironically, was closed off by the PSOE's subsequent policy, which resulted in a 'homogenization' or institutionalization: the reduction of Spanish film to politically progressive but aesthetically timid European models (180).

Thus they write that, in spite of the progressive disappearance of censorship, 'cuando España pugna por empezar a liberarse de un tutelaje estatal castrante, en Europa es especialmente más necesaria que nunca la protección cultural del cinematógrafo ante la crisis estructural de la industria' ['when Spain was fighting to being to free itself from a castrating dependence on the state, in Europe the cultural protection of cinema, faced with the structural crisis of its industry, was more necessary than ever'] (182). And if they propose an engagement with Reality (broadly defined to range from sociopolitical struggle to the exploration of the allegorical imagination) as the defining characteristic of the cinema of the Transition, they identify five incompatible political currents implicit in filmic texts: rejectionist reaction (Mariano Ozores), a moderate right reconciled to change (Pedro Lazaga), a moderate left 'pactista y posibilista' (Emilio Martínez Lázaro), a radical left unwilling to settle for bourgeois democracy (Eloy de la Iglesia), and, finally, an avant garde underground (which includes the first films of Pedro Almodóvar) (184). It should be noted here that the reputation of filmmakers at the time of the Transition is no guide to their perceived status today: Eloy de la Iglesia, who was (as we saw in the previous chapter) bitterly attacked in the 1970s for his crude cinematic 'pamphlets' on sex and politics by conservative commentators such as Vizcaíno Casas, is now held to be the definitive filmmaker of the Transition, fusing Leftist critique with popular success (197–201).

It is worth pausing for a moment over the controversial figure of de la Iglesia, who made no fewer than twenty-one feature films, including some of the biggest grossing titles of all time, between 1966 and 1986. While notorious during the Transition as a leading exponent of the *destape* (the new nudity which, in his unique case, was focused more on young male than female bodies), de la Iglesia was also deeply engaged in social issues that had been prohibited just a few years earlier. Thus in *Los placeres ocultos* ('Hidden Pleasures', 1976) a bourgeois business man falls for a working class youth; in *El diputado* ('The Congressman', 1976) a married Socialist politician is involved with a male prostitute in the pay of the extreme Right; and in *El pico* (1983) the sons of a Civil Guard and a Basque separatist politician become enmeshed in the drug subculture of Bilbao. Reviled by the press on both Left and Right, de la Iglesia's cinema of excess was accused by *El Alcázar* of belittling the armed forces and praising 'queers' (Martialay 1983) and attacked by the newly founded *El País* for its 'commercialism' in mixing sex and politics into a 'cocktail' that proved all too easy to sell (Trueba 1979). Yet, as I have written elsewhere, de la Iglesia's cinema marked a unique moment in which the twin themes of homosexuality and Basque separatism, previously unspeakable in Spanish film, achieved a mass audience (Smith, *Laws of Desire* 129); and in Spain it was not until as late as 1996, when he was honoured with a retrospective at the San Sebastián–Donostia Film Festival, that de la Iglesia was acclaimed as the creator of a 'new genre'. His 'high risk cinema', showing as it did what Spanish film had never before shown, is said to have incited the rage of the censors and the irritation of critics, even as it attracted the fervour of contemporary audiences (Aguilar et al. 11).

It is striking that Pérez Rubio and Hernández Ruiz's unusually detailed and comprehensive typology, which assigns de la Iglesia to the most radical of its political categories, fails to coincide with the typologies of previous studies. For example in her *Spanish National Cinema* of 2003 Nuria Triana Toribio begins by noting, uncontroversially, that it was 'popularly held that the new democratic Spain needed a new democratic national cinema which would announce and explain to the world at large the death of the old Spain and bring the nation together' (Triana Toribio 109). But she goes on to claim that films of the era followed three strategies: they either promoted literary and cultural heritage, or exploited the (supposedly) authentic Spanishness of *costumbrismo* ('local colour'), or advocated heterogeneity and eclecticism (110–11). All of these tendencies are rooted in the recent cinematic past (invoking as they do relevant precedents such as the *nuevo cine español* (the 'new Spanish [art] cinema' of the 1960s), Berlanga, and 'subgéneros' ('popular genre films'), respectively) and will extend into the Socialist era of the 1980s. Crucially, however, they do not map easily onto political positions: for example the second trend of *costumbrismo* was taken up by both conservatives and those to the left of the PSOE.

Given this critical controversy, I would like to sketch out four preliminary observations that will frame my argument in this third chapter. Firstly, industrial factors must be considered together with formal or ideological ones. Secondly (as I suggested earlier), cinema of the Transition (and beyond) does not reinforce the amnesia hypothesis and is indeed centrally engaged with the exploration of Spanish history. Thirdly, film is inextricable from television, its twin sister in the audiovisual sector and whose history is much less studied by scholars even as it plays a greater role in popular memory. Finally, screen narrative must also be examined formally, not just for content: indeed the form may contradict that content, transforming the latter's overt meaning.

I will explore each of these areas in turn, before moving on to a case study of two audiovisual products from 1973, which (as we have seen) is for Pérez Rubio and Hernández Ruiz the first year of the Transition in the cinematic sector. The texts are Víctor Erice's *El espíritu de la colmena* ('The Spirit of the Beehive') and Antonio Mercero's *Crónicas de un pueblo* ('Chronicles of a Village'). As we shall see, the most celebrated art movie of the time and its best-loved TV drama share unexpected and significant characteristics. I end with a close analysis of a valuable source of testimony to the role of cinema and television in the construction of popular memory in the Transition and beyond: Antonio Muñoz Molina's prize-winning novel *El jinete polaco* ('The Polish Horseman', 1991).

Exhibiting history and pedagogy

Before examining our chosen texts, let us consider the question of the film industry. While scholars tend to focus on production, stressing the sheer number of features made, they tend to neglect exhibition. And here it is the case that the Transition coincided with the continuing collapse of cinema going as a mass activity in Spain. Thus in the twenty years from 1968 to the low point of 1988, the number of screens fell from eight thousand to two thousand, the number of admissions from 376 million to 69 million, and the rate of annual visits per person from 11.22 to 1.79 (SGAE 2003, 307). The figures for the decade of the Transition itself (1973–83) are for screens, 5632 to 3510; for admissions, 278 million to 141 million; and for annual visits, 7.99 to 3.7. While the exhibitors' reluctance to renovate decrepit theatres must take some of the blame, the rise of television is clearly influential here: between 1966 and 1969 the number of sets had already doubled from 1.5 to 3 million and over half of the population claimed to watch 'regularly' (Palacio 2001, 58, 64).

Second comes the engagement with history. As is well known, the view is widely held in Spain today that the Transition was founded on a willed (and culpable) amnesia to the crimes of the past. However, as I have noted in earlier chapters, Jo Labanyi argues that 'the Transition process was achieved precisely by leaving to one side — not "forgetting", I would insist — any discussion of political responsibilities for [the] past' (Labanyi, 'Introduction' 123). While the past was thus not allowed to determine the course of the present and future, it remains the case that both film and television in the period explicitly and frequently reflected on Spain's recent and violent history.

Thus within the declining sector of cinema, both producers and audiences favoured historical titles. Against the 'pact of forgetting' hypothesis once more, so called 'cine histórico' ('period pictures') was prominent and popular with audiences even as they lost the habit of cinema attendance. *El desencanto*, Jaime Chávarri's somewhat austere documentary on the consecrated poet of the Francoist regime, Leopoldo Panero, attracted a quarter of a million spectators in 1976 (Ministerio de Cultura database 2007), while the supposedly unpopular and elitist *El espíritu*, set in the 1940s, won half a million (Ministerio de Cultura database). Saura's *Cría cuervos*, an oblique and demanding allegory of the regime, set in the present but obsessed with reworking the traumas of the past, gained over one million spectators in 1976 (Ministerio de Cultura database). By the mid 1980s, with the coming of the first

Socialist government, historical drama with a progressive politics (often adapted from prestigious literary originals) would become a canonic, even dominant, genre in Spanish cinema (Triana Toribio 122). Moreover the trend continued after the Transition. According to the data in Carlos Heredero's impeccable survey of the 1990s, there were no fewer than thirty-six features set in the Spanish past during that decade (Heredero 76–79).

Likewise television, adopting what Manuel Palacio has called 'pedagogy', set out both to educate Spaniards in democracy and to explore their past. Palacio has given a pioneering account of the medium and its content in the period (Palacio 91–121). Democratic education was of course carried out above all through informational programming: respected news weekly *Informe semanal* ('Weekly Report') began as early as 1973, while *La clave* ('The Key'), which ran from 1976–83, used an unusual format (discussion after the screening of a film on a relevant topic) to offer live and uncensored debate on previously taboo social and political issues of the moment (Marxism, the *autonomías* [historic nationalities in Spain], homosexuality, single mothers).

As Palacio writes, these news programmes remain firmly lodged in the 'collective memory of televisual nostalgia' today (96), in part perhaps because, in the absence of private competition, state-run RTVE could count on monopolizing the mass audience, however educational the tone of its programming. But historical pedagogy also worked through television fiction, especially the big budget series shot on film that had never before been produced for the medium. Coinciding with the 'heritage' trend seen in cinema, prestige projects such as the lavish *Fortunata y Jacinta* (1980) exploited a historical setting to argue for reconciliation and consensus amongst modern Spaniards in a way clearly legible to audiences of the period (Palacio 94, 154; Smith, *Television in Spain* 43–48).

Meanwhile, in spite of the reformist Charter for RTVE finally approved in 1980, the financial reliance of public broadcasting on the government, barely resolved even today, posed yet more crudely than the argument over a national cinema the paradox of state dependence and creative freedom in a new democracy. The early campaign of *El País* against the state broadcaster's corruption and political servility set the tone for the *telebasura* ('trash TV') debate that was to follow much later, in which television would be dismissed by the press on the basis of individual programmes that were conflated with the medium as a whole.

The argument for television, so neglected and scorned as a medium, can however be made theoretically as well as empirically on the basis of the audience's greater engagement with the small screen than the large. John Caughie, a British media scholar, has raised six general questions of TV studies which, distinguishing film from television, will inform our case studies below. First Caughie argues for the 'specificity' of the medium and its 'possibilities of meaning and subjectivity', even while it is accused of banality and familiarity. The second problem is history. While the cinematic canon is readily accessible and regularly revived (New York's Criterion have recently edited luxury editions of both *El espíritu* and *Cría*), television's past is often wiped or forgotten. TV, nonetheless, 'establishes commonalities of shared experience and communities of memory' (13) that may be more intimate than film.

Caughie's third question is the national. Domestic in all senses, television may seem parochial (17), but it remains a more sensitive barometer to local sensibilities than internationally targeted cinema. Text is a fourth problem, exhibiting structural differences with film. 'Television drama', writes Caughie, 'uses the word to tell us about the world.' 'Film', he says, 'allows us to dream; television drama invites us to be responsible' (18).

Moreover, TV, consumed in the home, is (in a fifth problem) everyday (20), but not to be dismissed as unending electronic 'flow'. The final problem is value. 'A significant part of [TV] pleasure', writes Caughie, 'seems to lie in repetition, recognition, and familiarity' (23), not characteristics that are traditionally prized aesthetically. Caughie argues that TV drama 'gives us a certain purchase on certain questions of theory and criticism, meaning and value [...] important for an understanding of the recent history of British culture' (23–24). In spite of journalists' and intellectuals' contempt for the medium (arguably more intense than in Britain), the same may well prove to be true of Spain.

Schools for scandal? 'El espíritu de la colmena' and 'Crónicas de un pueblo'

Let us turn now to our two audiovisual case studies. Pérez Rubio and Hernández Ruiz place *El espíritu de la colmena* in the category of 'rehabilitation of history' or 'the present past', apparently part of their third strand of 'moderate Leftism' (Pérez Rubio and Hernández Ruiz 205). Triana, more focused on the recuperation of popular cinema as an unexamined index of social change, prefers to ignore the film altogether. Moreover, in spite of its period setting *El espíritu de la colmena* has little in common with the heritage films that followed it. Certainly the most prestigious film of late Francoism or the early Transition, *El espíritu de la colmena* is generally taken to embody a universal, abstract, or purely subjective point of view, what screenwriter Angel Fernández Santos called 'the look behind the eyes'. As the first feature by the quintessential auteur maudit Víctor Erice it is also held to be a uniquely personal vision, stamped with an individual aesthetic. Yet, industrially, it is the product of producer Elías Querejeta and his artistic team, crucially cinematographer Luis Cuadrado, whose collaborations with other directors such as Saura clearly share a family resemblance with Erice's debut. By setting the vogue for 'quality' or 'art' cinema, albeit in a different style to that later promoted by the Socialists under the Miró law, *El espíritu de la colmena* also anticipates the growing disconnection between Spanish film production and domestic audiences of the Transition, who did not always take kindly to what producers and governments took to be the priorities of a new national cinema.

Given the film's reputation over some thirty years as an exemplum of poetic lyricism, it is instructive to return to its reception on release. The Francoist daily press such as *El Alcázar*, often (like the popular audience) hostile to *El espíritu de la colmena*, associates its 'dangerous obscurity' with a 'modernity' of style and 'foreign influences' (Martialay). The progressive monthly cinephile magazines stress rather the historicity of the film, claiming it represents 'the spirit of Spanish society in 1940' (Feito 48), and (paradoxically, perhaps) its connection to a modern audience:

the elusive enigmas or 'puzzles' of the film require the 'active participation' of the public (Genover 25). I myself have argued that the film's engagement with history and politics is embedded in its mise en scene: in the weathered textures of its landscape (the bleak meseta), authentic locations (the ruinous houses and streets), and faces (the careworn local extras) (Smith, *The Moderns* 34–35).

Far from being seen as a universal masterpiece of art cinema, then, *El espíritu de la colmena* was experienced in its own time, by both conservative detractors and progressive supporters alike, as a specific intervention in national history and contemporary politics. Moreover I would argue that in its stress on everyday domesticity (what Vicente Molina Foix called 'the war behind the windows' [Molina Foix 112–18]), *El espíritu de la colmena* coincides to some extent with a televisual aesthetic even as it exploits the familiar shooting and cutting style of art cinema (most especially, the fixed camera, long take, and leisurely pace).

But what were Spanish audiences watching as they retreated from rundown cinemas to consumerist homes that were now reorganized to centre on the TV set? *Crónicas de un pueblo* was the most popular drama on TVE from 1971–73. Commissioned directly by the regime (by second-in-command Carrero Blanco, no less) with a propagandistic brief to explain to audiences the Fuero de los españoles ('The Spaniards' Charter', one of the seven Fundamental Laws of the regime), the show, which remains embedded in popular memory today and is currently available on DVD, has been disavowed even by its creator Antonio Mercero (Smith, *Television in Spain* 66). Perhaps the only Spanish professional in the medium to deserve the label 'auteur', Mercero went on to create definitive dramas of the end of the Transition (*Verano azul* ['Blue Summer', TVE, 1981–82]) and, for commercial Antena 3, the full democracy (*Farmacia de guardia* ['All Night Chemist', 1991–95]). In spite of the unavoidably collective production process (*Crónicas* itself boasted several directors and writers), Mercero displays no less consistency than the individualist Erice in both thematics and style: his dramas consistently focus on collective protagonists and communal processes (a rural village facing the challenge of modernization, a group of teenagers on holiday, the staff and customers at an urban chemists), often focusing on children as unwitting witnesses to social change.

The overt didacticism of *Crónicas*, with clunky dialogue citing the Fuero (which dates back as far as 1945), often placed somewhat uncomfortably in the mouth of the tolerant and permissive schoolteacher, might be seen as a precursor of the government-led 'pedagogy' adopted by successive Director Generals of TVE under the Transition and beyond. Certainly it is reinforced by the plot structures of the weekly half-hour shows: typically, social tensions are set in play by outsiders from the city (whether wealthy businessmen, sleazy conmen, or criminal teens in miniskirts and sports cars) only to be resolved by the village's figures of authority: the young mayor, the kindly priest, and the teacher, once more. Seduced into complicity by their weekly contact with such figures, surely newly urbanized Spanish viewers were simply engaging in comforting, regressive nostalgia at a time of preoccupying change?

Crónicas' technique, however, clearly contradicts its intermittently didactic scripts. Mercero borrows from neo-realism: shooting wholly on location in 14 mm and with live sound, he documents everyday life in a Castilian village which does not seem to have changed since *El espíritu de la colmena*'s 1940s. The ironically named Puebla Nueva del Rey Sancho ('New Town of King Sancho') is as desolate as it is picturesque and the surrounding Castilian countryside is as bleakly sterile as in Erice's feature film (some episodes document repeated, and fruitless, attempts to drill for water or purify the polluted stream). As in Erice once more, implicit political critique (easily legible at the time) is embedded in the worn textures of landscape, built environment, and the lined faces of extras, non-professional actors ably integrated with principal players who had hitherto been little known supporting actors themselves.

Exploiting the national specificity of the TV medium (not to mention its banality and familiarity), Mercero thus raised new possibilities of meaning, telling Spaniards about their world and asking them to take responsibility for it in a continuing, collective process that now gives us a certain purchase on recent Spanish history that we do not necessarily find in film. Ironically, however, Mercero used techniques parallel to those of Erice's art movie: the fixed camera, the long take, and the leisurely rhythm that require the active participation of the audience in the production of meaning.

Let use compare two sequences in *El espíritu de la colmena* and *Crónicas* that are set in a schoolroom and thus explicitly engage in audiovisual pedagogy. Erice's anatomy lesson takes place early in the film. Apparently based on the personal memory of his screenwriter collaborator, this well-known scene is deeply engaged with the poetic exploration of point of view (of fantasy and subjectivity) that is a key theme in his film. The scene stages a collective and relatively democratic dynamic between the kindly teacher and active pupils, who are encouraged to participate in the class. However, audiences of the period would have no difficulty recognizing those elements of mise en scene placed in the background that gesture towards historical reference and political repression: the ruinous state of the exterior streets; the raising of the flag before lessons begin; the twin maps of Spain hanging at the back of the room (Fig. 4). Surprisingly, perhaps, Erice's shooting style is here quite conventional or classical, breaking down the sequence (and the space) from long to medium shots and close ups, and climaxing with little Ana's point of view, as she replaces the eyes in the slightly sinister wooden male figure who is called 'Don José' by the teacher.

Crónicas's classroom is more complex. The context is an episode ('La peseta de Dionisio'/'Dionisio's Peseta') in which an arrogant businessman, whose car breaks down in the village, is taught the values of humility and cooperation by the mechanic of the title, who will accept only the nominal fee of one peseta for his labour. Intense social conflicts (between town and country, modernity and tradition, capital and labour) are thus staged but, finally, contained by a reassuring narrative closure. This main plot strand is, as ever, complemented by the subplot in which the children act out a parallel story. Having misbehaved, they are kept after school by the teacher (the kindly 'Don Antonio', played by Emilio Rodríguez) who suggests they comment on stories in the newspaper.

While the overt message here is once more the dignity of labour and the mutual

FIG. 4. Francoist pedagogy (I): *El espíritu de la colmena*

responsibilities between government and people (the former provides paternalist guardianship or 'tutela' to the latter), the shooting and performance style tell us something different. Filmed in a single take of some three minutes, the schoolroom sequence presents us with a kind of forum for the staging of social problems with the children posed provisionally and perilously (one falls, another grins at the camera) around an institutional figure who is clearly only miming his authority, jokily putting implausible words into the mouths of his young charges (Fig. 5). What is important here is a sense of improvisation and collectivity where once there was rigidity and order.

Unlike that of Erice, Mercero's pedagogy may not invite us to dream, but it does seek to establish a commonality of shared experience which remains today a community of memory (*Crónicas* featured heavily in the celebration of fifty years of TVE that extended throughout 2006). Moreover the continuity and productivity of Mercero's televisual career, so different to Erice's halting and stunted filmic progress (just three features in over thirty years), suggests the possibility of a developing national narrative that has accompanied Spanish audiences from late Francoism, through the Transition, to the present day. While the value of such a narrative is founded on the typically televisual qualities of repetition, recognition, and familiarity (far from the unique and unforgettable artistic event that is *El espíritu de la colmena*), it deserves to be praised and prized nonetheless. If, as Palacio claims, TV consumption is one of the key bases of socialization and memories of the medium are amongst the most recognizable criteria for communal self-identity (Palacio 11), then audiovisual research on the Transition, as elsewhere, should no longer remain focused on a small number of canonic feature films.

Fig. 5. Francoist pedagogy (II): *Crónicas de un pueblo*

Visualizing the Transition: 'El jinete polaco'

Evidence for my proposal to expand the focus beyond art cinema to embrace the role of the audiovisual as a whole in the construction of history and memory comes from a perhaps unlikely source. Antonio Muñoz Molina's encyclopedic novel *El jinete polaco* is generally considered to be one of the most successful by this popular and respected novelist and was named the winner of the Planeta and National Literature Prizes in 1991 and 1992, respectively. Muñoz Molina (born in 1956) is also often cited as a pioneer in addressing the questions of history, memory, and modernity in democratic Spain in fictional form (see Labanyi, 'Memory and Modernity' 95).

The initial premise of his plot is perhaps worthy of a *telenovela*: an expatriate interpreter, who was born into rural poverty but has clearly benefited from the social mobility of the Transition, retells the story of his own life and that of his family under the Republic and Dictatorship. His story is told to a woman who is revealed, finally, to be the young girl he had once slept with and had subsequently forgotten many years before. While the novel is determinedly modern and cosmopolitan (much of the action takes place in New York, where the Rembrandt painting from which the book takes its name also hangs), it is founded nonetheless on a minute transcription of life in Spain through the course of the twentieth century, as represented by the central family's Andalusian hometown of Mágina (a barely disguised literary version of Muñoz Molina's own native Úbeda).

In its close attention to the everyday, and most especially to the experience of children as uncomprehending but impressionable witnesses of political conflict and social change, *El jinete polaco* clearly has something in common with the two audiovisual texts I studied earlier. And although the novel's premise is the retrieval of memory and history afforded by still images (a precious trunk of vintage photographs is discovered at its start) (see Fernández), it also contains a detailed and valuable account of the incursion of moving pictures into a setting that is initially as underdeveloped, even primitive, as the villages of *El espíritu de la colmena* and *Crónicas de un pueblo*.

Superficially, *El jinete polaco* would appear at first to make the case, familiar in Spain, for television as *telebasura*: a vehicle of distraction, alienation, and amnesia. Thus the nomadic narrator is shocked on his return to now democratic Spain to find his once active peasant parents 'hypnotized' by the small screen (Muñoz Molina 259) or his formerly astute grandmother indignant at the 'lies' told by the highly coloured characters in the Latin American *telenovelas* that became so popular in the 1980s (519). Elsewhere a TV set signals the new desolation of family life in modern Spain as it plays, too loud and unwatched, to the neglected residents of an old people's home (562). The mass culture of television is also compared unfavourably to the oral tales of popular memory, which seem at first to have inspired the free-flowing narrative of the novel itself (570).

Yet the narrator also reveals in spite of himself the hidden history of audiovisual media that is embedded in family narratives and social relationships. Watching a TV documentary on the Cuban War with his son, the narrator's father, normally uncommunicative, remarks that all the men they are seeing on screen are 'now dead' (a rare admission of his own mortality) (386); or again, watching the news in the new democracy the narrator catches sight of the man who had been his school teacher during the late Francoist period (and had had an affair with his young girlfriend), now a respected politician of the new government (427). Television thus provides an opportunity, however unpredictable and fragile, for making individual and collective connections at a time of rapid historical change.

Two passages that deal with audiovisual media seem the most significant in this context. The first narrates the repeated and almost fantastic arrival of television into Mágina in the late Francoist period, described in terms of the limited but intense and heightened perspective of a rural child. It is a 'shining, white thing', giving off a fire which is not red and yellow like the familiar burning wood but is rather 'blue': a 'circular domesticated hearth' (177). Or again on another occasion the child narrator is taken by the hand to what is clearly one of the 'TV clubs' common in the 1960s, where with his neighbours he watches a 'kind of radio', a 'tiny cinema' in which a blonde lady reads 'pronouncing all her 's'' (unlike in the child's local Andalusian dialect) only to give way, in the blink of an eye, to a matador finishing off a bull (177). Mass media soon give rise to a chaotic enumeration of diverse and unfamiliar names invading the restricted but familiar and safe space of the home: 'Madrid, London, Paris, His Excellency the Head of State, His Holiness the Pope, [singing star] Manolo Escobar, Fidel Castro, [bullfighter] Manuel Benítez el Cordobés, the cloak of [bandit] Luis Candelas, the jingle of [chocolate drink] Cola Cao' (178). Politics, religion, and entertainment mingle and merge in the child's past experience and present recollection of late Francoism, enabled, in spite of the narrator's overt hostility to the medium, by the compelling, but disturbing, blue light of television.

A second, much later, passage treats the Transition itself in this same fluid multimedia light. Here, mixing individual and collective memories, the narrator looks back over his lost years abroad, now reduced to women and cities he can no longer identify, as if seen 'through the window of a departing train or taxi' (400). In this second passage the founding metaphor is cinematic. The narrator's life has been 'como esas películas en las que el viento arrastra hojas de calendarios y se ven girar primeras páginas de periódicos y en dos minutos ha transcurrido una generación' ['like those films where you see the wind tearing off the pages of calendars and the front pages of newspapers turning over and in just two minutes a generation has passed'] (400). As in the case of the chaotic enumerations of the television of his childhood, the narrator offers (using a distancing impersonal pronoun) a hetero-geneous list of his own personal and political milestones of the Transition:

> ... se ha enamorado uno sucesivamente de y para siempre de cuatro o cinco mujeres... ha visto en la plaza de Oriente la cola fúnebre de los que acuden a despedirse del cadáver de Franco, ha votado por primera vez, se ha afeitado para siempre la barba, ha salido una mañana hacia su trabajo en París y al abrir el periódico ha encontrado la foto de un guardia civil con tricornio, bigotazo y pistola... y ha querido morirse de rabia y de vergüenza, ha recibido con retraso la invitación para la boda de su mejor amigo... (Muñoz Molina 400)

> [... you fell in love with four or five women one after the other and for ever... saw in the Plaza de Oriente the queue of people waiting to say goodbye to Franco's corpse, voted for the first time, shaved off your beard once and for all, went out to work in Paris and on opening the newspaper found a photo of a Civil Guard with a three cornered hat, a big moustache, and a pistol... and wanted to die of rage and shame, received too late an invitation to your best friend's wedding...]

Clearly there are celebrated literary precedents for such streams of consciousness, which are highly typical of the novel as a whole. What is striking here, however, is that the juxtaposition of the grand narrative of national history (the death of Franco in 1975; the attempted coup by Tejero on 23 February 1981) and the little story of personal biography (the shaving of the beard so typical of committed Leftists in the Transition; the love of a woman or the neglect of a friend) is anticipated by techniques that are identified in the novel itself with film and television: the accele-rated timeframes of montage sequences and the chaotic collage of televisual flow.

As we have seen, Pérez Rubio and Hernández Ruiz argue that the Transition, unlike other periods of tumultuous historical change, did not produce a revolution in cinematic language. Yet, as Pérez Rubio and Hernández Ruiz also acknowledge, the extensive corpus of films made in the period is diverse and challenging and cannot be restricted to a few famous titles such as *El espíritu de la colmena* and its self-consciously artistic successors. Indeed the recent critical re-evaluation of Eloy de la Iglesia, an urgently contemporary director who had as little interest in film form as he did in posterity, suggests that the time is ripe for a wider appreciation of feature films drawn from the less favoured categories mentioned by critics like Triana, such as the popular 'subgéneros'.

A healthy scepticism towards art movies as privileged witnesses to the historical process of the Transition could also be linked to the new interest in television as mirror of and actor in everyday life in Spain. There seems little doubt that Mercero's much-loved TV drama can be read, like Erice's celebrated film, as early participants in a long-lasting democratic pedagogy for Spanish audiences. But it may well be the case that it is in Muñoz Molina's novel (which is not so dissimilar to the memoirs of Tusquets studied in the previous chapter) that we find the subtlest account of the intimate roles played by the twin media of cinema and television in the individual experience of the collective process that was the Transition to democracy.

Works cited

AGUILAR, CARLOS, DOLORES DEVESA, CARLOS LOSILLA, FRANCISCO LLINÁS, JOSÉ LUIS MARQUÉS, ALICIA POTES, CASIMIRO TORREIRO (eds). *Conocer a Eloy de la Iglesia* (San Sebastián: Filmoteca Vasca, 1996)

CASTRO DE PAZ, JOSÉ LUIS, JULIO PÉREZ PERUCHA, SANTOS ZUNZUNEGUI (eds). *Historia(s) del cine español: la nueva memoria* (A Coruña: Vía Láctea, 2006)

CAUGHIE, JOHN. *Television Drama* (Oxford: Oxford University Press, 2000)

FEITO, ÁLVARO. REVIEW OF *El espíritu de la colmena*, *Cinestudio*, 127 (1973), 47–48

FERNÁNDEZ, MARÍA LUISA. 'El medio fotográfico en la narrativa de Antonio Muñoz Molina' (PhD dissertation, University of California, Irvine, 2008)

FERNÁNDEZ SANTOS, ANGEL. 'Una hermosa elegía inacabada', *El País*, 25 May 1985, no page no.

GENOVER, JAUME. Review of *El espíritu de la colmena*, *Dirigido por*, 25 January 1974, no page no.

HEREDERO, CARLOS. *Semillas de futuro: cine español 1990–2001* (Madrid: Nuevo Milenio, 2002)

LABANYI, JO. 'Memory and Modernity in Democratic Spain', *Poetics Today*, 28.1 (2007), 89–116.

——'Introduction: The Politics of Memory in Contemporary Spain', special issue of *Journal of Spanish Cultural Studies*, 9.2 (2008), 119–25

MARTIALAY, FÉLIX. Review of *El espíritu de la colmena*, *El Alcázar*, 12 October 1973, no page no.

——Review of *El pico*, *El Alcázar*, 15 October 1983, no page no.

MOLINA FOIX, VICENTE. 'La guerra detrás de la ventana', *Revista de Occidente*, October 1985, 112–18

MUÑOZ MOLINA, ANTONIO. *El jinete polaco* (Barcelona: Planeta, 1991)

PALACIO, MANUEL. *Historia de la televisión en España* (Barcelona: Gedisa, 2001)

PÉREZ RUBIO, PABLO, and JAVIER HERNÁNDEZ RUIZ. 'Esperanzas, compromisos, y desencantos. El cine durante la Transición española', in Castro de Paz et al., *Historia(s) del cine español*, pp. 178–253

SGAE [SOCIEDAD GENERAL DE AUTORES Y EDITORES]. *Anuario SGAE de las artes escénicas, musicales y audiovisuales* (Madrid: Fundación Autor, 2003)

SMITH, PAUL JULIAN. *Laws of Desire: Questions of Homosexuality in Spanish Writing and Film, 1960–90* (Oxford: Oxford University Press, 1992)

—— *The Moderns: Time, Space, and Subjectivity in Contemporary Spanish Culture* (Oxford: Oxford University Press, 2000)

—— *Television in Spain: From Franco to Almodóvar* (Woodbridge: Tamesis/Boydell and Brewer, 2006)

TRIANA TORIBIO, NURIA. *Spanish National Cinema* (New York and London: Routledge, 2003)

TRUEBA, FERNANDO. 'Sexo y política, un cóctel que vende' [review of *El diputado*], *El País*, 27 January 1979, no page no.

Web source

MINISTERIO DE CULTURA DATABASE, <http://www.mcu.es/bbddpeliculas/cargarFiltro.do?la yout=bbddpeliculas&cache=init&language=es/>, [accessed 10 May 2007]

PART II

Cinema: Authority and Society

CHAPTER 4

A Question of Queer Authorship

Almodóvar's Unpublished Short Stories (1973)

Institutions, aesthetics, and authority

There seems little doubt that Pedro Almodóvar is now amongst the most commercially and critically successful of European directors. In a career spanning three decades and seventeen features, from *Pepi, Luci, Bom* in 1980 to *Los abrazos rotos* (*Broken Embraces*) in 2009, all of his films have turned a profit and many of them have won the most prestigious of prizes, including Oscars for both Best Foreign-Language Film and (more importantly perhaps) Best Script. He is in the unique position of being celebrated by the Hollywood establishment, even as he holds tight to his native Spanish language and locations in Madrid and la Mancha. Marvin D'Lugo has recently read Almodóvar's oeuvre as a consistent and coherent reflection on his own career: 'through the evolution of a style and a conception of filmmaking, he has moved to a critique of his own past and the culture out of which his cinema has taken shape' (D'Lugo 129). Clearly none of the cultural producers I treat in the rest of this book (whether they work in literature, cinema, or television) have achieved comparable success both nationally and internationally.

Abroad this success story has been closely linked to homosexuality. In English-speaking countries Almodóvar is as regularly attributed the label of 'openly gay director' as he is the backhanded compliment of 'women's director'. Ironically this has not been the case in Spain, where Almodóvar's features, massively popular at the box office, have been frequently patronized by critics and snubbed at the Spanish Oscars or 'Goyas' (Triana-Toribio, *Spanish National Cinema* 146–47). And while other Spanish celebrities have openly negotiated recent shifts in the boundary between public and private (by willingly coming out or even celebrating the same-sex marriage that is relatively uncontroversial in Spain), Almodóvar remains silent on his private life, even as his political position, once ambiguous, has become overtly identified with that same governing Socialist party that extended marriage rights at the start of its first term (see Mira 43–45, 435–38). It is symptomatic that the English-language Wikipedia article on Almodóvar confidently lends him both the 'openly gay' and the 'women's director' labels, while the Spanish-language equivalent fails to mention either (Wikipedia).

Almodóvar has also received relatively limited academic attention in Spain itself, where it is no secret that most scholars of Spanish film are unsympathetic to his highly coloured narrative and mise en scene, preferring the rigours of social realism, a genre they identify with a distinctively Spanish tradition and aesthetic (Triana-Toribio, *Spanish National Cinema* 132–40). Conversely Almodóvar's favoured subjects (women and gays) fortuitously coincide with an Anglo-American academy in which film studies have historically been preoccupied with feminism and queer theory (see Maddison). The Anglophone cultural field has thus proved a more fertile ground for Almodóvar than his home territory, critically if not commercially, as he has, through the sheer force of his artistic vision, produced a new image of Spain that is more widely recognized overseas than it is in the Peninsula, as shown by Carlos Boyero's dismissive review of *Todo sobre mi madre* (*All About My Mother*) (Boyero).

I have argued elsewhere that, far from being repressed, there was an active desire for homosexuality in Almodóvar's cinema that facilitated its distribution abroad, as early as *La ley del deseo* (*The Law of Desire*, 1988) (see Smith, *Desire Unlimited* 80). Certainly there has existed a group of gay critics who explained, celebrated, and thus promoted, inadvertently or otherwise, his films to foreign audiences. This queer-friendly tendency runs from Almodóvar's earliest US interview, in which he showed a snapshot of his boyfriend to pioneer queer film historian Vito Russo (Russo), to the queer content of his penultimate film, *La mala educación* (*Bad Education*, 2004), received much more warmly and openly in New York and London than in Madrid or Barcelona (Holden, Fernández Santos).

The success of Almodóvar's most recent films (since 1995's *La flor de mi secreto* [*The Flower of My Secret*]), whose quality has been attested by a general critical consensus, is due in part to his resurrection of that highly contested category the 'art movie'. The three privileged themes of the later films have been: literarity (the self-conscious references to Djuna Barnes, Tennessee Williams, and Truman Capote); urbanism (the celebration of architectural monuments previously unseen in his cinema such as Madrid's Plaza Mayor or Barcelona's Sagrada Familia); and sexuality (the lesbians and trannies of *Todo sobre mi madre* [*All About My Mother*]; the paedophile priests and perverse youths of *La mala educación* [*Bad Education*]) (see Smith, 'Resurrecting' 155–66). Once again, such adult themes may well have been positively welcomed as signs of distinction by Almodóvar's emerging audience: newly upmarket at home, where rising ticket prices made moviegoers more wealthy, urban, and educated than ever before, and a self-selecting niche abroad, as foreign-language films found distribution increasingly difficult (SGAE 78).

The question remains as to how or, indeed, if Almodóvar can be considered as a queer auteur. Now auteurship has of course been discussed and critiqued even more than the related category of 'art cinema'. And this is not the place to summarize forty years of debate. But a brief citation from Pam Cook's *The Cinema Book* sets the scene for much current usage of the term:

> There is now a certain tendency to examine how particular sites and practices produce the author, a concentration on how films circulate, the contexts in which they are apprehended and the rules which govern their interpretation. This approach contends that authorship is produced through such cultural apparatuses and technologies as: interview, criticism, publicity, and curriculum, and that [...] one should try to take account of the different conditions of possibility for creative claims. (304)

Although Cook insists that the 'independence' of the auteur and their 'vision' are inextricable from industrial factors (314), her institutional understanding of auteurism (as sites and practices, contexts and rules, apparatuses and technologies) is, of course, far from the Romantic conception of creative genius that might once have been associated with the term.

Clearly each of these factors is relevant to Almodóvar's unique cultural career, although the most apposite would seem to be the textual: the skill of his production company El Deseo in orchestrating interview, criticism, publicity, and curriculum has been a necessary, if hardly sufficient, motive for his success and sets him apart from European rivals (see Triana Toribio 'Auteurism' and Grant). The conditions of possibility Cook cites include nationality ('changed global circumstances of film production, circulation, and exhibition'), gender (women remain in a tiny minority as directors), and cinephilia (the proliferation of festivals may well influence artistic agendas). But we would have to add homosexuality as a further, and perhaps ambivalent, condition of possibility for Almodóvar's creative claims. As in the case of women directors, rarely admitted to the select ranks of auteurdom, there seems to be a structural conflict between sexual preference and the perceived effortless authority of authorship. And it could be argued that one-time masters such as Pasolini and Fassbinder achieved their status in spite, rather than because, of their sexuality.

There is no doubt that even today a director's name above the title remains part of the film industry's repertoire of promotional strategies (Weiner). Rather than wholly dissolving auteurism, in postmodern fashion, into such commercial questions, however, I would like to argue for a broader approach that combines the institutional and the aesthetic. As is well known, Foucault's functionalist 'author function' identified three necessary conditions for a candidate to fulfil in order to qualify for privileged status: consistency of value (all works in the corpus must be equally worthy of serious consideration); conceptual coherence (however varied, the works must share a common theme); and stylistic unity (their artistic signature must be unmistakable) (Foucault 108–12). Now, it could be claimed that the Almodóvar 'signature' is akin to that of a fashion label, whose designer name magically adds 'distinction' to a previously anonymous cultural commodity (Bourdieu 171). But I would like, for a moment at least, to take seriously the possibility that the somewhat archaic virtues of consistency, coherence, and stylistic unity can still have critical purchase in the investigation of an oeuvre; and may indeed be significantly inflected by their placing within a queer context. And I intend to test this hypothesis by examining works by Almodóvar that have received no previous attention.

Reading the juvenilia

Almodóvar's seventeen features have been exhaustively studied. Indeed there are no fewer than six critical monographs on his work in English alone, of which the first edition of the first was published in 1994 (Smith *Desire*, Allinson, Edwards, Johnston, D'Lugo, and Acevedo Muñoz). There are also a large number of volumes of collected essays (e.g. Vernon and Morris) and interviews (e.g. Willoquet-

Maricondi) in many languages. But there remains a body of his early work that is wholly unknown and has received no scholarly (or, indeed, journalistic) attention: the short stories written in the 1970s that are held in fading, cyclostyled volumes in the manuscript room of Madrid's Biblioteca Nacional. I would like to give an account of one of these unpublished collections, 'Relatos' (shelf mark T49), attributed to 'Pedro Almodóvar Caballero' (a unique instance in which he uses his full name) and dated 19 July 1975, just four months before the death of the dictator Francisco Franco. As Almodóvar's earliest surviving work (his first feature would not be distributed theatrically until 1980; only one of his early super-8 shorts has been released on DVD), these narratives at the very least deserve proper scholarly attention and at most may give unique insight into their author's artistic development. The fact that one of those stories was further developed into an unproduced script that also survives in typescript makes it especially significant in examining Almodóvar's earliest modes of composition.

Six copies were made of the typescript 'Relatos'. It consists of eight stories of greatly varying length: the shortest is two folios, the longest nineteen. I shall give a brief account of each in the order in which they appear in the volume. In 'La vida por delante' ('The life ahead of you', 5 fols), which takes place in Almodóvar's native La Mancha, a young, romantic poet is killed in a traffic accident. His pragmatic girlfriend cheerfully escapes in the car with a stranger. The brief and sketchy 'La gorda Carmela' ('Fat Carmela', 2 fols) chronicles an obese woman's comic attempts at suicide, also in the countryside. In the lengthy and detailed 'Retrato superficial de la vida de Miguel' ('Superficial portrait of Miguel's life', 12 fols) we are told the life story of a man but with time running backwards. We thus begin with his emergence from the grave as a decrepit old man and end with his final retreat into his mother's womb as a baby. The longest text (19 fols), which I treat at the end of this chapter, has the clearest connections with Almodóvar's future cinema. 'La visita' ('The visit') tells the story of a beautiful drag queen who returns to her childhood seminary to confront the priest who had abused her as a young boy. 'La anunciación' ('The annunciation', 2 fols) is a sketch of a Virgin Mary who is updated as a housewife and receives the angel's visit while doing her laundry. 'La redención' ('Redemption', 14 fols) is a serious retelling of the story of Christ's Passion, which focuses on His relation with the thief Barrabas and ends with the two fleeing into the countryside before the Crucifixion has taken place. The briefest text, 'Las muletas olvidadas' ('Forgotten crutches', 1 fol.), shows the downside to a miracle cure: now the lame man can walk, the poor crutches are abandoned. Finally 'La anciana' ('The elderly lady', 4 fols), the story of an unlikely job opportunity, was rewritten as a short script. I return to this narrative in both its versions a little later.

There are some general points to be made here about these texts, which show evidence of four continuing and overlapping tensions. First, between the country and the city: although several stories treat the tedium of life in La Mancha (whose position in Almodóvar's imaginary is not so different to that of Andalusia in Muñoz Molina, that other cosmopolitan exile from the country) and 'La visita' takes place in rural Extremadura, the promise of an urban lifestyle is available even to the elderly lady in 'La anciana'. Secondly, the comic and the serious are crudely juxtaposed.

'La gorda Carmela' is based on farcical physical comedy that would be well received in the playground, while the existential angst of 'Retrato superficial' is worthy of Becket. Third come the secular and the religious. The replaying of Biblical narrative is surprisingly frequent here, in the young Almodóvar's versions of the Annunciation and the Passion (and perhaps of Christ's miraculous cures). The tone of these pieces echoes a contemporary work, the unexpectedly sober *Salomé* (1978), Almodóvar's only super-8 to be released on DVD. *Salomé* somehow manages to combine an unsalacious version of the titular story with a restaging of the sacrifice of Isaac. Finally, there is the question of narrative development and perspective. The most striking thing about 'Relato superficial' is of course its backward running plot, a technique that the young Pedro would share with established creators as diverse as Stephen Sondheim (*Merrily We Roll Along*), Harold Pinter (*Betrayal*), and Martin Amis (*Time's Arrow*). The distinctive feature of 'La redención' is that the perspective on the familiar Christ tale is the unfamiliar one of the thief who, in the Gospel at least, would be crucified beside him.

I would suggest, then, that these juvenilia reveal, in traditional auteurist style, continuing privileged themes that emerge fully fledged only in Almodóvar's latest and most sophisticated features. Thus having begun as a cinematic booster of Madrid, Almodóvar has latterly returned to his rural roots with some sensitivity, especially in *Volver* (2006). Having made his name with outrageous farces, he has increasingly acknowledged the tragic subtext of his features: *Hable con ella* (*Talk to Her*, 2002) ends in suicide, *La mala educación* in trauma and murder; no less than three recent films focus on the distressing condition of youthful coma or brain death (Kinder). The religious realm, disavowed in Almodóvar's early films of the Movida Madrileña (the cultural revolution of early 1980s Madrid), returns with a vengeance in *La mala educación*, which glories in the riches of Catholic iconography even as it attacks the hypocrisies of the Church. Likewise the washing of the inert body of the coma victim in *Hable con ella* clearly cites the deposition of Christ, a reference made explicit by the musical cue used in the sequence, which is entitled 'The Holy Sheet'. Finally, the formal concern for narrative structure and point of view has been fully exploited in the latest films. *Hable con ella* is told in a series of flashbacks within flashbacks; *La mala educación*'s tale of priestly abuse is told in a film within a film and from at least two conflicting points of view. And as a subtle and complex recreation of the horrors of the Dictatorship and the traumas of the Transition, this last film participates in that trend to 'resuscitate Franco' and replay recent history that we have seen in earlier chapters.

Two stories, two films, two prototypes

Having made a general argument for the importance of these unknown early and imperfect texts as plausible evidence for Almodóvar's auteur status (of the consistency, coherence, and unity of his work), we can go on to examine more closely the two stories that announce the queer current by which Almodóvar will be well known, abroad at least: 'La anciana' (the story that was rewritten as an early script) and 'La visita' (the story that was incorporated into both *La ley del deseo* of 1987 and *La mala educación* of 2004).

In the first story the opening situation of the unnamed protagonist is described as follows:

> Sentada en la cama, la anciana señora hojea con curiosidad el periódico. En la página de ofertas laborales hay algo que puede interesarla: SE NECESITAN SECRETARIAS DE 18 A 30 AÑOS — BUENA PRESENCIA — QUE TENGAN CONOCIMIENTOS DEL INGLÉS O FRANCÉS. SUELDOS A CONVENIR — PRESENTARSE EN ...
>
> — Esto puede ser lo que me conviene, piensa para sí, sonriendo pícaramente. Con el periódico entre las manos imagina, semidormida, lo que con toda seguridad se esconde bajo aquel anuncio. (fol 1)

> [Sitting on her bed the elderly lady curiously flicks through the newspaper. In the jobs vacant she finds something of interest: WANTED: SECRETARIES AGE 18–30 — GOOD APPEARANCE — KNOWLEDGE OF ENGLISH OR FRENCH. SALARY TO BE AGREED — PLEASE COME TO ...
>
> 'This could be just what I need,' she thinks to herself, smiling naughtily. Still holding the newspaper, and half asleep, she imagines what is surely hidden behind that advertisement.]

Note that there is no description of the location or contextual placing of the character here. Almodóvar moves straight on to her bizarre and touching fantasy: namely that this innocent advert is a cover for prostitution and the white slave trade in Beirut.

When the old lady goes for interview her attitude is described as 'suficiente y serena' ['self-controlled and calm'], but she is rudely dismissed by the employer: 'Largo de aquí, vieja loca [esto no es] un asilo' ['Get out of here, you crazy old woman. This isn't an old people's home'] (fol. 3). Almodóvar's conclusion is significant:

> Se siente desorientada, no quiere volver a su casa, donde la esperan sus criados, su viejo esposo enfermo, y la comodidad de una situación social privilegiada. Porque lo que ella desea es vivir, abandonar aquella rutina [...] decide volver a su casa pero sabe que en la primera ocasión lo dejará todo para siempre.
>
> — No es el único empleo interesante, ya encontraré otras cosas, la ciudad está llena de ocasiones ... FIN

> [She feels disorientated and doesn't want to go home, where she is awaited by her servants, her old sick husband, and the comforts of a socially privileged position. Because what she wants is to live, to abandon routine [...] she decides to go back home but she knows that the first chance she has she'll leave it all for ever.
>
> 'This isn't the only interesting job, I'll find something else, the city is full of opportunities ...' END]

This character is clearly the prototype for a recurrent figure in Almodóvar's features: the mature woman who seems to serve as a projection of gay male fantasies of escape from a repressive social order. We think of Luci in *Pepi, Luci, Bom*, the browbeaten housewife who leaves an abusive husband for masochistic ecstasy with teenage punkette Bom; the Mother Superior in *Entre tinieblas* (*Dark Habits*, 1983), engaged in a passionate romance with an unsuitable nightclub chanteuse; or even Carmen Maura's moving mother in *Volver*, who kills her husband, abusive once more, and impersonates a ghost for her estranged daughters.

Now, Almodóvar's sympathy for and empathy with such mature female characters are distinctive and transparent. But let us see how he develops this vestigial tale into a short script that remained unfilmed. 'El anuncio (título provisional)' (shelf mark T50247) is dated 14 June 1976 (i.e. one year after the collection of stories) and is divided into fourteen scenes. The first gives a much more elaborated and visualized account of the setting of the lady who is only now granted a name:

> Habitación de Doña Julia y su esposo. Hay dos camas separadas por una mesita. Doña Julia está en la cama más cercana a la ventana, recostada en su almohadón. Son las diez de la mañana, la luz propia de esta hora entra modosamente por la ventana. El matrimonio anda por los setenta años pero, por lo que puede verse, el tiempo ha tratado peor al marido que a la esposa. La habitación consta de rancios muebles, llenos de detalles familiares, religiosos, y 'deliciosamente femeninos'. La atmósfera de la casa es de una familia burguesa acomodada.
>
> Después de mirar varias páginas, la venerable señora encuentra algo que parece llamarle la atención. En la página de ofertas laborales hay un anuncio sobre el que la señora reposa pensativa la mirada... Doña Julia se quita las gafas y sonríe para sí como diciéndose, ya sé lo que se esconde detrás del anuncio. Dobla el periódico y semidormida deja vagar su imaginación (fol. 1)

> [The bedroom of Doña Julia and her husband. There are two beds separated by a table. Doña Julia is on the bed closer to the window, leaning up against her bolster. It's ten a.m. and the light appropriate to this time of day is smoothly coming through the window. The couple are about seventy but, as can be clearly seen, time has been less kind with the husband than it has with the wife. The bedroom is full of old-style furniture featuring details which are familiar, religious, and 'deliciously feminine'. The atmosphere is that of a comfortably off middle class family.
>
> After looking at a number of pages, the elderly lady finds something that seems to interest her. On the jobs vacant page there's an ad which the lady looks at pensively... Doña Julia takes off her glasses and smiles to herself, as if saying, 'I have a pretty good idea what's hidden behind this advertisement.' She folds the paper up and half-asleep lets her imagination wander.]

Here, unlike in the first version, precise details of mise en scene serve the purpose of not just class location (bourgeois comfort) but also of psychological explanation (the twin beds hinting at marital frustration, the 'deliciously feminine' details at an outdated style now available to be re-appropriated as camp).

At once more concretely objective and more emotionally subjective than the first version, this opening scene gives way to a detailed evocation of the old lady's fantasy: abducted from the interview room to a hotel in Morocco (fol. 6), soon Doña Julia is wowing the nightclub crowd as an unlikely diva: 'vestida explosivamente, sale a cantar Hava naguila' ['explosively dressed, she comes on stage singing Hava Nagila'] (fol. 7). A montage, the sequence most beloved of Hollywood biopic, shows Julia enjoying a diet of drugs, beatings, and triumphant musical performances that turn her into the 'reina de aquel antro' ['queen of that dive'] (fol. 9). She is rewarded with the passionate kisses of 'un apuesto joven' ['a strapping young man'] (fol. 10).

Awaking from her dream (minutely visualized by Almodóvar) Julia takes a taxi to the office, where she is, as before, rejected by the interviewer (11). Although she is close to tears Julia composes a letter to her husband before leaving home: 'Quiero llevar una vida independiente... espero que podamos seguir siendo buenos amigos' ['I want to lead an independent life... I hope we can still be friends'] (fol. 13). The script ends as follows: 'Se baja del taxi en la puerta de un hotel. Una nueva vida empieza para Doña Julia. FIN' ['She gets out of the taxi outside a hotel. A new life begins for Doña Julia. END'] (fol. 15).

What is fascinating here is to see how a premise that is rather unpromising from the cinematic point of view (tracing as it does a transformation that is internal and invisible) is now opened out by Almodóvar in strictly filmic terms through the newly precise mise en scene (the 'deliciously feminine' furniture), the explicit staging of fantasy (the Morocco sequences), the appeal to editing (classic montage), and the use of exterior locations (the taxi and hotel). It is telling that where before we were merely told that our heroine would at some point abandon the marital home, here we are actually shown her arriving at the hotel entrance, the gateway to a new life of urban opportunities. The sympathetic empathy of a twenty-something gay man for a seventy-year-old married lady is here combined with elements that now clearly belong to transnational camp: the divaesque performances and costumes that hark back to an era far indeed from the self-conscious modernity of contemporary Madrid. But this campy comedy is by no means cruel. As Almodóvar's subsequent career was to show, a genuine love for and admiration of heroines of a certain age will be a consistent feature of his signature style.

Let us go on to examine 'La visita', but beginning with the mature film versions of the narrative. In *La ley del deseo* (*The Law of Desire*, 1987) (Almodóvar's first self-production which lent its name to his production company, El Deseo), Carmen Maura's transsexual Tina returns to her old school chapel with her lesbian lover's daughter. With a tousled mane of hair, hoop earrings, and flamboyant red polka-dot dress, she is a vibrant parody of Spanish femininity. Advancing towards the camera which tracks back before her she sings, straight to camera, a hymn of praise to the Virgin, until the priest playing the organ comes into shot. As their dialogue begins the couple are held in two shot with the child playing behind. Almodóvar finally cuts into close up for more conventional shot reverse shot, as Tina reveals that she is that boy whom the over-affectionate priest has tried in vain to forget (Fig. 6).

There is some humour here (the priest asks Tina not to return to the chapel choir, please) and there is no evidence of real abuse. In Maura's subtle performance Tina is more melancholy than angry and, indeed, fiercely protective of the memories that are 'all [she] possesses'. Moreover she proclaims that she has not changed much since she was a boy, immune to the disappointment provoked by the men she loved, whether priests or fathers.

The revision of this scene in *La mala educación* is much more complex and sober. After drag queen Gael García Bernal's Zahara confronts Father Manolo in the chapel she pursues him to his office, where he is nostalgically studying a snapshot of the child Ignacio he abused. García Bernal's flowing locks seem to echo Maura's twenty years earlier and his performance is equally nuanced. Like Maura he advances towards the camera to confront the priest and their close-ups are nearly frontal in position (Fig. 7). A flashback within a flashback (or a script within a script) heralds

FIG. 6. Vengeful transvestites (I): Tina (Carmen Maura) in *La ley del deseo*

FIG. 7. Vengeful transvestites (II): Zahara (Gael García Bernal) in *La mala educación*

for the first time, however, a playing out of the primal scene of abuse itself. As the innocent child sings 'Moon River' (from the *Breakfast at Tiffany's* that Almodóvar so often cites as a camp classic), we cut to a slow-motion sequence of boys bathing in emerald water, a pastoral idyll whose brilliant light contrasts tellingly with the gloomy interior of the previous location. The point of view here is troublingly non-specific, but is best taken as the 'mindscreen' of the priest. Cutting back to the mismatched couple, Almodóvar chooses to hide the sexual act behind a clump of reeds. The fleeing child falls, cuts his forehead, and, in a showy digital effect, his face literally splits in two, the unambiguous sign of lasting psychic trauma.

Unlike in the earlier version there is no trace of comedy here. Ignacio-Zahara is also strangely unsympathetic, blackmailing the priest where Tina simply sought to relive her memories of past pleasures. And while Tina holds fast to that lost love, however disappointing, Ignacio-Zahara has rather been wounded by it, blaming her tragic destiny on that unwanted sexual aggression. That attitude will, moreover, become yet more complex when later in the film we discover that García Bernal's character is merely impersonating the abused child who was in fact the junky brother he will conspire to murder with another over-amorous priest. The play of reverse narrative movement and shifting perspective is one that we have glimpsed already in Almodóvar's early 'Relatos'.

How then do the mature movie versions of this compulsively repeated scene compare to their origin in the short story of 1975? Here there is a conspicuous defence of frivolity. The transvestite returns to the seminary to announce the death of his/her brother (as in *La mala educación*) but s/he is dressed as Dietrich in *The Devil is a Woman* (fol. 1). Later it is the priest who dons glitzy drag, wearing a 'red velvet gown' in the style of the 1950s (fol. 10) and kissing a *chulo* (a cute, cocky guy) at a party (fol. 16). Typically, however, this campy comedy is already cut with unexpected seriousness. The sexual abuse is explicit: in a flashback the child is forced to masturbate the priest, whose pubic hair is said to feel 'like dry grass in a field' (fol. 9), a disturbingly specific tactile reference. And Almodóvar provides us with two mutually contradictory endings: either the transvestite swishes out safely (like Tina in *La ley del deseo*) or (like Zahara in *La mala educación*) she is murdered by the priest who only then discovers s/he is the much-mourned brother (fol. 19). Almodóvar's ambivalence towards the scene, which permits no definitive ending, could hardly be more self-evident.

This constant cohabitation of comedy and tragedy is clearly one of Almodóvar's trademarks, even as his features became increasingly serious over the decades. And it is clear that this tendency, linked to his equally ambivalent feelings for his rural origins and Catholic education, form part of that formal continuity and thematic unity that would seem to qualify him as an old-fashioned auteur, even as he has exploited the commercially compromised resources of promotion and interview that is the sign of branding in contemporary cinema. Such commercial canniness may undercut Almodóvar's perceived cultural authority even as it supports his uniquely elevated media and social profile.

To conclude: I have argued that the two figures first found in the unpublished and rapidly fading typescripts of 'El anuncio' and 'La visita' (the mature, fantasizing woman and the glamorous, vengeful transvestite) can be read as structuring principles of Almodóvar's now extensive film corpus. But Almodóvar could hardly have anticipated that such idiosyncratic queer subject matter would provide the foundation for such a successful career. And, in spite of the compulsive repetition of some themes in his oeuvre (which, as we have seen, stretches over some thirty years) I am not suggesting that his extravagantly imaginative creations be reduced to mere symptoms of psychobiography. After all, many thousands of real victims of priestly sexual abuse have not succeeded in turning that trauma into artistic expression. More important perhaps is the evidence given by these unknown texts of Almodóvar's continuing exploration of fictional form: of narrative development and multiple points of view. If the child is indeed father to the man (as some of the more intrusive press interviews of Pedro have suggested [Mackenzie]), then the earliest creative works that survive by that man confirm that he is clearly a self-conscious artist as much as he is a successful self-publicist and reluctant queer auteur. And, as we shall see in the next chapter, Almodóvar's focus on the brutalized child is a key theme in contemporary Spanish cinema.

Works cited

ACEVEDO MUÑOZ, ERNESTO. *Pedro Almodóvar* (London: BFI, 2007)

ALLINSON, MARK. *A Spanish Labyrinth: The Films of Pedro Almodóvar* (London and New York: I. B. Tauris, 2001)

ALMODÓVAR CABALLERO, PEDRO. 'Relatos', unpub. ms. in Biblioteca Nacional, Madrid, 19 July 1975 (shelf mark T49)

——'El anuncio (título provisional)', unpub. ms. in Biblioteca Nacional, Madrid, 14 June 1976 (shelf mark T50247)

BOYERO, CARLOS. '¡Cuánto talento para la ortodoxia abusiva!' [review of *Todo sobre mi madre*] *El Mundo*, 16 April 1999

BOURDIEU, PIERRE. *The Rules of Art* (Oxford and Cambridge: Polity, 1996)

COOK, PAM. *The Cinema Book*, 2nd edn (London: BFI, 1991)

D'LUGO, MARVIN. *Pedro Almodóvar* (Urbana and Chicago: University of Illinois Press, 2006)

EDWARDS, GWYNNE. *Almodóvar: Labyrinths of Passion* (London: Peter Owen, 2001)

FOUCAULT, MICHEL. 'What is an Author?', in *The Foucault Reader*, ed. by Paul Rabinow (Harmondsworth: Penguin, 1986), pp. 101–20

GRANT, CATHERINE. 'www.auteur.com?' [*sic*], *Screen*, 41.1 (2000), 101–08

KINDER, MARSHA. 'Reinventing the Motherland: Almodóvar's Brain-Dead Trilogy', *Film Quarterly*, 58.2 (2004), 9–25

MACKENZIE, SUZIE. 'All About My Father', in Willoquet-Maricondi (ed.), pp. 154–61

MADDISON, STEPHEN. 'All About Women: Pedro Almodóvar and the Heterosocial Dynamic', *Textual Practice*, 14.2 (2000), 265–84

MIRA, ALBERTO. *Miradas insumisas: gays y lesbianas en el cine* (Barcelona and Madrid: Egales, 2008)

VERNON, KATHLEEN M., and BARBARA MORRIS (eds), *Post-Franco, Postmodern: The Films of Pedro Almodóvar* (Westport, CT: Greenwood, 1995)

RUSSO, VITO. 'Man of La Mania', *Film Comment*, 24.6 (November/December 1988), 13–17

SGAE [SOCIEDAD GENERAL DE AUTORES Y EDITORES]. *Hábitos de consumo cultural* (Madrid: SGAE, 2000)

SMITH, PAUL JULIAN. *Desire Unlimited: The Cinema of Pedro Almodóvar*, 2nd edn (London and New York: Verso, 2000) [1st edn 1994]

——'Resurrecting the Art Movie? Almodóvar's Blue Period', *Contemporary Spanish Culture: TV, Fashion, Art, and Film* (Oxford and Cambridge: Polity, 2003), pp. 144–68

TRIANA-TORIBIO, NÚRIA. *Spanish National Cinema* (London and New York: Routledge, 2003)

——'Auteurism and Commerce in Contemporary Spanish Cinema: *directores mediáticos*', *Screen*, 49.3 (2008), 259–76

WILLOQUET-MARICONDI, PAULA, ED. *Pedro Almodóvar: Interviews* (Jackson: University Press of Mississippi, 2004)

Web sources

FERNÁNDEZ SANTOS, ANGEL. Review of *La mala educación*, *El País*, 19 March 2004, <http://www.elpais.com/articulo/cine/perversidad/angel/elpepuculcin/20040319elpepicin_11/Tes)>, [accessed 20 October 2008]

HOLDEN, STEPHEN. Review of *La mala educación*, *New York Times*, 9 October 2004, <http://movies.nytimes.com/2004/10/09/movies/09bad.html?_r=1&oref=slogin>, [accessed 20 October 2008]

WEINER, ALLISON HOPE. 'Shyamalan's Hollywood Horror Story, with Twist', 2 June 2008, <http://www.nytimes.com/2008/06/02/business/media/02night.html>, [accessed 31 July 2010]

WIKIPEDIA. 'Pedro Almodóvar' [Eng.], <http://en.wikipedia.org/wiki/Pedro_Almodóvar>, [accessed 31 July 2010]

——'Pedro Almodóvar' [Sp.], <http://es.wikipedia.org/wiki/Pedro_Almodóvar>, [accessed 31 July 2010]

CHAPTER 5

Spanish Cinema's Missing Children

Juan Antonio Bayona's *El orfanato*
('The Orphanage', 2007) and
Jaime Rosales' *La soledad*
('Solitary Fragments', 2007)

Restoration and reflection

In her book *Cinema's Missing Children*, which treats films from across Europe and North America since 1990, Emma Wilson suggests that 'one of the central fears and compulsions explored in recent independent or art cinema is the death or loss of a child' (2). For Wilson this discrete topic opens out on to much wider fields of enquiry, posing questions 'about the protection and innocence of childhood, about parenthood and the family, about the past (as childhood is constructed in retrospect as nostalgic space of safety), and about the future (as fears for children reflect anxiety about the inheritance left to future generations)' (2). Although Wilson refers in her introduction to associations devoted to the plight of missing children in France and the United States (3), her concern is less social and political than psychic and emotional; and, neglecting popular films on the subject to focus on directors such as Egoyan, Almodóvar, and Todd Solondz, she is able to argue that her chosen texts 'conjure the fears and phantoms of our culture in ways that offer no easy solutions or redemptive closure' (4). The stylistic or narrative choices of such auteurs ('the refusal of (re)solution and often of action') correspond to specific modes of spectatorship ('a space for reflection and imaginative, emotive viewing') and indeed of ethics ('a mode of respect and reckoning with the difficulty of the subject treated') (4).

Now Wilson herself is highly sensitive to the concrete material implications of her topic, especially with regard to parents' sense of responsibility and even guilt at the loss of a child. Indeed in her analysis of the several and mutually contradictory critical accounts of Freud's 'dream of the burning child' (in Lacan, Žižek, and Cathy Caruth) she traces the inextricability of fantasy and reality, of dream and the waking state. And she relates the characteristic 'troubled vision' and 'hallucination' here (the parents' desire for an impossible animation after death) to the disavowals of cinema, which offers a 'material form' for the 'phantom of a missing child' (8).

Beyond wish fulfilment, however, Wilson's canon of art movies, which she subjects to subtle close readings in the ten chapters that follow, do not suggest 'relief, repair, or exit from the horror of the loss of a child'. Rather they seek to debate the meaning of such losses and to offer them 'cultural significance' (8). The popular 'restorative' fantasy of reunion with the child is thus contrasted with the 'reflective/ melancholic' vision of the auteur (14).

In this chapter, and basing myself on Wilson's pioneering study, I would like to address two Spanish films released in 2007 that lay claim to being, in their very different ways, the most representative of their nation and their year. J. A. Bayona's first feature *El orfanato*, generally taken to be a glossy horror film, was the biggest-grossing feature of the year (and the second biggest Spanish film of all time), with an audience of some four million that eclipsed even *Pirates of the Caribbean*. Jaime Rosales' second feature *La soledad*, a rigorous and experimental art movie, was seen on its first release by only 41,000 viewers, but, in the face of strong competition from the favourite *El orfanato*, it won the main Goyas awarded by the Spanish Film Academy for best feature and best director (*El orfanato* had to be content with craft awards and 'best new director') (Base de datos, 'El orfanato', 'La soledad').

As we shall see, in press coverage the two films were frequently mentioned in the same breath; and both became implicated in an unusually bitter debate on the nature and future of Spanish cinema as a whole. But I believe no critic noted that, in spite of transparent differences in the production, reception, and textual composition of the two films, they shared a common theme: the loss and death of a child, in both cases a small son. Opening out from Wilson's monograph on this theme, with its impeccable analyses of independent films, I intend to broaden discussion of the Spanish versions of her theme to embrace genre film, as well as art movie; and to reinsert psychic readings of loss, mourning, trauma, and (attempted) redemption (which clearly remain appropriate for both *El orfanato* and *La soledad*) within the industrial and institutional contexts which lent this mismatched couple of features such profound social meaning. Although I understand the missing child here primarily as symptomatic of contemporary social conditions (and both films are set in the present), critics have also linked the theme to the questions of memory and historicity that we have explored in literary, cinematic, and televisual texts treated in earlier chapters of this book.

An initial (and, I shall argue, erroneous) hypothesis is that the two films can be read as a simple dichotomy. Thus while *El orfanato* is held to represent commercialism and a powerful distribution strategy (it was exported to forty countries), *La soledad* embodies art and a solitary production process (it has, indeed, yet to secure theatrical distribution in the UK and USA, where it has been shown only in festivals). Or again, the first is thought to be a genre film, overly dependent on antecedents of the same ilk, while the second is thought to be auteurist, and thus held to be uniquely original (we set out some of these conditions of auteurism at length in Chapter 4). These preconceptions have further implications that are national and theoretical. The polished *El orfanato* is said, by Spanish critics at least, to be 'Hollywood-like' in form (although this term remains undefined), while the sober *La soledad* is thought to be faithful to the experience of everyday life in Spain (even though it aspires to the rarefied reaches of film art). Or again, the former film is said to be based on movement (hostile critics decry the mobility of Bayona's camera), while the latter is characterized by stillness, an immobility that forces the spectator to pay attention to the passing of time (in the theatre, as in the diegesis).

At this point one consecrated example of critical discourse will suffice: the post-Goya commentary by licensed maverick Carlos Boyero, the newly appointed senior film writer of *El País*, itself the most influential national daily and, as we saw in the previous chapter, a high profile detractor of Almodóvar (5 February 2008). Under a headline that makes rather puzzling use of an Anglicism ('La Academia se hace "cool"'), Boyero claims that *La soledad* is both 'insólita, poderosa, turbadora' ['unusual, powerful, disturbing'] and wholly ignored by the public ('no [la] ha visto ni dios' ['not a soul has seen it']), even though it had gained 'prestige' from critical praise and acceptance at Cannes. Conversely *El orfanato* is described dismissively as follows: 'Ese deslumbrante éxito comercial [...] un astuto cóctel de situaciones, personajes, e historias con transparente y molesto aroma a déjà vu' ['This dazzling commercial success [...] a canny cocktail of situations, characters, and stories with a strong and nasty whiff of déjà vu']. Boyero goes on to claim that 'ese éxito disfraza la eterna crisis del cine español' ['this success merely masks the endless crisis in Spanish cinema'] and to mock 'la sagrada excepción cultural' ['the holy cow of cultural exception'] much invoked by industry professionals. Hence while Boyero makes a strong statement of the superiority of the aesthetic over the commercial, he also laments the failure of the Spanish film industry, perpetually in crisis, and of state efforts to support it, generally held to be ineffectual.

While these distinctions (art vs commerce, etc.) remain themselves distinct, they coalesce in a broad critical consensus: *El orfanato*, for all its apparent novelty, engages in the repetition or recognition of preceding generic archetypes, while *La soledad* appeals to uniqueness and distinction both in its subject matter, however deceptively everyday, and its technique, however deceptively simple. My argument here is that, even as the press discussion of the films sought to give each a separate and stable social meaning, this hierarchized opposition (or struggle for cultural authority) was already under pressure in the Spanish cultural field; and that, on closer analysis, the founding opposition of art and commerce cannot account for either the production processes or the textual composition of the films themselves. As we shall see, the lost child becomes somehow conflated with Spanish cinema, a cherished but contested object whose very future is thought to be under threat.

Art, commerce, and temporality

It is of course Pierre Bourdieu who has treated at greatest length and with greatest subtlety the assumed conflict in the cultural field between art and commerce and the hierarchized oppositions to which that conflict gives rise. In *The Rules of Art*, his exhaustive study of French cultural industries in the nineteenth and twentieth centuries, Bourdieu calls attention to the 'antagonistic coexistence of two modes of production and circulation' that manifest an 'inverse logic' (143). The first is the 'anti-economic [i.e. anti-financial] economy of pure art' whose 'disinterestedness' reveals itself in the 'denial of economics'. Here short-term profits are rejected in favour of an autonomous production process that results, over time, in the 'accumulation of symbolic capital'. Conversely the 'economic' logic of artistic industries insists that trade in cultural goods is by no means exceptional and is 'just another trade'. Here the focus is on mass distribution, with 'immediate and temporary success' meeting the 'pre-existing demand of [an undemanding] clientele' (143).

As a social scientist, Bourdieu categorically rejects that rapturous aesthetic enthusiasm (the 'astonished abandon to the work [...] in its inexpressible singularity' [xv]) that Boyero expresses with regard to *La soledad*. And he traces the 'historical genesis' in the nineteenth century of the pure aesthetic and the heroic figure of the struggling autonomous artist, who makes an ethical break first with the bourgeoisie (61) and latterly with sponsorship even from the state (139). Seeking no moral or political reference or relevance, the pure artist becomes, for the first time, 'responsible only to himself', exploiting an 'inverted economy' in which the (monetary) loser takes all the symbolic profit (216).

On the one hand, then, there is no longer a correspondence between external hierarchization (social or financial success) and its internal equivalent (peer consecration) (217). But on the other hand, this institutional autonomy is inseparable from aesthetic purity: painting becomes 'a play with forms, values, and colours independent of any reference to transcendent meanings' (289). But institutional conflict and aesthetic evolution are not of course fixed but rather played out in and over time in rather complex ways. Bourdieu writes that 'agents and institutions engaged in the [cultural] game are simultaneously contemporaries and temporally discordant'; and that 'the appearance of a group capable of leaving its mark by establishing an advanced position is rendered by a shifting of the structure of the field of the present' (158). Or again: 'To impose a new producer, a new product, and a new system of taste on the market at a given moment means to relegate to the past a whole set of producers, products, and systems of taste', with 'each artistic act which leaves its mark [...] "displac[ing]" the entire series of previous artistic acts' (160).

These acts are described to Bourdieu by a contemporary painter as 'winks inside a milieu'. He himself glosses this phrase as 'silent and hidden references to other artists [...] affirm[ing] in and through the games of distinction a complicity the interrelations and interactions of which the work is just a silent trace' (161). There is thus a 'homology' or 'pre-established harmony' between artists, critics, and consumers made manifest in such unquestioned beliefs as the opposition between art and money: 'avant-gardism often offers no other guarantee of its conviction than its indifference to money and it spirit of contestation' (162).

Although Bourdieu briefly refers in this context to cinema (alongside theatre, painting, and literature) he does not treat the medium in any detail. Yet there is no doubt that Spanish film critics continue to reiterate the unthinking discursive limits (or 'habitus') explored in *The Rules of Art*. Thus, over the course of six months in which the paper repeatedly returned to the film (*El País*, Archivo: *El orfanato*) the best *El País* was willing to say of *El orfanato* was that it 'saved the Spanish box office from disaster' (4 February 2008), that it was chosen as the Spanish contender for the foreign-language Oscar (28 September 2007), and that it was to be remade in the US (6 October 2007). When the film failed to make the short list of those nominated by the US Academy, the decision was said by *El País* to be based on 'prejudices against genre films' (22 February 2008). Elsewhere the 'technical brilliance' of *El orfanato* was contrasted with the 'cine radical, cine de emociones, cine alejado de la concesión' ['radical and emotional cinema, a cinema that makes no concessions'] of *La soledad*, said to be an 'underdog' compared to its commercial rival (4 February 2008).

The horror film's impure aesthetic was even presented in terms reminiscent of Frankenstein's monster: 'un cuerpo hecho de piezas ensambladas [...] gratuitos samplers' ['a body made of pieces patched together [...] unmotivated samples'] (10 December 2007). The same piece assures discerning consumers that, based as it was on an original script that was not written by its director, *El orfanato* 'no es una obra de autor' ['is not the work of an auteur']. Another piece claims the two films cannot even be compared: while one is a 'perfect commercial product' the other demonstrates 'the rigour of life.' In its unremitting depiction of everyday activities shown almost in real time (queueing and cooking, arguing and ironing) *La soledad* simply 'speaks of life' (8 February 2008).

In a report on Jaime Rosales's acceptance speech at the Goyas, the director, who is described as 'sober and valiant' (10 February 2008), presented himself as part of a generation of experimental filmmakers from Catalonia at the 'antipodes of Hollywood' that included older auteurs Marc Recha and José Luis Guerín. Rosales is also said to be more concerned with time in cinema than with the time his films last at the box office. The auteur himself thus coincides with the rhetoric of *El País*'s various journalists, who are strikingly consistent in their accounts. In this inverted cinematic economy, it was the losers (Rosales and his downtrodden heroines) who took all the symbolic, if not the financial, capital.

Yet there are hints in the press itself of another more complex model of the cultural field in which art and commerce are not mutually exclusive and 'Spanish cinema', no longer taken for granted, can be called into question. In a piece called 'Esa cosa llamada "cine español"' ['That Thing Called "Spanish Cinema"'] (4 September 2007) Rosales himself notes that, like the arch commercialists Almodóvar and Amenábar, he benefits from working with his own production company (elsewhere he admits to having attended business school). One short piece decries the Spanish Academy's 'allergy' to box-office success (5 February 2008). Another reminds us of the lengthy and financially disadvantageous production process of *El orfanato* (19 November 2007) which confirms that Spanish screenwriters are subject to 'the law of the jungle'. After nine years of work Sergio Sánchez earned just 30,000 euros for writing a feature that had grossed 19 million by the time of the article. A 'red alert' over 'empty box offices' reminded Spaniards that, in a bad year like 2007, a national cinema can be dependent on a single title. While there was an unseemly battle between producer Tele 5 and the Ministry of Culture as to the accuracy of figures for *El orfanato*, it was reported that over a third of admissions to Spanish films in 2007 were for that one film (5 March 2008), even as the number of screens fell from 936 to 889 (16 January 2008). Curiously, as audiences retreated, a record 172 Spanish features were produced in that year, too many for the local market to absorb. Spanish cinema was thus said to be experiencing a 'Groundhog day':

recurrent isolated hits, such as *El orfanato* or Amenábar's *The Others*, with which it was frequently compared, built no momentum for the industry as a whole, which was obliged repeatedly to reinvent itself (3 December 2007).

This discussion, which acknowledged the necessary complicity between art and commerce (most especially in an industry still dependent on the public investment for which taxpayers were entitled to see evidence of accountability), fed into an acrimonious debate on the future of Spanish cinema. After *El País* published a bitter anonymous attack on a filmmaking establishment that failed to connect with local audiences, directors were given ample space to reply. In his spirited defence of Spanish cinema Alex de la Iglesia praised *El orfanato* for its outstanding commercial success (6 February 2008); and in a piece that asked what would happen 'if there were no Spanish cinema', Icíar Bollaín also lauded the film for attracting spectators who were only 'occasional' viewers of their own cinema (7 February 2008). Interestingly, Bollaín argues in terms of cultural exceptionalism (Spanish cinema should not be abandoned to American producers who have 'nothing to do with us'), yet she also appeals to purely commercial criteria (the alleged 'hundreds of thousands' of jobs dependent on the industry).

It is an ambivalence that can also be seen in *Fotogramas*, Spain's best-known cinephile magazine. Thus in November 2007 Sergi Sánchez welcomed the Academy's choice of *El orfanato*, a first-time director's audience-friendly feature, as Spain's Oscar hope, asking if the decision signified a 'radical change' from the past. In previous years Academicians had opted for consecrated directors who often treated nostalgic or historical themes. Here it is not the self-consciously avant-garde Rosales but the more reticent Bayona who is proclaimed the 'great hope of Spanish cinema'. Yet Sánchez also calls the film (like Amenábar's winning *Mar adentro* [*The Sea Inside*]) 'Spielbergized', claiming it is identical in its aesthetic to mainstream US horror films.

Fotogramas' review the previous month (Trashorras) had been equally ambivalent. First, it proclaimed that *El orfanato* pointed the way forward to the 'marriage' between industry and creativity that is 'necessary' in any national cinema; second, it attacked the film's 'Hollywood-style pseudo-mimesis' which aimed to please all sectors of the public; and third, it claimed that this unrepentant commercialism was relieved by three factors: Bayona's 'faith' in his dramatic material; his technical talent and boldness (as shown by a daring circular tracking shot); and his star Belén Rueda's passionately 'hormonal' performance (Fig. 8). Significantly, in interviews published in the same issue of the magazine, both Bayona (de Fez) and Rueda (Piña) attempt to distance their film from genre clichés. Thus Bayona argues that he and his screenwriter radically reworked horror conventions, adding depth and backstory (97). And Rueda is asked, somewhat intrusively, if the fact that she had in real life lost a small child made her performance in the film more 'painful' (94). Commercial filmmaking, it is suggested here, relies both on professional craft and personal commitment, the unique contributions offered by a group of creators rather than a single auteur.

Ironically, in interview with the French *Positif* (Peleato), the most auteurist of periodicals, Jaime Rosales acknowledges the vital contribution of his co-screenwriter

FIG. 8. Mourning mothers (I): Laura (Belén Rueda) in *El orfanato*

Enric Rufas (32–33). In canonic style, *Positif* recounts the apprenticeship of the heroic artist, who left bourgeois Barcelona for the 'third world' film school of Havana (31); contrasts his 'artistic way' with that of 'entertainment'; and confirms his discovery of the 'non-Hollywood canon' of Ozu, Bresson, Pasolini, and Tarkovsky.

What is striking here in the article and accompanying review (Ferrari) is that Rosales' pure aesthetic is consistently defined in negative terms that suggest the stripping away of resources. Denying depth of field, the image is made 'flat' (Ferrari 28–29); and rejecting camera movement, music, and dramatic action, the spectator is compelled to contemplate life as it is lived. Even a positive innovation (the rare use of split screen to give simultaneous, but distinct, perspectives on a scene) is presented negatively, as a refusal to impose a point of view (Pelleato 34). Similarly, the ideas of the film are 'hidden': a bus bomb in which a child dies goes unexplained, obscurely invoking the very different terrorist attacks on Madrid trains in 2004. We are also obliged to experience 'temporality' in takes that are wilfully held beyond their usual length (Pelleato 34). This apparent impersonality (shots are said to be 'neutral' and 'open') is, however, proclaimed a 'portrait of its author', who confesses that since the birth of his child he is newly preoccupied with the tension between life and death (Pelleato 35). As in Bourdieu, the autonomous author (the auteur) is inextricable from the purity of his aesthetic.

Before looking at the films themselves we can then briefly reread this critical discourse, which lends the films social life and meaning, in the light of Bourdieu's analysis of the cultural field. Rosales would at first seem to embody the 'anti-economic economy of pure art' with a vengeance. Yet he does not deny economics. Indeed, he is his own producer and insists that he draws up the budget himself. And his accumulation of symbolic capital has been unusually rapid (*La soledad* is just his second feature). Moreover, in spite of the absence of a mass audience for his work, there is clearly a pre-existing demand for his films, as shown by the ready acceptance of them by the most prestigious critics. In traditional avant-garde style, his purist aesthetics tends to reduce the art object to a play of light and form (critics discuss his frame compositions at length) and renders political and social reference problematic (even a terrorist outrage is somehow made non-specific).

It is characteristic that *La soledad* refuses to engage directly with the death of the child, leaving an ellipse where the most emotional scenes (the aftermath of the bombing, the funeral) might have been expected. With no transcendent meaning allowed to surface, we are thus left, ironically perhaps, with the evidence of everyday life as it plays out in time, a somewhat surprising subject for a film that through its consecrated references to European masters aspires to the status of timeless art.

This latter aspect raises the question of temporality so central to Bourdieu. While it could be argued that Rosales and his faithful critics attempt to impose a new system of taste on an unwilling market, the mute references in *La soledad* to Ozu and Bresson affirm a complicity with the old masters, rather than an attempt to dispatch them to the past. Indeed it might be suggested that it is not Rosales but Bayona who is attempting to introduce a new aesthetic regime to the Spanish audiovisual establishment, one which champions an impure aesthetic and unconsecrated genre filmmaking over the European art-house tradition. Given the new awareness of the commercial dimension of cinema which we have seen intermittently in the press and the heightened concern that state-sponsored cultural industries should give taxpayers value for money, such a project would involve a shifting of the structure of the field of the present rather similar to that once mounted by the avant-garde. Certainly the violent reactions of some critics to Bayona's success would suggest that *El orfanato* constitutes something of a challenge to the 'pre-established harmony' between artists, critics, and (the more distinguished) consumers which had hitherto been taken for granted.

Evidence for this emerging shift in the field thus comes from Spain, where Bayona's film received all but the most prestigious prizes and hence managed to combine to a large extent, and in spite of loud complaints from *El País*, external and internal hierarchization (financial success and peer consecration). But it also comes from abroad. Launched in the wake of the highly successful *El laberinto del fauno* (*Pan's Labyrinth*), and aided by Guillermo del Toro's status as the film's 'presenter', *El orfanato* was successfully marketed by canny British distributors to both youthful genre aficionados and the mature audiences who favour specialist foreign movies (Gant). The dual logic of art and commerce was thus suspended at a time when changes in the distribution of foreign films were widely debated.

Moreover, according to the US co-producers of *El orfanato*, the old opposition between America and Europe no longer held in current industrial practice. In a report titled 'Hollywood Looks for Local Heroes', part of its 'Review of the Year', trade journal *Screen International* wrote in December 2007 that the trend for major studios to play 'an integral part in the production process' of foreign language features was now 'poised to explode' (Kay 26). The first example cited is precisely *El orfanato* (others come from Mexico, India and Japan). One executive says that 'we believe in each territory and never want to homogenize product'; and that the broad 'mandate is to make local product with local people and talent in each territory' (27). In the specific case of *El orfanato*, Warner Bros' executive vice-president of international also claims that the focus was from the start on the home market, not the global. The film's modest budget (given here as $4 million) was adjusted to 'the [financial] range appropriate' for Spain; and the aim is always to 'do whatever is good for that country'. It thus follows that the primary reason for a Hollywood co-production in a foreign territory is no longer the film's potential to 'travel' abroad (27).

Screen International's praise of Warner's 'vast experience with local-language co-production', which had helped *El orfanato* to a gross of $33 million at that time, tends to downplay the role of Spanish partner Tele 5, which has an enviable track record with local audiences in both television and film (I treat three successful series broadcast by the private web in Chapters 8 and 9). But it is clear, that even at the level of the purely economic, the 'Spielbergization' of Spanish film, which *Fotogramas* still claims to recognize in *El orfanato*, is no longer an attractive strategy for multinational studios. With the North American market 'stabilized', they now attempt to tailor their product to fit the tastes of still growing international audiences.

Conversely, a home-grown production like *La soledad* (made, we remember, by the director's own production company) is highly dependent on the 'winks' to international auteurs that the more distinguished art-house audiences and critics (in *Positif*, as in *El País*) can pride themselves on recognizing. Arguably, it is less clearly integrated into a national cinema (less precisely calibrated to local audiences and local tastes) than an apparently delocalized genre piece like *El orfanato*. It is telling that the limited distribution history in the UK of *La soledad*, feted as a 'masterpiece' in Spain, reveals a certain tension over national origin. The film was first shown at three select venues (London, Liverpool, and Bath) under the rubric 'A Celebration of European Cinema', in a scheme funded by the EU's MEDIA programme. One aim of MEDIA is to raise the market share of 'non-national European films' in neighbouring countries beyond the current stubbornly low rate of 10%. The small season was called 'Common Language' and claimed to 'celebrate the universal language of film' ('Common Language').

Conversely, *La soledad* was also shown just days later at the fourth edition of the London Spanish Film Festival. Here it was said to belong to 'a 'new wave' in Spanish cinema — low-key, low-budget indie films dealing with contemporary themes' (4th London). Like Rosales himself, the festival organizer also cites the veteran José Luis Guerín in this context. The abstract minimalism of *La soledad* thus proved to be surprisingly mobile, presented by rival exhibitors in the same month and the same city as an example of international art-house (indeed, as a 'non-national' film) and as a localist indie addressing social issues.

Evidence for Spanish consumer reception of the two films comes from specialist website hoyCinema ('Comentarios'). One year after the films' release, it is no surprise that *El orfanato* has received many more comments than *La soledad* (1255 versus 437); nor that viewers, most of whom have watched DVDs at home, are by a large majority hostile to the second film, attacking its slow pace and everyday subject matter, and expressing their anger or embarrassment that such a film should be named best picture at the Goyas and be subsidized by the Spanish taxpayer.

What is striking, however, is that the consumer comments, mainly positive, on *El orfanato* testify to a closer attention and analysis of the film on the part of ordinary spectators. Viewers state that they watched it several times and engage in vigorous debate over their favoured and competing interpretations of its enigmatic plot. In parallel with the mixed signals we saw in Spanish press responses (which showed some awareness that art and commerce were not necessarily incompatible), so evidence from Spanish audiences (or at least from those active enough to post their comments on internet forums) reveal that a popular genre film can elicit a more active engagement than an austere art movie.

Having examined the production and reception of these two very different features we can now return to the films themselves. My aim is both to integrate Bourdieu-style institutional analysis with close readings in the style of Wilson; and to read details of textual composition (of narrative and film form) in the light of the films' common and problematic premise: the missing child.

The aesthetics of lost objects

> Laura regresa con su familia al orfanato en el que creció de niña con la intención de abrir una residencia para niños discapacitados. La película es un viaje emocional, el del personaje de Laura, más que una película de terror. En este viaje, Laura rememora recuerdos de su niñez [...]. El nuevo entorno despierta la imaginación de su hijo que comienza a dejarse llevar por juegos de fantasía cada vez más intensos. Estos van inquietando a Laura progresivamente hasta el punto en el que llega a pensar que hay algo en la casa está amenazando a su familia. (hoyCinema, 'El orfanato')

> [Laura returns with her family to the orphanage where she grew up as a child intending to open a home for children with special needs. More than a horror movie, the film is an emotional journey, following the character of Laura. During this journey Laura re-experiences memories of her childhood [...]. The new environment awakens the imagination of her son who starts to be carried away by fantasy games that grow more and more intense. These games disturb Laura so much that she begins to think that something in the house is threatening her family.]

> Adela, una joven separada y con un hijo de un año de edad, está cansada de la vida que lleva en su pequeño pueblo natal al norte de León. Deja atrás las montañas y los paseos por los prados para trasladarse a Madrid donde todo es ruido, tráfico y un continuo vaivén de un lado a otro. Para salir adelante se busca un trabajo de azafata y se muda a un apartamento junto a Carlos e Inés, dos jóvenes muy agradables. Los tres se llevan muy bien en seguida, compartiendo comidas, dudas y ratos de ocio. Antonia, la madre de Inés, tiene un pequeño supermercado de barrio. Lleva una vida bastante tranquila junto a su novio, Manolo, y sus tres hijas: Inés, Nieves y Helena, la mayor. Sin embargo, poco a poco, su placentera vida empieza a tambalearse. Primero, los médicos detectan un cáncer incipiente en su hija Nieves. Más tarde, la ya tensa relación entre sus hijas se complica aún más cuando Helena le pide prestado dinero a su madre para comprarse un piso en la playa. Adela no ha tenido grandes dificultades para adaptarse a la vida urbana, a pesar de que el padre de Miguelito no le ayuda demasiado económicamente. Un atentado terrorista, mientras viaja en autobús,

dejará su vida hecha añicos. A partir de ese momento deberá encontrar la fuerza para regresar a una vida normal. (hoyCinema, 'La soledad')

[Adela, a young woman separated from her partner and with a son just one year old, is fed up with life in her small home town in the north of León. Leaving behind the mountains and country walks she moves to Madrid, which is full of noise, traffic, and constant bustle. To eke out a living she gets a job as a hostess and shares a flat with Carlos and Inés, two very nice young people. The three get along well together from the start, sharing meals, problems, and spare time. Antonia, Inés's mother, owns a small neighborhood supermarket. She lives quite a quiet life with her partner Manolo and her three daughters: Inés, Nieves, and the eldest Helena. However, little by little, her pleasant life starts to fall apart. First, doctors detect an early-stage cancer in daughter Nieves. Later the tense relationship between the sisters gets even more complicated when Helena asks to borrow money from her mother to buy a flat by the seaside. Adela hasn't had much trouble adapting to life in the big city, in spite of the fact that Miguelito's father doesn't help her much with money. A terrorist attack on a bus will shatter her life into tiny pieces. From that moment she'll have to find the strength to get back to a normal life.]

Over the course of 2007–08, when *El orfanato* and *La soledad* were released, short-listed for various prizes and awards, and repeatedly discussed in the cultural press, there was continuing coverage in Spain of real-life issues concerning the loss, abandonment, and trafficking of children (*El País*, Archivo: 'orfanato'). The majority of these news stories originated in distant lands. Thus, following Madonna's contested adoption of a child from Malawi (29 August 2007), *El País* reported on 'anomalies' in the care for and adoption of orphans in Ethiopia (17 December 2007; 5 February 2008) and on a French NGO's attempt to export children from an orphanage in Chad (29 October 2007; 16 January 2008). Colombian terrorists were found to have placed the stolen child of a kidnap victim in an orphanage (7 January 2008), while the long-running investigation into sexual abuse and murder at an orphanage in the Channel Islands was headlined 'Torture in Paradise' (3 December 2007). Ukrainian orphans were treated to holidays in Catalan homes (30 July 2007), but, less gratifyingly, Chinese authorities imposed new restrictions on international adoptions from local orphanages (4 May 2008). (Similar anxieties over population movements also register in the Spanish cinema and television on immigration, as we shall see in the next chapter.)

Some stories came closer to home. Adopted Spanish kids were said to 'stumble' at school, with every four months in an orphanage leading to one month's loss of educational level (4 March 2008). Other children were alleged to have been 'returned' to Spanish orphanages by adoptive parents who had encountered 'heartbreaking misunderstandings' with their new charges (16 January 2008). An abandoned son, raised in a Spanish orphanage, requested the exhumation of his presumed dead father for DNA analysis (13 June 2008), while the Isla de San Simón, a notorious Francoist detention centre and latterly orphanage in Galicia, was newly opened up to guided tours (7 June 2008). Finally, the practice in Spanish hospitals of separating the newborn from their mothers for the first hours of life was criticized by a pressure group, which claimed that skin-to-skin contact was vital even for vulnerable premature babies (13 July 2008). Disconcertingly, this sympathetic piece on their campaign was run under a headline that asked whether a mother's love was 'only chemical' (i.e. based on bonds forged by physical contact immediately after birth).

The different forms of separation between mother and child, however temporary in this last case, thus gave rise in the press to more general anxieties about parenthood and the family, about the troubled legacy of the past and the problematic promise of the future. And they also focused on the relation between a changing Spain and a developing world seen as the source of a traffic in or a transfer of missing children. Newly visible, the latter seemed not just vulnerable but also disturbingly mobile. While a British critic like María Delgado reads *El orfanato* within the metaphorical context of the ghosts of the Civil War and the exhumation of collective graves (uncited in the film itself), it could be argued that the heightened contemporary awareness of the actual plight of missing, dead, or displaced children, abroad as in Spain, is an equally relevant and resonant context for the premise of *El orfanato*, as of *La soledad*.

Let us look more closely at the narrative structure and film form of both features. As we have seen, in the case of *El orfanato*, a first feature from the director, stress was placed in publicity on the lengthy apprenticeship of the creative team, including the screenplay, which was subject to repeated revisions. Although the plot can be read it terms of a dynamic three-act structure (and contains opening and closing sequences that 'frame' the main action), it is also characterized by symmetries and repetitions. Thus in the prologue to the film the child Laura plays tag with her young companions, while at the end the adult Laura summons up their ghosts with the same ritual words and gestures. Or again, the treasure hunt with adopted son Simón, in which resonant objects (a doorknob, a key) are vertiginously substituted for one another, is repeated by mother Laura alone when she believes it will solve the riddle of his disappearance. And of course the uncanny revenant (the deformed child Tomás, who wears a sack over his head) is seen both in the faded home movies of a distant era and in the lushly shadowed and digitally tweaked photography of the present.

But the most complex aspect of the script was its attempt to sustain ambiguity (the 'intellectual uncertainty' also cited by Freud in context of the uncanny [341]) until the very end: all of the events we are shown can be read as either supernatural or susceptible to rational explanation. Bayona and Sánchez took care to balance Rueda's increasingly disturbed mother (and Geraldine Chaplin's terrifying psychic) with more sceptical witnesses, such as Laura's ineffectual husband and the pragmatic social worker who joins the hunt for the missing child.

The 'making of' documentary on the DVD stresses the sheer labour involved in the visual side of the production, as in its script. And it is no accident that the film won awards in craft categories, such as the special effects make-up created by Catalan company DDT (winner of the Oscar for *El laberinto del fauno* in the previous year). This sense of a collective commitment to excellence is shown in the press, where star, screenwriter, and director are each respectfully interviewed (Rosales, on the other hand, is generally given full credit as auteur for *La soledad*). Rueda in particular, familiar as a jobbing actress in television (she starred in *Los Serrano* which I treat in Chapter 8), was praised for her new achievement as a performer: no longer the 'good time girl' of TV drama and sitcom, she had transformed herself into a fully fledged dramatic actress, profiting from a full three months of rehearsal before the shoot. A carefully crafted script, a meticulous production design more typical of serious drama than horror, virtuoso performance and shooting style (that mobile camera), and a lush orchestral score thus all come together to suggest a 'quality' work that surpasses its lowly genre origins.

Consistent with this sobriety is the final twist to a complex plot. Where distinguished predecessors such as *The Sixth Sense* (M. Night Shyamalan, 1999) and *The Others* (Alejandro Amenábar, 2001) revealed, finally, that the characters that the audience took to be real (Bruce Willis's reassuring psychotherapist, Nicole Kidman's overprotective mother) were in fact themselves fantastic apparitions, *El orfanato* takes the opposite route. A quick cut montage late in the film reveals that the missing child was not abducted by ghostly companions but had simply been trapped in a cellar from which he could not escape (that missing doorknob, once more).

Moreover in a move more typical of Wilson's art-movie corpus than of crowd pleasing genre pictures, there is no attempt at restoration of the broken family and no reparation for the now definitive loss of the son. With the help of the pills she is shown to be taking in great numbers, Laura escapes into psychosis and death, comforted only (as in Freud's dream) by the fantasized reanimation of the dead child. While this conclusion suggests perhaps that the emotional is as much part of the real as the prosaically rational (Laura is consistently more compelling than her doubting husband), the banal cruelty of the cause of the tragedy, unguessed at even by Geraldine Chaplin's psychic, suggests a return to the everyday world of domestic accidents and a farewell to the fantastic realm of invisible friends and ghostly enemies.

El orfanato, then, is relatively reticent. Certainly, unlike other horror films released at the same time, it features almost no explicit gore. Yet it is not surprising that Bayona's earnest professionalism did not win it greater peer consecration and critical kudos. As Bourdieu notes, at least since Duchamp signed a urinal and thus transformed a found object into an artwork, craft has not been recognized as a criterion for creative originality. On the contrary the 'pure aesthetic' of the avant-garde had progressively denuded art of the opportunities in which the academic painter could display his hard won professional skills.

La soledad, on the other hand, seems to confirm the avant-gardist rejection of the technical virtuosity that is celebrated in and by *El orfanato*. Its apparently casual plot juxtaposes two strands that, spurning the complex causal connections of *El orfanato*, barely coincide. In the first, young mother Adela, separated from her partner Pedro, relocates from the provinces to Madrid with her son Miguelito. There she moves in with Inés, the daughter of the widowed Antonia, who has two other daughters. The relationship between Antonia and her three children constitutes the second plotline.

Although the leisurely pace and slow unfolding of the narrative at first seem random, *Variety* noted parallels between the stories of the two mothers (Holland).

For example the neglectful father Pedro asks his ex-partner Adela (played by the little known Sonia Almarcha) for money (he fails to pay child support) and daughter Helena asks the same of her mother Inés (with the frivolous aim of buying a holiday home). In the 'carefully wrought script', each strand, writes *Variety*, 'becomes a commentary on the other, dealing with issues such as selfishness, greed, ambition, and emotional manipulation.' Inaccurately predicting that the 'pic [was] likely to find some companionship in offshore arthouses', the US trade paper coincides with the Spanish dailies and French monthly cinephile magazines in praising the 'beauty' and emotional 'intensity' of the film.

There is a contradiction here, however. On the one hand (and in line with the rigours of a pure aesthetic) 'all of the drama is under the surface'. And the fact that, unlike Rueda, actresses of *La soledad* are relatively unknown makes it easier for their performances to be read as perfectly naturalistic. But on the other hand, some aspects of the film's narrative and technique (critiqued by *Variety*, amongst others) are almost embarrassingly self-evident. Thus Adela's initially aimless plotline turns on a bus bombing in which her baby son Miguelito is killed. However abstractly this event is depicted and however indefinitely it is framed (we never discover if the perpetrators are Al Qaeda or ETA), the attack clearly alludes to the most dramatic and bloody event in recent Spanish history, the train bombings of 2004 that are known in shorthand as '11-M'.

Moreover much of this lengthy and leisurely film (some thirty minutes longer than *El orfanato*) is shot with what *Variety* calls 'determined experimentalism' in split screen (Spanish 'polivisión'). It is a technique more showy than any in *El orfanato* and one which lends the everyday activities so minutely depicted a gloss of self-conscious avant-gardism. Indeed more than one critic compares this rare technique to Cubism. Breaking with what he dismisses as the 'Fordism' of the conventional shot/counter shot, Rosales strips down feature film to a bare minimum of resources. But while he refuses to allow his audience narrative conflict and development, camera movement and close ups, actorly performance and music, he still employs ostentatious distancing techniques which tend to alienate the spectator from the fictional world his camera observes so patiently. Moreover the sudden intrusion of traumatic violence into daily routine risks becoming an auteuristic tic. Rosales's debut, the carefully named *Las horas del día*, juxtaposed the banal financial and personal problems of its unexceptional hero with the brutally sudden and unmotivated murders that he inexplicably commits.

How is it, then, that critics speak so consistently of the emotional effect of a film that relies so heavily on the negative qualities of absence, distance, and ellipsis? One answer comes once more from Bourdieu. In the uncharacteristic close reading of Faulkner that closes *The Rules of Art*, Bourdieu argues that the novelist institutes a new kind of chronology that has to be reconstructed by the reader (327). In a rather similar way, Rosales relies on his patient and complicit viewers (familiar like *Positif* with Deleuzian time-image) to supply the action and the feeling that he has so rigorously excluded from the film itself. Emblematic here are the so-called 'empty shots' which begin and end the film (depopulated rural and urban landscapes) which are 'filled' by competent viewers who recognize them as an homage (in Bourdieu's word a 'wink') to Ozu. Certainly such spectators deserve some kind of reward for surviving Rosales's punishingly long takes. While *El orfanato* is surprisingly austere, its cinematic craft still provides all viewers with transparent visual and narrative pleasures. Conversely, it is *La soledad*'s uncompromising (or 'determined') refusal of gratification that inspires elite spectators to join the director in proclaiming it a masterpiece.

It was Freud who wrote, in the essay on the uncanny once more, that repetition is a 'compulsion powerful enough to overrule the pleasure principle' (360). Prolonged and repeated exposure to films such as those by Rosales confirms that unpleasurable sensations can become a reliable source of pleasure for some spectators, if only they are repeated often enough. Certainly it requires a lengthy, if self-regarding, apprenticeship in cinephilia to enjoy recognizing Rosales' references and thus to transform his minimalist version of the everyday into an aesthetic which is 'privileged' in both the artistic and the social senses of the word. But it is the two films' treatment of the climactic moment of the death of the child that shows the most revealing differences and leads us back to Wilson's study, with which I began.

The refusal of resolution

> Cuando algo muy terrible ocurre en un lugar a veces queda una huella, una herida, que sirve de nudo entre dos líneas de tiempo — como un eco que se repite una y otra vez.
>
> [When something terrible happens in a house there remains a trace, a wound that serves as a knot between two timelines — like an echo repeated over and over again.] (Aurora, the psychic, in *El orfanato*)

In neither *El orfanato* nor *La soledad* do we see the death of the child, the event that has a good claim to be the most significant turning point in both narratives. After the young Simón disappears, we are shown Laura's fierce distress, plunging into the waves when she fears he is with his imaginary friend in a cave cut off by the rising sea. In the second half of the film, maternal emotion is more constrained as Laura retreats deeper into fantasy and memory. When she finally discovers Simón's body in the classical 'terrible place' that it the cellar, Bayona alternates between subjective and objective points of view. Thus, in heartrending fantasy, the child at first appears identical to when he disappeared and addresses his mother as she cradles him. He then returns to the all too physical corpse that he has in fact become. Finally the lost object is regained once more, as Laura gathers to her the ghostly children, including her own child and the disfigured Tomás. While readily legible by an attentive audience, this editing technique has something in common with *La soledad*'s 'Cubist polyvision', in its presentation of a double perspective that resists simple resolution.

The mother's guilt over the death of the child thus appears to provoke a restorative fantasy of reunion. But it is one that is possible only in death, as is underscored by the final sequence in which Laura's now widowed husband lays flowers on the common grave of his wife and adopted son. The phantom of the missing child's

FIG. 9. Mourning mothers (II): Adela (Sonia Almarcha) in *La soledad*

return in (apparently) physical form (of his impossible animation after death) is thus a clear example of the 'troubled vision' characteristic of the disavowals and wish-fulfilments of dream and of cinema. But Laura's desire to protect her child is also her desire to regress and be a child: the lost children, murdered and incinerated by a crazed worker, recognize her as one of their own when they reassemble at the film's close. *El orfanato* is thus sceptical of a nostalgia for childhood that can leave no legacy to the future and takes care to open a space for reflection on the mortal dangers of confusing fantasy and reality.

In *La soledad* we are privy neither to the death of the child nor to his potential rebirth in memory and fantasy. After a lengthy and typically inconclusive scene in which Adela meets an acquaintance on the bus as she holds Miguelito on her lap, Rosales cuts to an extreme long shot of the bus from outside. From this distance we see only a puff of smoke and anonymous figures fleeing out of frame and hear only a muted explosion and indistinct shouts. While the shooting style denies the material reality of a terrorist attack (shown all too graphically in TV footage of the real-life 11-M) and avoids the perhaps coercive emotivity of the fictional recreation of mutilated bodies, it attempts to reinsert the deadly, exceptional event into the flow of everyday temporality. Indeed Rosales himself claims that the film's modest moral is one of survival, that 'life goes on', for some, if not all.

After a lengthy and disconcerting ellipsis (the child's death is never openly mentioned), we are shown the unspeakable violence only in the wounds it has left in the mother's body and psyche at an unspecified time later. Solemnly she showers, keeping her braced and injured arm out of the flow of water. And a renewed attempt at sociability first proves fruitless: Adela's flatmates struggle to keep conversation going at the dinner they have kindly prepared for her (Fig. 9).

Here, as elsewhere, Rosales' definition of 'solitude' is existential rather than social. It is striking that the city is not held responsible for urban isolation or, indeed, for a terrorist violence that seems more a random force of nature than a politically motivated act. Rosales' refusal of (re)solution and, indeed, of dramatic action even *in extremis* (so reminiscent of Wilson's auteurs) thus leaves open a yet wider and more challenging space for reflection and imaginative, emotive viewing than that offered by *El orfanato*. It is one that is implicitly ethical in its respect for the difficulty of the subject treated and is made manifest by his camera's refusal to intrude on public tragedy and private grief.

But the deaths of the children in each film are not the only ones. Simón's loss and fantasized reanimation are juxtaposed with the fate of his mother Laura, with her retreat into psychosis and suicide. Miguelito's unseen murder is paralleled in *La soledad*'s second narrative strand by the death of the older widow Antonia. In split-screen once more we are made to watch at length as she takes in the washing from the balcony. Almost out of shot, she then slowly collapses on the bedroom floor, her limbs trembling in the mute agitation that seems to signal stroke. There is no camera movement, no music, and (because of the discreet distance kept by the camera once more) no view of her face. This 'natural' death, which is once more integrated into the sights and sounds of the everyday life that unthinkingly continues around it, contrasts with the clearly 'unnatural' death of Laura, experienced in a drug-fuelled fantasy that is bathed in uncanny light and lushly underscored. But in spite of his rejection of transcendent meaning, so typical of the avant-garde, it is Rosales and not the more rapturous Bayona who gestures towards a modest overcoming of traumatic circumstance: the temporality of the everyday is implicitly dignified by the awareness of mortality, in acknowledgement of the inevitable loss of loved objects, whatever their age.

One final point of contact between the films is that neither uses the death of the child to suggest, in conservative style, that social change is a threat to the family (Wilson 154). For in both, traditional family structures are always already lost: Laura is an orphan who has adopted another orphan, and one who already faces mortal illness (Simón is HIV-positive); Adela is separated from Miguelito's neglectful father even before the film begins. And as a grieving mother, she is shown to depend more on the kindness of urban strangers (the flatmates she has met only recently) than on her rural family back home. There is even a hesitant renewal of urban sociability by the end of the film. Laura revisits the park café where she had once gone with her child and chats with the waitress. Her irreparable loss is thus folded back into a collective social world that, inevitably, fails to recognize it. The difference with *El orfanato*'s spectral tea party, when a crazed Laura attempts to summon the lost children back to *The Orphanage*, is striking. Unlike Bayona, Rosales allows us the possibility of individual survival after loss and trauma, however fragile and fragmented the society in which that survival must take place.

Hence while Rosales, in line with Bourdieu's autonomous artists, makes no overt political statement, he does gesture towards a certain ethical humanism that goes beyond the purist formalism of light, line, and colour. It is at the very least a contribution that his audience has proved willing to make to a film that remains so wilfully unresolved. Yet it is not clear how *La soledad* can, as some have claimed, mark the beginning of a new movement or generation in Spanish cinema, when it is clearly indebted to the transnational avant-garde that is so familiar to critics and cinephiles, if not to mass audiences. And I have argued that Bayona's vindication of the impure aesthetics of the genre film, newly allied to the painstaking professional craft that was acknowledged by audiences and Academicians alike, might better embody Bourdieu's 'logic of change' in the field of the present. Certainly both films silently employ 'winks' inside their milieux, affirming through their different games of distinction or quest for cultural authority a certain complicity with their respective audiences.

We should thus look critically at the forms of consecration and legitimation employed by the Spanish press, even as those subjective dispositions change over time in step with objective industrial and artistic conditions. But it is by no means clear what can count as 'evidence' for social trends in texts whose meaning is produced within the cultural field. In the next chapter I will argue that it is television, not cinema, that has greater authority to embody the private life of a society, whether addressing missing children or equally troubling migrants. But the fact that *El orfanato* and *La soledad*, two films that are at once so different and so similar, treat an identical theme makes it possible to argue, following and expanding on Wilson's thesis, that the death or loss of a child is indeed one of the central fears and compulsions explored in Spanish popular and art cinema. Moreover, the critical response to the two films suggests that, as a quintessential genre film and art movie, each represents a form of reparative fantasy for that cherished and contested object which is so regularly lost and re-found: Spanish national cinema.

Works cited

BOURDIEU, PIERRE. *The Rules of Art* (Cambridge: Polity, 1996)
'Common Language: A Celebration of European Film' [Programme], 30 May–5 June 2008
DE FEZ, DESIRÉE. 'Entrevista: J. A. Bayona', *Fotogramas*, October 2007, p. 97
DELGADO, MARÍA. Review of *El orfanato*, *Sight & Sound*, April 2008, pp. 44–45
FERRARI, JEAN-CHISTOPHE. Review of *La soledad*, *Positif*, June 2008, pp. 28–30
4TH LONDON SPANISH FILM FESTIVAL, *Programme*, 6–20 June 2008
FREUD, SIGMUND. 'The 'Uncanny', in *Art and Literature*, ed. by James Strachey (London: Penguin, 1985), pp. 335–76
GANT, CHARLES. 'Tell No One It's Subtitled', *Sight & Sound*, June 2008, p. 13
KAY, JEREMY. 'Hollywood Looks for Local Heroes', *Screen International*, 21 December 2007, pp. 26–27
PELEATO, FLOREAL. 'Entretien avec Jaime Rosales', *Positif*, June 2008, pp. 31–35
PIÑA, BELÉN. 'Entrevista: Belén Rueda', *Fotogramas*, October 2007, pp. 92–97
SÁNCHEZ, SERGI. 'La firma invitada: cambio ¿radical?', *Fotogramas*, November 2007, p. 11
TRASHORRAS, ANTONIO. Review of *El orfanato*, *Fotogramas*, October 2007, p. 14
WILSON, EMMA. *Cinema's Missing Children* (London: Wallflower, 2003)

Web sources all accessed 16 December 2008:

Base de datos, 'El orfanato', Ministerio de Cultura, <http://www.mcu.es/bbddpeliculas/ buscarDetallePeliculas.do?brscgi_DOCN=000041562&brscgi_BCSID=9bdcaodo& language=es&prev_layout=bbddpeliculasResultado&layout=bbddpeliculasDetalle>
——'La soledad', Ministerio de Cultura, <http://www.mcu.es/bbddpeliculas/buscar DetallePeliculas.do?brscgi_DOCN=000041367&brscgi_BCSID=3b870be7& language=es&prev_layout=bbddpeliculasResultado&layout=bbddpeliculasDetalle>

BOLLAÍN, ICÍAR. 'Si no hubiera cine español', *El País*, 7 February 2008, <http://www.elpais.com/articulo/cultura/hubiera/cine/espanol/elpepicul/20080207elpepicul_4/Tes>

BOYERO, CARLOS. 'La Academia se hace "cool"', *El País*, 5 February 2008, <http://www.elpais.com/articulo/cultura/Academia/hace/cool/elpepicul/20080205elpepicul_4/Tes>

DE LA IGLESIA, ALEX. 'Carta a *El País* de un cineasta del país', *El País*, 6 February 2008, <http://www.elpais.com/articulo/opinion/Carta/PAIS/cineasta/pais/elpepiopi/20080206elpepiopi_11/Tes>

HOLLAND, JONATHAN. Review of *La soledad*, *Variety*, 24 September 2007, <http://www.variety.com/review/VE1117933710.html?categoryid=31&cs=1&p=0>

HOYCINEMA. 'Comentarios', <http://www.hoycinema.com/comentarios/orfanato-2007.htm> and <http://www.hoycinema.com/comentarios/soledad-2007.htm>

——— 'El orfanato: sinopsis', <http://www.hoycinema.com/sinopsis/orfanato-2007.htm>

——— 'La soledad: sinopsis', <http://www.hoycinema.com/sinopsis/soledad-2007.htm>

País, El. Archivo: *El orfanato*, September 2007–February 2008, <http://www.elpais.com/archivo/buscador.html#>

——— Archivo: 'orfanato', July 2007–July 2008, <http://www.elpais.com/archivo/buscador.html#>

ROSALES, JAIME. 'Esa cosa llamada "cine español"', *El País*, 4 September 2007, <http://www.elpais.com/articulo/opinion/cosa/llamada/cine/espanol/elpepuopi/20070904elpepiopi_5/Tes>

CHAPTER 6

Re-presenting the Others

Cinema and Television on Ethnicity and Immigration

Domestic, exotic, and familiar

Of all the social issues that have come to the fore in Spanish cultural studies, the one that seems perhaps the most urgent is the theme of the ethnic or immigrant other in Spanish cinema. Isabel Santaolalla's major book of 2005, called precisely *Los 'otros': etnicidad y 'raza' en el cine español contemporáneo* ('The "Others": Ethnicity and "Race" in Contemporary Spanish Cinema'), remains vital here, both as a sweeping survey of the field and as an example of close readings of auteurist films that have come to constitute something of an authoritative canon in this context. As a unique and groundbreaking full-length study, it thus deserves to be addressed at some length and compared with a more recent monograph on the same theme (but addressing a wider range of media and periods) by Susan Martin Márquez.

What I go on to argue in this sixth chapter (leading on to the final section of this book, which focuses most closely on television) is that analysis should go beyond this relatively limited canon of social-realist films, which, while widely studied abroad, is hardly representative of the Spanish audiovisual field as a whole. To this end I examine in the second half of this chapter TV drama, which (in spite of its lack of cultural authority or, in Bourdieu's word, 'distinction') stakes a claim to being the true national narrative of Spain and the privileged forum for the working out of domestic issues such as ethnicity and immigration. I focus on two long-running professional series, *El comisario* ('The Police Commander', Tele 5, 1999–2009) and *Hospital Central* ('Central Hospital', Tele 5, 2000–).

In the introduction to her book Santaolalla traces some concepts of race and ethnicity in film, drawing on both black British scholars such as Stuart Hall and on Foucault. She specifies, however, that although images of ethnic groups share a fundamental feature (namely the construction of an objectified 'them' different from the assumed community of 'us'), each group carries different meanings with it and receives a different treatment from that of its fellows (22). And at a time when Britain, Germany, and France already had some tradition of films on this theme, Spain, belated as ever, had to wait until the 1990s for a changing social reality to be reflected on screen (23). Thus the *annus mirabilis* of 1996 produced no fewer than six feature films on the theme (including two by the major directors Imanol Uribe and Carlos Saura), partly in response to recent initiatives by the PSOE government: 1994 and 1995 had seen the Plan para la Integración Social de los Inmigrantes ('Plan for the Social Integration of Immigrants'), the Observatorio Permanente de la Inmigración ('Standing Commission on Immigration'), and the Foro para la Inmigración ('Forum for Immigration'). Since that date, writes Santaolalla, there has been a continuous 'trickle' of films on the theme of immigration, although they are artistically uneven and often commercially unsuccessful (23).

Santaolalla's main aims are to trace the typology of images in her corpus; to place them within cultural and ideological discourses; and to read those discourses in turn within debates on identities, both individual and communal, in contemporary Spain (24–25). With respect to that corpus, gypsies, resident for so long in Spain, are held to be a 'domestic Other'; less known Africans and Asians are the exotic 'Other par excellence'; and Latin Americans are the 'familiar Other', helped (or hindered) by a lengthy legacy of representations in Spanish film. Each sub-group thus bears a 'distinct charge [or degree] of alterity' within it (25).

In the body of her book Santaolalla explores her case studies, which prove more complex and contradictory than might have been thought. Thus in Chus Gutiérrez's *Alma gitana* ('Gipsy Soul', 1996), the story of a Romeo-and-Juliet affair between a hedonistic and (probably) non-Roma dancer and a more conservative and bourgeois gypsy girl, the viewpoint of the masculine *payo* subject is privileged over that of the feminine Roma love object (109); and gypsy society is 'normalized' in a way that stresses its conservativism and machismo (11). Yet the film ends (as I have noted myself) with an ambiguous and inconclusive shot (117) of the open road: the male protagonist pursues on his motorbike the bus in which the young woman has been sent away from him by her overprotective family.

Bwana (1996), Imanol Uribe's adaptation of a play about a Spanish family confronting an illegal migrant on the beach, is less amenable to progressive rereading, as here the absolute African Other is both deprived of speech and, in the Spanish woman's fantasy, stereotypically eroticized (indeed, he is frequently naked in the film). Moreover the family abandon the African to murderous fascist thugs at the film's end. Santaolalla notes that although the film, selected as the Spanish Oscar entry, was harshly criticized in the US for its negative images, it provoked no controversy in Spain, where such debates on the representation of ethnic minorities had hardly begun (158). Unselfconsciously, the film thus stages a 'clash' between self and Other, in which the Spanish family are richly particularized (in language, class, and even gastronomy) while the exotic African remains marginal, abstracted, and, eventually, brutalized (159).

Finally, Icíar Bollaín's *Flores de otro mundo* ('Flowers from Another World', 1999), based on a real-life story of the 'importing' of Caribbean women as potential wives for the men in a depopulated Castilian village, is much more complex. Beginning as it does with a shot of the bus arriving with the immigrant women, the film at first appears to stage once more the 'clash' of two different worlds: Caribbean warmth and exuberance vs. the cold sobriety of Castile. But, as it develops, *Flores* consistently troubles the expectations of what is familiar and what is strange, facilitating through its style of shooting and storytelling our identification with the Latin American newcomers and making the domestic audience look 'with strangeness' on everyday life in rural Spain (199). The local inhabitants are thus seen as 'Others' and the familiar is rendered 'distant' (204).

It is to a yet more vertiginous switch in perspective that Santaolalla alludes in her title. The twist in the tail of Alejandro Amenábar's English-language ghost movie *The Others* (a clear influence on J. A. Bayona's *El orfanato* ['The Orphanage', 2007], which we studied in the previous chapter) was that it was Nicole Kidman's fearful family who were the undead phantasms, while the ghostly intruders were the everyday mortals. And while Santaolalla concludes that we still await films made not about ethnic others but by members of these growing communities (260), Susan Martin Márquez has given in her later study some account of narratives, if not films, created by African immigrants in Spain, such as the Moroccan-Catalan Najat El Hachmi's memoirs *Jo també sóc catalana* ('I'm Catalan Too', 346–54). In *Disorientations: Spanish Colonialism in Africa and the Performance of Identity* (2008), drawing on both visual and textual sources, she examines the 'reformulations of Spanish identity' in response to the colonization and wars in sub-Saharan Africa and Morocco and 'unmasks family values' in the Franco-era colonies. The last chapter is most relevant to our topic, treating as it does contemporary 'Performance anxieties on the edge of Fortress Europe' (300–54).

Like Santaolalla, Martin Márquez privileges a single feature film in this analysis (and one made by a native born Spaniard or Catalan), José Luis Guerín's prize winning *En construcción* ('Under Construction', 2001). This documentary, which is, like Santaolalla's case studies once more, a favourite text for foreign critics, treats the building of a luxury apartment block in Barcelona's inner city Raval district. While the fiction films studied by Santaolalla staged 'clashes' between host communities and foreigners (even if some tended in the process to destabilize simple oppositions between self and other), the documentary stages for Martin Márquez the 'negotiation' of multiple identities based as much on class and language as on ethnicity and religion.

Focusing on a scene in which the discovery of a Roman cemetery delays building work as archaeologists mount a rescue dig, Martin Márquez notes how 'snippets of conversation [amongst bystanders] are woven together to suggest that throughout history ostensible "outsiders" have been essential to constructions of Spanishness' (310). For the Catalan, Castilian, and Arabic speakers alike, who are shown contemplating this newly disclosed 'place of memory', the exposed skeletons evoke persistent and uncompromising 'spectres of violence', in various periods and places. Yet it remains the case for Martin Márquez that 'the different groups of people who gather to view the cemetery do manage to connect meaningfully with one another, often through recognition of the commonality of human suffering and mortality' (311).

This language of what has been called (after Derrida) 'hauntology' (Labanyi), cited in earlier chapters of this book, recurs at the end of Martin Márquez's monograph, where she writes that the growing awareness of real-life immigrants in Spain renders traditional fantasies of the Other no longer tenable: 'African immigrants' incursions into the Spanish cultural sphere effectively bury the ghosts of the medieval past, so strategically employed by Spaniards over the previous two centuries' (354); or again 'the increasing presence of immigrants in Spanish life and cultural production is leading to a new form of "disorientation", as communities in Spain are forced to confront the realities of a modern–day *convivencia*, rather than indulge fantasies of a *convivencia* associated with a remote past' (355). We can now go on to see how this clash of (or negotiation between) phantasmatic and real others is played out on television.

TV fiction: overview

Recent television scholars have argued for the medium's privileged engagement with the social life of European nations. Thus John Caughie has shown how UK TV drama prizes the local and domestic (*Television Drama*); John Ellis has claimed that television is a mode of 'working through' social issues that have no definitive conclusion (*Seeing Things*); and Milly Buonanno has revealed that even the 'travelling fictions' of international franchises are rendered distinct and distinctive in media territories such as Italy (*The Age of Television*).

The argument for the privileged status of Spanish television as an index of national life is also clear. The annual audience for Spanish film is less than the nightly audience of a local television series. And, since the 1990s, such series have been dominant in prime time, pushing US shows to the margin of the schedule in a country where Hollywood films have always been dominant at the box office. Unlike in the case of cinema once more, TV audiences are not skewed towards the young, but embrace all the demographic fragments of the Spanish population. And in spite of growing competition from the internet, Spaniards have continued to devote increasing periods of time to television, making theirs one of the highest rates in Europe (Smith, *Television* 1). Given the intimate feedback loop between producers and audience in the television sector (with new strands either cancelled if they meet a poor response or retuned to gain the public's favour from week to week), a clear case can thus be made for television, not cinema, as the national narrative of Spain, in spite of the medium's low status in the cultural hierarchy and the scorn it still suffers from the print media. Certainly Spain is one of the few countries to have achieved an industrial mode of production comparable to that of the United States when it comes to long–form, primetime, quality series fiction. This is a phenomenon that deserves to be both studied and celebrated.

Television seems from the start to have been more open than cinema to foreign influence in Spain. While Santaolalla complains in the 2000s that no immigrants have had access to the means of filmmaking production, even under Franco two of the three pioneers of the electronic medium were foreigners (Palacio 148–50). Romanian Valerio Lazarov, known as the 'king of the zoom', revolutionized variety programming in the 1960s. Uruguay-born Narciso Ibáñez Serrador founded in the same decade the best-known and loved brand in Spanish audiovisual narrative: *Historias para no dormir* ('Stories to Keep You Awake', 1964), which was revived thirty years later by devoted filmmaker fans as *Películas para no dormir* ('Films to

Keep You Awake', 2005). Ibáñez Serrador's original studio-shot dramas embraced 'aliens' in both senses, starring as they did his ambiguously accented father in exotic locations that frequently involved encounters with extraterrestrials.

The third founding auteur of Spanish TV is often held to be the longest lasting of all creators in the medium: Basque Antonio Mercero, who created the classic fictions of the 1970s and 1980s and was examined in Chapter 3 of this book. As we have seen, the late Francoist *Crónicas de un pueblo* ('Chronicles of a Village', 1971–74), shot on location in a village quite as desolate as that of *Flores de otro mundo*, depicts an organic rural community repeatedly confronted by the shock of the other. While the alien intruder is generally marked not as ethnically different but rather as an untrustworthy ambassador of urban modernity, he or she can also play the part of divine messenger. The mysterious 'traveller with the smile' in one Christmas episode thus recalls the villagers to their ancient traditions and heals the social conflicts amongst them (Smith, *Television in Spain* 65–73).

Verano azul ('Blue Summer', 1981), Mercero's equally legendary series of the Transition, is based on a yet smaller community: a group of adolescents holidaying in Andalucía. Once more their idyll is threatened by alien intruders, bearers of disconcerting indices of modernization (including divorce, property development, and pollution). But outsiders can, as in *Crónicas*, also bring enlightenment. In one episode an otherworldly Christ- or yogi-like figure, complete with a tattooed Hindu motif, descends to the beach to teach the kids life lessons. The Other is thus in Mercero both under- and over-valued, feared for his disruptiveness and respected for his superior intuition.

Mercero's Christian ethics, generally unstressed in his series, tend even in *Crónicas* to propose a democratic tolerance of the other in a period when, of course, ethnic minorities were barely visible in Spain. For example in one episode local children are shown to be mistaken in their fears that a foreign resident is a dangerous criminal. And if in another they paint a black lamb white it is because they are concerned that it will be ostracized by the white majority of the flock. But it is a surprise to see that even a notoriously domestic and saccharine series such as Tele 5's *Médico de familia* ('Family Doctor', 1995–99), widely credited with pioneering the locally made fictions that have since dominated Spanish prime time (Lacalle 59), also began with a narrative of tolerance towards the ethnic other.

In the very first episode of this the most highly rated series of its decade the eponymous family migrate to the suburbs from the city centre. Main character Nacho (played by Emilio Aragón, who is both a doctor and a father in the series) is faced with a case of a young Roma girl who is withdrawn from school by her father. Visiting them in the encampment, he is told that tradition and family are everything to the gypsy community and girls thus require no education. The episode ends with Nacho explaining to his own daughter that sometimes nothing can be done to right a wrong, even when one has, as in the case of the earnest and well-meaning Nacho, the very best of intentions (see Smith, *Spanish Visual Culture* 32–39).

The workplace dramas that followed *Médico de familia* in the 1990s, such as the equally pioneering *Periodistas* ('Journalists', Tele 5, 1998–2002), also treat the ethnic theme as one of the topical issues for which their complex narratives were newly known. But it is striking that the new ensemble casts of such series, heavily biased towards urban women, found places for representatives of the historic nationalities (Catalans and Basques), but not for the new ethnic communities. Likewise in the top-rated comedies at the start of the millennium (7 *vidas* ['Seven Lives', Tele 5, 1999–2006], *Aquí no hay quien viva* ['No One Can Live Here', Antena 3, 2003–06]), it proved easier to incorporate sympathetic gay and lesbian characters into the regular casts than it did gypsies, Arabs, or Africans. Both comedies went so far as to run same-sex marriage or adoption plotlines for regular characters even as they relegated ethnic minority characters (such as 7 *vidas*'s exploited Latin American greengrocer's assistant) to the sidelines. It remains the case, however, that if a character is (rarely) allowed to give voice to racist opinions (7 *vidas*'s foulmouthed greengrocer once more) they are clearly disavowed within the context of the programme as a whole (see Smith, *Spanish Visual Culture* 39–46).

It seems likely, then, that, as in the better known case of cinema, the representation of 'race' and immigration in Spanish TV series is generally positive and sympathetic, even as it fails to provide a forum for ethnic minorities to express themselves. Indeed this is one of the conclusions of a meticulous monograph that offers a detailed content analysis of immigrant characters in recent Spanish television drama, analogous to Santaolalla's study for film: Charo Lacalle's *El discurso televisivo sobre la inmigración* (2008).

Lacalle begins by stating that, beyond quantitative studies, her aim is to draw a 'conceptual map of the relations between identity and alterity' in the depiction of foreigners or immigrants in Spanish TV fiction (3). And like Santaolalla she stresses the increasing 'domestication' of the exotic or ethnic subject, citing Stuart Hall on this development (4). In the process of the 'social construction of the other', the increasing visibility of immigration in Spain (11) intersects with the growing 'hyperrealism' of the television medium (14), with drama drawing ever closer to non-fictional and reality programming. On a more theoretical level, if identity must be 'rethought' in this new context (23), then subject and object (Spaniard and immigrant) will become inextricable from one another (27).

Lacalle takes as her corpus thirty series broadcast between 1998 and 2006 on national networks TVE1, Tele 5, and Antena 3, and on the Catalan TV3. When it comes to 'non-western European' immigrants, these shows feature no fewer than 146 narratives involving guest characters and 127 plotlines relating to permanent members of the casts (66). This is of course a much larger body of work than is to be found in the feature films I looked at in the first half of this chapter.

Yet more valuable than Lacalle's sketch of this vast field (which embraces both comedy and drama and representatives of African, Arab, Latin American, and Eastern European, but not Spanish gypsy, communities), is her documentation of changes in representation during her chosen period. Thus the depiction of immigrants as transient criminals and victims at the start of the decade declines markedly at the end, where such characters increasingly take on the privileged role of permanent cast members with whose more complex dilemmas viewers can identify (124). Negative depictions likewise give way to overwhelmingly positive characterizations, with an initial fear and repulsion replaced by sympathy and empathy (125). Ultimately this process is for Lacalle founded on an emergent 'mutuality': the 'fusion' of identity and alterity in narratives that replace exclusion and segregation by assimilation and integration (125).

Lacalle's survey of this huge field is as exhaustive as is possible: Spanish series typically run for twenty-five episodes a year and are scheduled in timeslots of well over an hour. And she singles out my own chosen dramas, *El comisario* and *Hospital Central*, as those that have most consistently engaged with the theme of immigration, identifying no fewer than sixty relevant episodes of the first series and forty-nine of the second that treat the subject (77–82).

Yet Lacalle offers no close analysis of individual narratives. I therefore propose to examine these longest-running series dramas on Spanish television by focusing on single episodes that address the ethnic theme in an especially significant manner. We can then compare and contrast these top-rated and prize-winning series with the better-studied feature films on the same subject analysed by Santaolalla and Martin Márquez, which are of course far more familiar to foreign scholars. Time-tied as the great majority of television is, the individual episodes will of course have been forgotten in Spain itself, and barely register even in Lacalle's specialist analysis (there is a brief reference to one of my episodes on page 81). My intention is to retrieve these narratives from the all too fleeting, electronic flow.

Case studies: 'El comisario' (1999–2009) and 'Hospital Central' (2000–)

El comisario (1999–2009) and *Hospital Central* (2000–), both of which are broadcast weekly in prime time on the top-rated national private channel Tele 5, belong to the 'super-genre' of 'professional television' (Bailey). As fictions set in institutions (legal and medical, respectively) they are ideally placed to articulate social issues and to mediate between the public and private perceptions of those issues. Attracting audiences in the millions for a decade and boasting characters with whom the public is clearly deeply engaged, both series have made a distinctive and long-lasting contribution to public life in Spain, even as they engage their faithful audiences' most private emotions.

In their second seasons at the start of the millennium both series devoted two episodes each to ethnic themes. In one plotline from *El comisario*, which I have studied elsewhere ('Crime Scenes'), a young Westernized Moroccan woman, the girlfriend of the son of Spanish police officers, is beaten by her father into a forced marriage to an older man 'back home.' And in another narrative thread from *Hospital Central*, an Arab man is concerned that his prosthesis is made from a product derived from pigs. I have preferred to concentrate on the following two episodes, which show interesting parallels with at least two of the feature films mentioned earlier, *Alma gitana* and *Bwana*, respectively. The official synopses are as follows:

> *El comisario* 2.09 (first shown 28 February 2000)
> 'La jaula del grillo'
> Javier Colmenar, un hombre que cumplió condena por una violación que no había cometido, está dispuesto a hacerle pagar a Casqueiro, quien lo detuvo, por los años de ofensa. Mientras tanto, un extraño accidente de coche y una serie de robos complican más la tarea del comisario y sus ayudantes.

['The cricket's cage'
Javier Colmenar, a man who has served a prison term for a rape he did not
commit, is determined to make Casqueiro, who had arrested him, pay for
the years he has lost. Meanwhile a strange car crash and a series of robberies
[wrongly attributed by racist Spaniards to a gypsy] complicate still more the job
of the police commissioner and his colleagues.]

Hospital Central 2.25 (first shown 24 June 2002)
'Un día cualquiera'
En la bodega de un avión los del Sámur se encuentran los cuerpos de dos
polizones: uno está muerto, la otra presenta una fuerte hemorragia en la
pierna; cuando la llevan al hospital descubren que es portadora del Ébola,
se dispara la alarma y Vilches, haciéndose cargo de la situación, incomunica
las dependencias. Una huelga de limpieza y auxiliares pone más trabas a la
situación, los medicamentos escasean y los piquetes no dejan pasar a nadie. Elisa
rompe aguas, pero dada la situación y la falta de medios, el parto será vaginal,
en contra de lo que se había estipulado.

['A day like any other'
In the hold of a plane the paramedics find the bodies of two stowaways: while
the man is dead, the woman is bleeding heavily from the leg. When they take
her to the hospital it is discovered that she is a carrier of the Ebola virus. The
alarm is given and Vilches, taking control of the situation, isolates the hospital
wards. A strike by cleaning and auxiliary staff further complicates the situation,
as medical supplies are running low and pickets won't let anyone through.
Elisa's waters break, but given the situation and the lack of resources, she cannot
have the Caesarian that was recommended for her.]

Both based and shot in Madrid, these two series stake a claim to being national
narratives in that week by week they compete to address and work through
topical issues that have no definitive solution. As professional dramas, they are also
both travelling fictions, originally derived from the influential North American
templates of police and medical series. But there is no doubt that, given their great
and continuing popularity with local audiences, they have (in Buonanno's word)
'indigenized' those originals in a way that clearly differentiates them from lower-
rated imports.

Like *Alma gitana*, the episode of *El comisario* that I have chosen favours a cross-
ethnic 'Romeo-and-Juliet' romance (indeed, one policeman mockingly addresses
the Roma lover as 'Romeo'). In this case, however, the sexes of the star-cross'd
lovers are reversed, with the male suitor a gypsy and the female beloved a *paya* (non-
gypsy). It could be argued that the former is to some extent objectified as an ethnic
other, since he is never shown within his own familial or social context. Darkly
handsome, he seems to stand increasingly isolated as the episode develops.

The plotline begins with a nosy neighbour calling the police to a moneyed
suburban area with a history of break-ins. She has seen a 'gypsy' entering a chalet
through the window. Although the daughter of the house professes to have seen and
heard nothing, the young man is taken away by the police, harshly interrogated, and
confined to a holding cell for the night when he remains silent as to his presence in
the house (Fig. 10). The next day the girl comes alone to the police station. After
she testifies that the couple are lovers and that the boy's refusal to speak to the police

FIG. 10. Roma boy behind bars: *El comisario*

is an attempt to protect her (her conservative parents know nothing of the affair), the boy is finally released. But at the end of the episode the police are called once more to the suburb where the youth has been brutally beaten. Although the father claims at first that he hit him with a golf club because he believed him to be an intruder, his daughter tells the truth: her father is a 'murderer' who, now notified of his daughter's affair, attempted to rid his family of the Roma suitor by any means necessary.

Unlike in *Alma gitana*, then, the two lovers have equal prominence. Indeed, it appears that the young woman, sexually active in spite of the fact that she is underage, is more vocal than her faithful young lover, who is condemned to silence. The episode thus stages a negotiation of or conversation on the intersection of multiple and intersecting themes: ethnicity, class, gender, and age. It also takes care to give voice to varied and mutually incompatible opinions. Thus the girl simply declares her love in public, and is apparently indifferent to ethnicity; the bad cop Telmo (Francesc Orella) taunts the boy with ethnic stereotypes; and the good cop Charlie (Juanjo Artero) interrupts the interrogation, fearing an innocent youth is being abused. Finally the father voices the prejudices of a Spanish bourgeois patriarch, exclaiming as he is arrested that he did not give his daughter everything to have her 'taken away' from him by a gypsy. Anxious to combat stereotypes of Roma as thieves (stereotypes voiced in the episode by unsympathetic neighbours and police alike), the series also neatly reverses the more traditional image we find in *Alma gitana*: it is not the gypsy family but rather the *payo* that is overprotective of its young daughter's honour.

This plotline, complete in one episode and played by guest actors who will not be seen again, is of course integrated into deep-level stories and focalized through the viewpoints and reactions of the now familiar regular cast. This complicates our response to the Roma micro-narrative. Thus the bad cop Telmo is coping in this series with marital separation and a diagnosis of HIV (*Hospital Central* also inflicted this plotline on a regular character at about the same time). The good cop, on the other hand, is often shown as feckless and irresponsible, and is currently carrying on an inconclusive affair with a colleague who will prove to be pregnant. The elemental passions of teenage romance are thus embedded within the more complex and graduated emotions of everyday adult life.

But, as is generally the case with police drama, we are invited not just to be moved but also to exercise our judgement. The episode's other plotlines thus provide either confirmation or qualification of the young lovers' story. In the main plot an innocent man, inadvertently jailed for rape years ago on the testimony of regular character Chief Inspector Casqueiro (Jaime Pujol), wreaks revenge on the policeman in a series of acts that culminate in the kidnapping of his father. We are clearly asked to compare the jailed cricket of the episode's title (a threatening gift from the vengeful prisoner) with the jailed gypsy, who is equally silent. But we are also provoked to meditate on the consequences of injustice and the possibilities for redress for both wrongly accused characters, the supposed rapist and the young lover, who is also viewed as a sexual threat. A third plotline, reminiscent of the classic neorealist feature *Muerte de un ciclista* ('Death of a Cyclist', Juan Antonio Bardem, 1955), reveals once more the deadly violence of the apparently irreproachable bourgeoisie: just as the girl's father will batter the gypsy with a golf club, so a wealthy motorist will leave the young cyclist he has run over unattended by the road side. As in the case of the feature films analysed by Santaolalla and Martin Márquez, the liberal or progressive outlook of the series is transparent here.

The released prisoner sends Casqueiro a caged cricket with the riddle: 'Why doesn't the cricket chirp?' The menacing answer comes later: 'Because it is dead.' As the father of the underage girl is read his rights by a clearly unsympathetic policewoman, the young Roma, spattered with blood, is taken away in an ambulance. Although it is clear (in Lacalle's terms) that the ethnic subject plays the familiar role of victim, he has been expressly cleared of criminality. Indeed this exculpation has taken a form that facilitates both the viewer's sympathy and empathy and the character's (attempted) assimilation and integration.

While it is not clear at the episode's end if he is dead or not, it remains the case that the traumatized body of the ethnic other, however domesticated he may have proved in this case, has provoked a continuing, if fragmented and inconclusive, conversation around ethnicity. The familiar (the middle class and suburban) has been rendered distant and the unfamiliar (the impoverished gypsy) all too close. In a very different context and medium, the procedure followed in this TV episode is not dissimilar to the strategies of the feature films *Alma gitana*, *Flores de otro mundo*, and *En construcción*.

The traumatized (and traumatizing) body of the ethnic other is much more prominent in the episode of *Hospital Central* that I have chosen for analysis. And the episode itself is also more complex, weaving together around a dozen plotlines (one for each of its featured cast) and providing some spectacular action sequences and exteriors befitting the episode's status as a cliff-hanging season finale.

The main narrative focuses not on a Roma, relatively familiar, but on the exotic ethnic Other par excellence: as in *Bwana*, it is the African immigrant. And as in *Bwana* once more, she has arrived illegally with a companion who has died in the

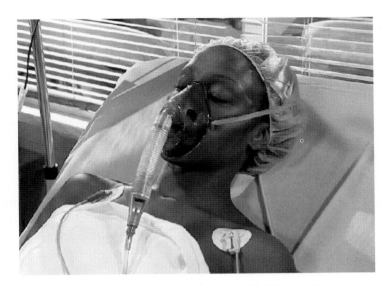

FIG. 11. African woman behind mask: *Hospital Central*

process, albeit here in the hold of a cargo plane, rather than in a raft crossing the sea. As no black or immigrant doctors or nurses are shown in the episode (indeed every one of the huge regular ensemble cast is a native-born Spaniard), the silent and near motionless stowaway, whose nationality is never identified beyond the plane's origin in Zaire, thus seems to stand in for her racial group in the most elemental and undifferentiated of ways.

Immobilized on the hospital bed with her face covered by an oxygen mask and body festooned with tubes (Fig. 11), she 'speaks' only through fluids: at one point her blood spills, darkly, menacingly, on the white floor. Moreover this black woman's death agony is framed by two white women giving birth. The 80-minute episode (almost the length of a feature film) opens with a Spanish passenger suffering a breech birth on the plane and ends with a regular character, the middle-aged cancer-survivor Elisa, having a healthy son in the exceptionally chaotic hospital. Given that the reason for this chaos is the emergency isolation procedures enforced by the African woman's diagnosis with the Ebola virus, it would seem that the Other represents a deadly threat indeed to the life-giving native Spaniards.

Yet this potentially melodramatic, even paranoid, plotline is carefully qualified by its placing within a discussion of the differing demands of social justice and public health. A strike by admin and cleaning staff is presented with some sympathy (they demand a living wage), even as it is shown to have a grave effect on patient care. And the many individual cases attended by the doctors are placed within a single broad institutional framework: should the cranky Dr Vilches (Jordi Rebellón), whose harsh treatment of a lawyer with a dislocated shoulder is clearly undiplomatic, be promoted to the sensitive administrative position of Head of the Emergency Room? As in *El comisario*, such institutional questions, drawing as they do on differing definitions of professional ethics and social responsibility, can have no simple resolution.

Moreover, although the presence of the black body provokes a health emergency, it also provides a test case for a public health service's duty of care to all, regardless of payment or origin, and most especially in the straitened circumstances provoked by the strike. The African, devotedly tended by doctors and nurses in spite of the risk of infection to themselves, is thus a kind of limit case for Spanish patients with less serious conditions. Indeed the episode focuses on the disconcerting practice of triage, or the prioritizing of care according to the urgency of patients' needs, even as it notes (even as the lawyer loudly proclaims) that all citizens have an equal legal right to treatment in public hospitals, and cannot be abandoned on trolleys however exceptional circumstances may be in the hospital.

As in police drama once more, these cognitive questions (such the efficient use of limited resources) are infused and confused by the disorderly emotional investments of the professionals called on to respond to them. Thus one female doctor discovers that the little girl she is treating is the daughter of the colleague with whom she (the doctor) is having an adulterous affair. Or again a surgeon is forced to carry out a kidney transplant when the patient's husband holds a knife to the throat of the psychologist who is his secret lover. In such cases, as with the tricky questions of race and immigration, cognition is coloured and qualified by emotion, public judgement by private affect.

Towards the end of the episode the African patient is missing from her bed. It is the most vulnerable regular character (Elisa, the cancerous pregnant doctor) whom the Ebola patient confronts: she staggers unsteadily towards her, with one arm raised as if making a greeting or pleading for help. As she collapses dead on the floor, there is little doubt that this moment of extreme body trauma (rare in the Spanish series, but typical of much recent medical drama in the US), speaks obscurely of a generalized social anxiety around race, health, and immigration.

Yet I would prefer to read the confrontation between the two women, who are both marked by deadly disease, as an example of respect for the other in all its unfathomable difference or in Lacalle's terms of mutuality within and across alterity. Certainly the ironic episode title ('Un día cualquiera' or 'A day like any other') shows that an exceptional, indeed unique, event (an outbreak of Ebola), provoked by an illegal immigrant, can indeed be incorporated into the social and personal life of the indigenous community that is embodied and represented by the hospital and, by extension, that of the TV audience.

Internal affairs

Television, of course, does not stand still. Before it was cancelled in 2009, after ten years on the air, later seasons of *El comisario*, perhaps aware of renewed US competition to local drama from the *CSI* franchise, incorporated aspects of 'body trauma TV' in new pathology-led plotlines; and *Hospital Central* explicitly staged its concern for health in the developing world by shooting special episodes on location in Latin America and India. And, testifying to Lacalle's argument that TV series in the second half of the last decade tended towards greater assimilation of and identification with immigrants, later seasons of the latter programme incorporated permanent foreign national characters. This is in marked contrast to the great majority of Spanish film production (from Almodóvar to genre films and art movies) in which major immigrant actors and characters, with the exception of Latin Americans, are vanishingly small in number. Both series remain proud of their commitment to quality and to the exploration of urgent social issues within the framework of continuing personal relations, often referring to such issues in the news sections of their official websites (Tele 5).

While we have seen that in Spanish television fiction the workplace (both police station and health centre) is subject to troubling spectres of violence, which originate from both inside and outside its limits, the 'precinct' (as Ellis calls the primary location of such dramas [*TV FAQ* 99–105]) is far from being a fortress. The professional sphere serves rather, in these top-rated fictions at least, as a permeable public space in which there is a possibility for the continuing and mutual recognition of human commonality, of love and of death. The assumed community of 'us' is thus modified, however slightly, by contact with the more or less objectified 'them' with whom it is shown to clash or, more typically, to negotiate in continuing and inconclusive conversation.

While the cinematic narratives studied by scholars such as Santaolalla and Martin Márquez are clearly significant and of more than academic interest, in contemporary Spain, as elsewhere, film is safely restricted to dedicated public places and experienced only on special occasions, some three or four times a year. The very rarity of the experience of cinema going thus helps to secure its cultural authority, both at home and abroad, where its serves, through festivals, as the legitimate representative of the nation. Yet, as Lacalle has shown, TV is a ubiquitous medium that treats the topic of immigration on a weekly basis. Hence it is not simply television's quantity of production but also its specific mode of consumption, namely its seamless integration into the spaces and rhythms of daily domestic life, that renders its invitation of the ethnic other into Spanish homes all the more valuable and salutary, however disorientating that presence may be.

Works cited

BAILEY, STEVE. ' "Professional Television: Three (Super)texts and a (Super)genre', *The Velvet Light Trap*, 47 (1 April 2001), 45–61

BUONANNO, MILLY. *The Age of Television: Experiences and Theories* (London: Intellect, 2008)

CAUGHIE, JOHN. *Television Drama* (Oxford: Oxford University Press, 2000)

ELLIS, JOHN. *Seeing Things: Television in the Age of Uncertainty* (London: I. B. Tauris, 2002)

—— *TV FAQ: Uncommon Answers to Common Questions about TV* (London: I. B. Tauris, 2007)

LABANYI, JO. 'Memory and Modernity in Democratic Spain', *Poetics Today*, 28.1 (2007), 89–116

LACALLE, CHARO. *El discurso televisivo sobre la inmigración* (Barcelona: Omega, 2008)

MARTIN MÁRQUEZ, SUSAN. *Disorientations: Spanish Colonialism in Africa and the Performance of Identity* (New Haven, CT: Yale University Press, 2008)

PALACIO, MANUEL. *Historia de la televisión en España* (Barcelona: Gedisa, 2001)

SANTAOLALLA, ISABEL. *Los 'otros': etnicidad y 'raza' en el cine español* (Zaragoza: Prensas Universitarias, 2005)

SMITH, PAUL JULIAN. *Spanish Visual Culture: Cinema, Television, Internet* (Manchester: Manchester University Press, 2006)
—— *Television in Spain* (London: Tamesis, 2006)
—— 'Crime Scenes: Police Drama on Spanish Television', *Journal of Spanish Cultural Studies*, 8.1 (2007), 55–70

Web sources both accessed 27 March 2008

Tele 5. Official website of news on *Hospital Central*, <http://www.telecinco.es/hospitalcentral/archivos/noticias.shtml>
—— Official website of news on *El comisario*, <http://www.telecinco.es/elcomisario/archivos/noticias.shtml>

PART III

Television: Genre and Transitivity

CHAPTER 7

❖

Re-visions of Teresa

Josefina Molina's *Teresa de Jesús* (TVE, 1984) and Ray Loriga's *Teresa: el cuerpo de Cristo* ('Teresa, the Body of Christ', 2007)

The biopic as genre and public history

This chapter, the first in my final section on genre and transitivity, treats two screen versions of the life of Santa Teresa de Ávila which cross the media divide: the TV miniseries directed by Josefina Molina and starring Concha Velasco, *Teresa de Jesús* (1984) and the feature film directed by Ray Loriga and starring Paz Vega, *Teresa, el cuerpo de Cristo* (2007). Embracing both the particular and the general, the chapter will analyse the use of mise en scene (of costume and art design) in the two works; address the sometimes discordant meanings inevitably brought to the projects by the careers and personae of directors and stars; and examine the extent to which the visual and narrative rhetoric of each can be derived from the distinct characteristics of their respective media. We thus return to the question of the representation of history that we saw in the first section of this book (which treated the Dictatorship and Transition to democracy), but going back to a much more distant period, which has, nonetheless, clear but contradictory implications for the present.

The historical Teresa is distinctive as a subject for the screen as she constitutes a test case for the interpenetration of the factual and the fantastic, if not fictional. In spite of the prominence in these modern versions of the concrete mise en scene (including the use, wherever possible, of authentic locations) that is so vital to the heritage genre, so much of Teresa's original story is subjective, taking place as it does in the inaccessible sphere of the mystical vision, that it blurs the distinction between the real and the imaginative from the very start. I shall argue that in their re-visions of this familiar story, the two texts thus make comparable truth claims with regard to the historical past, but also reinscribe those truth claims within the very different film and television ecologies of the contemporary moments in which they were produced.

Evidently, Teresa poses further specific and acute political problems. Championed as a rebel by some feminist theorists and theologians, she remains a highly institutionalized figure in Catholicism and was proclaimed the first female Doctor of the Church in 1970. Moreover in Spain she is closely associated not only with the distant Counterreformation but with the more recent regime of Francisco Franco. Already in 1937 painter José María Sert's monumental 'Intercesión de Santa Teresa de Jesús en la Guerra Civil Española', which shows the Saint soaring up from a war torn landscape to clasp hands with a hovering crucified Christ, was exhibited at the Pontifical Pavilion at the Paris World Fare (Llorente 187). The discovery or recovery during the Civil War of a relic of the Saint (her immaculate hand) was exploited as part of what Paul Preston calls the 'providential' narrative of Franco's crusade (220). In spite of repeated requests from the nuns for its return, the relic remained with the Caudillo until his death, so attached was he to it.

Teresa was also enshrined by Francoist cinema, in the reverent version of her life made in 1961 by Juan de Orduña and starring Aurora Bautista, the last in their cycle of collaborations on historical female figures that began with the hysterical Juana la Loca, *Locura de amor* ('Mad Love', 1948), and included the feisty *Agustina de Aragón* (1950). All screen versions of historical lives inevitably raise questions as to the conflict between history and narrative, between textuality and visuality, and between fidelity to the past subject and relevance to the present audience. However Teresa de Jesús or de Ávila poses those questions with unusually troubling persistence. And her story is transitive in two senses: its meaning clearly changes as it moves through successive historical periods; and it is highly adept at crossing boundaries between media: literature, cinema, and television.

Students of US biopics are fortunate in having access to an exhaustive and sophisticated study of the classic Hollywood corpus. In the absence of such a study for Spain, I suggest that George F. Custen's *Bio/pics: How Hollywood Constructed Public History* (1992) can serve as a template for later Spanish versions of the genre, throwing into relief the distinctive features of the latter. Let us look in some detail, then, at Custen's argument.

Attempting to combine approaches drawn from the humanities and the social sciences, Custen give a detailed content analysis of a full third of the three hundred biopics made in the studio era (1927–60), but also draws on archival sources that document industrial practices, star systems, and publicity processes of the period (3). He stresses that even though his chosen films may now seem 'naïve', they are the result of a 'complex social organization' with its own rules (4). Moreover the biopic, sometimes dismissed by critics and audience alike, is a privileged genre that dates back to the beginnings of cinema. Even in the silent era, it had many variants (hagiographical, psychological, autobiographical) and was already 'embroiled in controversies about truth, accuracy, and interpretation' (6).

For Custen to study Hollywood biopic is to 'reconstruct a shifting public notion of fame' which moved slowly, over decades, from the 'structural famous' (such as royalty) to a 'democratization' that included anyone in the news (6–7). The question 'How "realistic" is Hollywood biography?' is thus unanswerable for reasons that are at once institutional and textual. Custen cites Hayden White for whom 'demands for verisimilitude in film [...] stem from a confusion of historical individuals with the kinds of "characterization" of them required for discursive purposes' (7). Although this problem of 'translatability' (of the movement from an event to its telling or description) is not unique to film, we should nonetheless distinguish between historiography and 'historiophoty': 'What gets lost in the translation of the event from its verbal state to a visual/pictorial one' (9). Historical accuracy is thus not to be confused with facticity (10) for (following White again) all history, whether written or filmed, is 'a product of processes of condensation, displacement, symbolization, and qualification' (11).

It remains the case, however, that visual media (once cinema, now television) have tended to serve the purpose of 'enculturation' or creating 'public history' for national and international audiences. Custen documents how Hollywood biopics were quite literally 'validated as legitimate carriers of the lessons of history' through pedagogical tie-ins intended for school children (13). But if such materials transparently supported the maintenance of social order in general, the values of individualism promoted in such films also reflected back quite precisely on the star system and the autobiographies of Hollywood moguls (18). And the standardization of such narratives required that, ironically, 'the very novelty that makes the celebrated person famous, different from the viewer, must be packaged in a guise familiar to many viewers' (18). Thus legendary producer Darryl Zanuck consistently insisted that all protagonists should display a clear motivation for their exceptional achievement (a motivation that was established in a telegraphic scene early on in the picture) and that biopics should provide a 'rooting interest' that was 'congruent with audiences' own [unexceptional] experiences and expectations' (18).

Heroes were thus permitted to be unusual only in their area of special expertise: Edison was shown taking time out to enjoy apple pie with his family, while Alexander Graham Bell was spurred on to invent the telephone to alleviate his wife's deafness (19). In such 'secular saints', history was thus humanized, the public made private. Such a process was not of course unique to film. Custen cites Leo Lowenthal's seminal work on celebrity biographies in popular magazines, which 'like the earlier "Lives of the Saints" helped prepare average people to accept their place in the social order by valorizing a common, distant, and elevated set of lives that readers could hope to emulate.' (33)

In the interests of both efficiency and ideology, then, studios shaped the making of history: 'through standardization of the great man narrative, through ritualized use of certain actors in certain parts, through control of publicity, and through adherence to legal standards of what could be pictured about the famous' (22). But such formulae were not themselves immune to historical change. With the decline of the studio system, film biopics no longer found an audience: 'the ability to shape public history had [...] been seized by television and the smaller screen constructed the self with a very different image from film' (29). We can now go on to examine the reflection and refraction of the Hollywood model, so convincingly presented by Custen, in twin Spanish versions of a great life made for TV and film.

'Teresa de Jesús' (1984): the secular sanctity of an everyday classic

The television miniseries *Teresa de Jesús* was released on DVD in 2006 as part of a collection of 'classic series', a genre that was employed to celebrate the fiftieth anniversary of state producer and broadcaster Televisión Española. These 'commemorative editions' (labelled 'the best works in the history of our television' and including Teresa's near contemporary *Cervantes* of 1980) were said to mark 'a historical moment'. There could be no clearer sign that television, often despised, could now present itself as the vehicle of a public history that it did not simply represent but rather embodied. And while TVE, as a generalist broadcaster, may have been too diverse to boast the distinctive 'house style' of Custen's Hollywood studios, still it had a complex social organisation that attempted to legitimize itself as a carrier of historical knowledge. *Teresa* clearly falls within what Manuel Palacio has called the 'pedagogy' of TVE in the Transition and which we noted in Chapter 3. In this case this strategy is manifest in the attempt to use prestige drama, shot on film and on location, to work through privileged moments of the past in the service of a new democratic present (*Historia* 91–121).

Intended to coincide with the four-hundredth anniversary of the Saint's death, the series premiered on 12 March 1984 and its eight hour-long episodes continued to play weekly on Monday nights until 30 April (Quílez Esteve 102). Although TVE had as yet no competition for viewers (commercial television remained a decade away) it did not stint in promoting the series, insisting on the quality of this special event programming.

A respectful 'making of' with the emblematic title 'Producción española' ('Spanish Production') was aired on 31 July 1983. Here the series' budget is given as 200 million pesetas, a figure Josefina Molina says is 'adequate' (although, she adds, period productions require extensive preparation). Emilio Gutiérrez Caba, already a respected actor for some twenty years, offers a nuanced version of historical fidelity: while he may not embody the physical type of his character, the frail San Juan de la Cruz, he still aims to give a faithful account of his inner life. Protagonist Concha Velasco stresses the 'simpatía' ['friendliness'] of the Saint (rather than her holiness) and the responsibility she felt in playing a character who ages from a youthful 23 to an infirm 67. In such publicity materials Velasco's performance is presented and accepted by all as an example of that self-conscious 'star acting', which Custen identifies as a crucial element in the Hollywood biopic (62). This is in spite of the fact that Velasco's lengthy career as a feisty comedienne offered few precedents for a role as serious and demanding as this.

A more nuanced discussion with the then respected presenter Mercedes Milá (much later to host Spain's *Big Brother*), broadcast just days before the first episode, saw the director and star joined by Salamanca professor Víctor García de la Concha, the historical consultant, and novelist Carmen Martín Gaite, credited as writer of the series' dialogue. Molina, a distinguished veteran of TV literary adaptations since the 1960s, who stressed as late as 2006 her continued commitment to educational television, emphasizes first of all the 'research' that went into the project, a kind of labour also vigorously promoted as proof of quality by the producers of Custen's biopics, however fanciful such pictures may appear today. While Molina concedes the impossibility of direct access to the historical reality of the sixteenth century (for example, many original locations have been lost or altered), she insists that she has aimed not for easy 'consumption' on the part of the viewer, but rather for 'reflection.' When Milá asks, finally, how the director feels after so much effort has culminated in just eight hours of television, Molina attempts to redefine and defend the medium: now, especially with the advent of home video, TV is no longer merely 'consumed' but rather watched, as if in a cinema, with proper attention. It was a prediction that would be confirmed by *Teresa*'s lavish DVD re-release more than twenty years later.

Ironically, it is the academic García de la Concha who makes a claim for the immediacy of the series, beyond its historical authenticity. While the three women skirt embarrassedly around the subject of gender, he replies that Teresa was 'of course' a feminist who struggled for women's rights (and, equally, was 'of course' from a family of converted Jews, although this genealogy cannot serve as an explanation of her life and works). Teresa, he insists, was as much engaged by the world as she was by God and her life spanned a historical arc from reform to reaction that exemplifies the two Spains that still clash today. García de la Concha thus explicitly embraces the enculturation function of the biopic, its ability to shape public history in the interests of the present, even as he insists (like Molina) on the primacy of research in the creative process.

Reception of the series mirrored its producers' aims. Indeed, as was common in the period, press previews simply reproduced TVE's self-serving promotion, citing the location shooting (which roamed from Avila and Toledo to Úbeda and Seville), the meticulously recreated sets (almost ten thousand square metres in size), and the lengthy production process (three months of rehearsal and ten of filming) (Quílez Esteve 102). Premiered in situ in Avila, *Teresa* was explicitly authorized by the Church (as was the perhaps unexpected casting of Velasco in the central role). Reviews were likewise reverent, with the exception of licensed heretic Francisco Umbral, who claimed dismissively that television could never capture the subtleties of the Saint's prose (this in spite of the fact that consultant de la Concha was the academic who had done most to vindicate Teresa's reputation as a literary, as opposed to devotional, classic of the Golden Age).

At first sight, the series' narrative and visual style seems to fall well within the classic tradition of film biopic that Custen rightly calls 'hagiographic'. The credits consist of a single lengthy take in long shot. Overshadowed by the celebrated city walls of Avila, framed by a picturesque tree, and accompanied by an ominous French horn and stirring strings, tiny black figures make their way on foot and in wagons towards the viewer, as if travelling towards us through history. After the credits have rolled (Velasco's star name precedes Teresa's), the stately procession then proceeds in the first sequence of episode 1 along rutted roads lined by modest stone houses. When a title announces with ostentatious precision 'Gotarrendura, Avila, Autumn 1538', the wan-faced and shining-eyed Teresa descends from a rather sinister sedan chair to be greeted by her affectionate uncle and father (the distinguished Héctor Alterio and Paco Rabal will be given surprisingly little to do over the next eight hours' screen time). As the men discuss the state of the world (the ruinous politics and economics of Castile) and hint darkly at past trials (law suits against their father), Teresa retires to bed, wracked by the first of a lengthy series of inexplicable (and unexplained) illnesses that will dominate several episodes.

While the series does not open, like the classical film biopic, with an authoritative voice-over (known appropriately as 'voice of God') or with on-screen titles proclaiming the truth and accuracy of the story to be told, it does start (like the Hollywood template) in medias res: Teresa has already entered her first convent and is returning home to recuperate from illness. As Custen describes also, the fact that the screen life begins with an adult protagonist means that the family is deprived of a much of its formative function on that protagonist's personality: it is characteristic that Teresa's *conversa* (Jewish convert) ancestry is not explicitly mentioned until much later in the series. Genealogy is thus not destiny. Rather, repeated shots of the bleak wintry landscape and harsh built environment (even at Mass the congregation sit on a cold stone floor) suggest that environment will be a more decisive factor in the future Saint's hard won achievement.

Like her Hollywood sisters once more, Teresa is provided from the start with a close friend. Sister Juana will serve as a mirror, a confidant, and, latterly, a critic, throwing into relief through her timidity the courage of the Saint in defending her visions and initiating her reform of the Carmelite order. Already, a certain distance between them is established in spite of the intimacy of their female friendship: Teresa tells the concerned Juana that there are 'things that [she] cannot explain' to her.

While dwelling on this passionate companionship, the first episode also appears to offer Teresa a male romantic partner in the small town of Becedes, where she continues to recuperate. The first of Teresa's many confessors is a darkly troubled young man who himself confesses his mortal sin of concubinage to Teresa. This scene takes place in the unusually pastoral setting of a verdant forest, complete with babbling brook and buzzing bees. Teresa boldly tears off the magical amulet he wears around his neck, thus establishing the centrality of her initiative (a vital element in the biopic career). But the minor character of the bewitched priest remains strangely prominent: the episode ends with him watching tearfully as the Saint leaves his small town for Avila.

If Teresa is provided, like the great majority of biopic heroes, with family, friends, and a (vestigial) romance (which serve in traditional style to both dramatize and validate her exceptional destiny), the series, given its extended length and measured pace, lacks the strict causality required of a classic ninety minute feature film. Molina, de la Concha, and Martín Gaite do indeed seem to propose in the first episode a turning point for Teresa, the decisive moment with which the biopic normally opens and on which its narrative turns. This, we are told, is the discovery of Juan de Osuna's *Abecedario espiritual* ('Spiritual Alphabet'), a manual Teresa is later obliged by the Inquisition to burn. But this supposed revelation remains strictly internal: Velasco reads in voice over lines of text that require her character to work, and suffer, in the strictest of silence.

Similarly the series fails to use flashbacks to depict popular episodes from the autobiography *Su vida* ('Her Life') that cry out for dramatization: the child Teresa's flight from home in a bid to convert the Moors is (like her *conversa* heritage) mentioned only obliquely. Typically it is told, not shown. Moreover the scenes of Teresa's refusal to eat and her daily vomiting suggest to the modern viewer a potential psychological narrative (of hysteria or neurosis) that is in competition with the spiritual career that is so hard to translate from word to image. As incidents proceed at apparently random intervals in the second episode (successive titles read 'Two Years Later', 'One Year Later', 'Twelve Years Later') it is difficult to discern much sense of dramatic urgency and shaping. Indeed much of this episode is taken up with the young Teresa's apparent death and resurrection at her father's house, an event that brings her spiritual career to a lengthy halt.

Custen identifies three motifs in performer biopics: 'resistance by the establishment of the field, advice from a older colleague, and a dramatic breakthrough [...] — often in the nick of time — for the novice' (70). The indispensable 'public reception of talent' (71) is here long delayed. Confessor Gaspar Daza is just the first in a line of male authority figures who resist Teresa's innovations, claiming that her (as yet unshown) visions are diabolical illusions, the product of the emotions and not the intelligence. But fellow nuns are equally sceptical, with Teresa provided with a full-blown antagonist in the venomous Sister Teodora, in a conflict that is schematically opposed to her growing intimate friendship with wealthy lay supporter, doña Guiomar. While the creators put an unusually feminist message into Teresa's lips at the end of this episode (she claims that a wife's existence is mere submission to her husband and repeated pregnancy), the alternative satisfactions of convent life and female comradeship have as yet by no means been established. As Custen writes, for female subjects of biopics above all, the 'price of being different' (of innovating) is retribution and misfortune: 'men are defined by their gift, women by their gender or their gendered use of their gift' (106).

Significantly, Molina's depiction of Teresa's mystical visions, which begins in episode 3, is as hesitant and circumspect as the historical Teresa's accounts of them to her confessors and readers, as if the director too feared resistance and rejection by her public. While Teresa is permitted an unusually direct commentary on the Inquisition-inspired book burning (she sardonically suggests the unsympathetic Teodora 'enjoy' the conflagration), her mystical experiences are represented obliquely through a series of formal framing devices. Thus in a first vision of Christ, Teresa is shown in prayer, reciting in voice-over a poem on the fusion of love and pain. Out of the darkness appears what is clearly not a physical person, but a painting of her Beloved. Or again, a little later the Transverberation is not shown to us directly, but rather told to Guiomar as a surrogate for the audience. Hearing the saint's ecstatic cries, the laywoman enters her cell and cradles Teresa in a Bernini-like pietà (Fig. 12). Using the exact words of *Su vida* (including such distinctive details as the 'small size' and 'shining countenance' of the angel) Velasco breathlessly recites the description of how an angel pierced her heart with an arrow. The lighting dims behind them to leave the two women in luminous isolation. After Teresa's tale the sympathetic Guiomar provides confirmation of its truth claim: 'I know that you are not lying.' It remains the case, however, that the viewer has, like the character, not been a witness to this most celebrated of scenes.

Finally, a single sequence showing hell as a dark tunnel, caked with mud (but lacking the creepy-crawlies or 'sabandijas' of the original text) is introduced by a slow tracking shot into the back of Teresa's black hood and a dissolve, which reads as the transition to a dream sequence. Even in a brief scene of levitation, the only example of the supernatural in the whole series that is shown in a clearly objective

FIG. 12. Visions of Teresa (Concha Velasco, left) (I): *Teresa de Jesús*

shot, sceptical detractors such as Teodora are absent, leaving only Teresa's fervent supporters to spread the word of the miracle around the convent.

In the second half of the series Teresa's reform is shown as a balancing act between innovation and tradition, confirming Custen's comment that in the biopic innovation leads inevitably to the establishment of a new tradition (153). But the production team of *Teresa* walk a similar tightrope. While they give some credence to revisionist accounts of the Saint that viewers in the democratizing and increasingly secular Spain of the Transition might be expected to support (Teresa is shown to be a feminist and anti-racist), they must also deliver a series that is historically accurate (as shown by frequent titles indicating dates and places) and devotionally inoffensive (as shown by the swelling strings that accompany Teresa's visions, however circumspectly the latter are shot). There is some ideological confusion here. But the rooting interest beloved of Zanuck is transparent. Spurred on by resistance, the Saint establishes her foundations against all the odds, receiving the essential acknowledgement from older colleagues only at the end of episode 4, when Daza grudgingly announces: 'You have done it.'

But if there are moments of dramatic breakthrough under pressure of time (the convent at Medina del Campo is set up literally overnight in episode 5), motivation and causation are less clear. Indeed Teresa herself is made to voice the 'battle' between the twin impulses she feels to meditation and to foundation (her twin loyalties to Mary and Martha). But the depiction of worldly works, easier to translate from textual to visual than ineffable visions, is itself somewhat ambivalent. A montage of domestic labour in one new convent illustrates Teresa's most famous saying ('God lives amongst the pots and pans') and offers a chance to show that the exceptional person is (like Edison or Bell) reassuringly normal outside his or her special gift. But the sequence is capped by the Saint vomiting after attempting to gut fish (4). If the televisual *Teresa* can embrace democratic sociability as well as Catholic spirituality (and the star persona of Velasco is clearly more at home with the first than the second), it has difficulty encompassing the psychological reading of Teresa as neurotic or hysteric which briefly breaks surface here once more.

In spite of this ideological incoherence, so alien to classic Hollywood, *Teresa* does hold fast to two more of Custen's biopic conventions: reflexivity and the trial. In the second half of the series there is a continuing commentary on the nature of fame, which might be called Cervantine. Like Don Quixote, Teresa is now acclaimed by the populace when arriving in a new town; and, like the Knight once more, her acquaintances are eager to read her story. The capricious Princess of Eboli asks for a copy of *Su vida* and is shown sceptically laughing over it with her ladies in waiting (episode 5). Later she and other society figures, spurned by Teresa, will betray the author of the manuscript to the Inquisition. When the aged Teresa returns to her first convent as a Prioress who is imposed by the authorities against the nuns' will, younger women ask 'What was she like?', as if Teresa were a historical figure even before her death. It is no surprise that the last episode should begin with Teresa, now a seasoned author, giving dictation to a young nun. Life is becoming biography before our very eyes.

Teresa's growing fame does lead, finally, to unambiguous acclaim, not just from the future Saint John of the Cross (whom Teresa recognizes as a fellow 'bicho raro' or 'odd ball') but from an institutional supporter in the form of the loyal and attractive Padre Jerónimo Gracián (episode 6). Seville, the setting for a late foundation, is at first presented as profoundly alien to the industrious and abstemious Castilian Saint: watching the Orientalist spectacle of veiled women and turbaned men and the display of glazed pottery and finely embroidered cloth, Teresa remarks wearily 'Here they are always on holiday' (episode 7). But it is also in Andalusia, far from the Castile that she says is 'closer to heaven', that Teresa receives the most visible accolade of fame as the embodiment of community judgement (Custen 149). After a procession that is unusually picturesque for a historical series that is typically somewhat austere in its mise en scene, the Archbishop of Seville kneels in the street to be blessed by the future Saint. This scene corresponds to a classic moment in the performer's biopic: the artistic triumph that magically transforms innovation and transgression into tradition and legitimation. In such reflexive scenes, *Teresa* becomes in part a commentary on that same construction of fame that is the origin of, and justification for, the biopic as genre.

Pointedly, this public acclamation comes immediately after Teresa's gravest and most explicitly staged trial, where she is interrogated by three Jesuits from the Inquisition (episode 7). It is striking that this is the first time that Teresa has faced her accusers directly: when the Town Council of Avila debated her first foundation she was not shown to be present, nor was she when enraged townspeople tried to force their way into the convent (episode 4). As Custen notes, trial scenes were so central to the biopic that, even if the studio's researchers found no historical evidence for them, they were frequently fabricated (187). A 'powerful condensing device', the trial affords 'a stage for the drama of fame' with 'a clear rooting interest in the roles of defendant and prosecutor' (186). Moreover the trial serves as 'a kind of meta-structure of fame [...] vindicating the cause with a finality seldom seen in other real-life contexts' (187).

In the case of Teresa, however, although trial does indeed lead to public triumph (a walk-on by the King will pronounce Teresa a 'jewel in [his] crown'), vindication is by no means definitive. Already her Discalced order has been sabotaged by rival Carmelites. And in the final episode the young nuns no longer accept Teresa when she returns to her first foundation; she quarrels bitterly with her family over an inheritance; and her increasing infirmity is disrespected by aristocratic patrons who demand she pay them visits. Although an extended deathbed scene is framed by supernatural portents (a wintry almond tree bursts into bloom, a final voice over recounts her posthumous triumphs), the focus at the end of the series, as throughout, is on the sheer suffering of the physical body.

It is perhaps here that *Teresa*, a series that strains like so many of TVE's in the period for the quality and dignity of film, coincides most closely with the medium for which it was actually made. For, as Custen notes once more, TV movies and miniseries have focused more heavily than classic cinema on female protagonists who are often presented as victims, not infrequently of unknown maladies. While the tradition of 'woman ennobled by suffering' is inherited from the studio era, the focus on 'the woman's body ravaged by illness' is distinctively televisual (227). Now, Concha Velasco's early career as the quintessential 'chica ye-ye' (the modern girl of the 1960s who danced and sang with more enthusiasm than professionalism) hardly paved the way for her depiction of the ever frail Teresa. But it had begun to earn her the intimate and lasting familiarity with Spanish audiences she had won by the 1980s. Inadvertently, perhaps, by placing such emphasis on Teresa's everyday physical travails and neglecting her exceptional spiritual vocation, Molina and Velasco coincided with a certain 'populism of fame' (224) and 'egalitarian mode of representation' (225) that are typical of television, even as their Teresa drew so heavily on the more hallowed template of the cinematic biopic.

'Teresa, el cuerpo de Cristo' (2007): from historiography to historiophoty

The first feature film on Saint Teresa for over thirty years, *El cuerpo de Cristo* seems to set itself up as irreverent and transgressive from the start. Ray Loriga, who takes the credit for both direction and screenwriting, came to fame as a tattooed and bleached haired generation X novelist, with a reputation for sex, drugs, and rock and roll. With just one feature to his name to date (*La pistola de mi hermano* ['My Brother's Gun', 1997] was based on a self-penned novel), he had also co-written one of Almodóvar's most disciplined scripts: the noirish *Carne trémula* ('Live Flesh', 1997). His chosen leading lady, Seville-born Paz Vega, had made her name on television in early seasons of street-smart sitcom *7 Vidas* ('Seven Lives', 1999–2000), where her character was a daffy, but adorable, Andalusian in Madrid. By now, however, her star persona was less domestic, having achieved her highest profile in Julio Medem's erotic art movie *Lucía y el sexo* ('Sex and Lucía', 2001) and musical sex comedy Emilio Martínez Lázaro's *El otro lado de la cama* ('The Other Side of the Bed', 2002), a film whose premise could hardly be further from his *Las 13 rosas*, which we examined in Chapter 1. The one sheet poster for her *Teresa* set the tone for the film: Vega, chestnut hair flowing free and nude from the waist up (albeit seen from the side) looks coyly down as a man's hand, clearly bearing the trace of Christ's stigma, caresses her bare arm and shoulder. Given the profile of both director and author, surely this feature would be a wilfully controversial and irreverent version of the Saint's life, intended to wound the sensibilities of the faithful in the service of box office success?

The Church took the bait. Before the film even opened a bishop attacked it for carnality and for its improper reduction of mystical experience to psycho-sexual complexes. Producer Andrés Vicente Gómez, whose lengthy career embraces both commercial blockbusters (*Torrente* [1998] and *Isi & Disi* [2004]) and period pictures with some pretension to quality (*Belle époque* [1992], *Libertarias* ['Freedom Fighters', 1996] and *La niña de tus ojos* ['The Girl of Your Dreams', 1998]), rejected this anathematization, noting that the film had at that time only been seen by a select group of critics, who proclaimed it 'unscandalous': more respectful than daring, more classical than innovative (Ocaña).

Moreover the track record of the rest of the creative team suggests (like that of Vicente Gómez) a certain balance between innovation and tradition that, ironically perhaps, is also typical of the biopic as genre. Thus the lush costumes were by Eiko Ishioka, a Japanese designer best known for her equally extravagant wardrobe for *Bram Stoker's Dracula*. In the film's official 'making of' she cheerfully confesses to ignorance of Catholicism, although admits to having conducted some research in museums. Veteran José Luis Alcaine, perhaps Spain's most respected cinematographer, claims rather that his work was based directly on contemporary painting (which was, of course, highly stylized) and on his historical knowledge of light sources in the period. Art director Rafael Palmero, who says that he aimed to create 'dramatic' and 'emotional' spaces, not faithful reconstruction, had actually worked on the austere *Teresa* TVE series twenty years earlier. Emilio Ruiz (whom Loriga calls a 'legend' of Spanish cinema) had constructed his distinctive foreground transparencies (known in Spanish somewhat misleadingly as 'maquetas') for the same Francoist biopics that the TV *Teresa* of the Transition had been so anxious to distance itself from. Iconoclasm thus held hands with traditional cinematic craft.

In this documentary both director and star, treading a tightrope once more, avoid overt polemics and tend to secularize the historical figure in a way that was already apparent in the statements of Molina and Velasco back in 1984. Thus Loriga claims that Teresa was an 'exceptional person, woman' whose story is one of both 'struggle' against her problems and of 'love' and 'carnality'. Vega enthusiastically calls her subject a 'revolutionary' who was 'ahead of her time.' Female supporting players are anxious (again like the team of the TV Teresa) to reassure contemporary audiences that their characters are not so distant from modern values. Geraldine Chaplin's chilly Prioress is 'not bad', but bored, frustrated, and isolated. Leonor Watling's Guiomar is no *beata* (sanctimonious busybody), but rather an active and vigorous woman. Alluding perhaps to Vega's hyper-sexualized star persona, Chaplin notes ingenuously that the crew was 'surprised' by her performance: Paz, she says, found a 'balance between the two sides' (of spirituality and carnality).

The film itself reveals, surprisingly once more, an even closer link to the classic biopic template than the TV version, and not simply because a limited screen time of just 97 minutes imposed a greater requirement for narrative condensation. *El cuerpo* opens in traditional style with a 'voice of God' scene-setting narration, albeit less precise than the TV series' meticulous titles (we are told the action takes place in 'Castille, in the second half of the sixteenth century'). The male voice-over (like *Teresa de Jesús*'s male relatives in the opening sequence of the series) highlights the paradoxes of the period: the riches of the Indies and the poverty of the people. It adds that 'our Church' was assailed both from outside, by the Reformation, and from inside, by heretics and the Inquisition. What is distinctive here, however (and it is already found in what Andrew Higson, following Claire Monck, calls the British 'post-heritage' films such as *Elizabeth* (Shekhar Kapur, 1998) (Higson 197)), is that we are from the start presented with graphic scenes of supposed Illuminist orgies and Inquisitional torture chambers.

This shift from textuality to visuality (or from historiography to 'historiophoty') will prove to be the significant difference between the Teresa of the Transition and that of the millennium. But, I would argue, the latter is not necessarily less historically accurate or theologically reverent than the former. Indeed in the process of translatability from word to image there is much to be gained, as well as lost, by taking leave of the text. Thus while the TV credit sequence was anchored in the concrete physicality of an authentic location (the familiar walls of Avila), the film credits offer a kaleidoscopic evocation of the mystical experience. Richly dressed in a scarlet gown, Vega's young and beautiful Teresa (no attempt to echo the 'authentic' moles drawn on Concha Velasco's pallid face), glides into frame with rays of light and doves superimposed. Abstract tactile patterns (fire or fur?) bleed into sensual details (female fingers and richly decorated rosaries).

In spite of this over-laden mise en scene (Teresa's first convent is full of gorgeously dressed young society ladies), the film holds fast to traditional narrative conventions. It begins, once more, in medias res with the confessor Daza (here played by veteran Eusebio Poncela) telling Teresa to abandon the 'madness' of calling Christ her 'husband'. We at once dissolve, in a technique also characteristic of classic biopic, to a flashback of Teresa caressed by a first boyfriend, her cousin: a rose thorn suggestively pierces her skin. Cut to the father who, believing that her honour is now blighted, packs Teresa off to the nunnery. In telegraphic dialogue he tells her: 'No man will love you now'; to which she replies: 'I know One who will.' This brief episode serves as both psychological motivation (Teresa is now free to embrace the love of Christ) and causation (she has no choice but the convent). It thus serves as the classic turning point of biopic in which the subject's exceptional achievement is both glimpsed at the start and presented as a 'rooting point' for an audience primed to accompany that subject in her struggle for vindication against hostile authority.

Rejecting the austere landscapes of the TV series, the feature film focuses on interiors that are often lush and sensuous spaces, festooned with Eiko Ishioka's fantastical costumes. The visuality of Catholic practice is celebrated in one early sequence where Teresa is crowned with a lavish garland of flowers. But this visual

FIG. 13. Visions of Teresa (Paz Vega, right) (II): *Teresa: el cuerpo de Cristo*

extravagance is also to some extent functional. Teresa is, as before, gifted with a best friend called Juana. However here she is a threadbare 'servant' who, contradicting Teresa's claim that 'We are all equal [in the convent]', goes barefoot out of poverty not piety.

But if Loriga raises the social question of class more evidently than Molina, he also presents Teresa's visions in a form that is much more direct, more tangible, than on TV. The scene on the poster is indeed briefly shown: bathed in golden light, Christ caresses Teresa's naked back. The Transverberation is shown, briefly but directly once more, with no angel but with the Saint's scarlet bodice pierced by a myriad of golden arrows. Later the visions are presented as pictorial tableaux, embodied by actors who, although immobile, are clearly physical beings and not (as in Molina's version) merely representations. Thus Teresa as the Magdalene (in scarlet, once more) mourns over a handsome Christ, deposed from the Cross, as the Virgin looks on, cloaked in blue (Fig. 13). Or again Teresa rises from her bed to fall at the feet of a life-size and very corporeal crucified Christ. Elsewhere a foreshortened Christ, laid on a table, clearly cites Masaccio. Unlike in Molina's version, such scenes are not framed by distancing devices such as the retelling of the story by the Saint or the dissolve that conventionally signals a dream sequence. Loriga is notably more graphic once more in recreating the queasy abjection that is a disquieting characteristic of *Su vida*: at one point worms and slugs (Teresa's 'sabandijas') swarm over Christ's immaculate body.

Although there is one brief scene of Teresa walking by Avila's walls, shot in the same spot as the TV series' credits, Loriga rejects the 'heritage' shots of landscape and monuments. But he does not neglect the feminist interpretation already promoted on television twenty years before. Teresa has no real female antagonist here (even Chaplin's icy prioress finally cries out 'I want to be you!') and her struggle is focused on male authority figure the Provincial de Avila, played by Manuel Morán, best known as the abusive father in Goya-winning social realist drama *El bola* (2000). He mutters darkly about Teresa's *conversa* lineage and alleges that women have 'too much imagination and too little order'. Leonor Watling's youthful Guiomar hosts what appears to be female-centred salon, supported by liberal clerics. Given that academic García de la Concha had proclaimed Teresa a feminist twenty years earlier, this interpretation hardly seems controversial today. And feminist heroics is once more reinforced by the trial motif that is beloved of the biopic. Although the emphasis in the feature film, unlike in the miniseries, is on visions not foundations (on Mary not Martha), Teresa is from the opening sequence attacked by those who resist her innovations and faces an explicit trial sequence halfway through the film. Interrogated by male accusers as to how she can be sure that her visions are true, she can only reply in the paradoxical terms of *Su vida*: passionately defending (in Vega's incongruous Andalusian accent) the 'sweet wounds' Christ has gifted her with. We are also shown the trial in absentia, where the hostile town council attempts, unsuccessfully, to block Teresa's first foundation.

Teresa's final and public triumph is, however, unambiguous. Swapping her rich gown for a more sober habit, she treks over a bleak landscape to ring the old bell of her new convent (the impressively realized image is the product of Ruiz's 'maqueta'). A swelling orchestra instructs to be moved by Teresa's success, while the traditional titles (familiar from the earliest days of the biopic) reaffirm her legacy: not only did the fragile foundation survive but Teresa went on to be a Doctor of the church and a 'fundamental' figure in Golden Age literature. The feature film, given the restricted period it spans, does not treat the reflexivity of fame addressed by the TV series. But nor does it focus on the physicality of the female body, wracked by mysterious illness, which, I have argued with Custen, is so characteristic of the rival medium of television. Molina's more prosaic presentation may lay claim to a more egalitarian mode of representation; but Loriga's heightened visuality (his use of the quick cutting and disorientating superimpositions, held to be typical of an 'MTV' style) attempt to reproduce more immediately the mystic rapture over which Molina, more modest or more timid, prefers to draw a veil.

Suddenly Last Supper

In spite of press support from the Left-leaning *El País*, *Teresa, el cuerpo de Cristo* did not find a large audience. Official figures say it was seen by just 122,460 people (Base de datos). It seems that the devotional public that, encouraged by the Church's support, still enjoy Molina's 'classic' series did not take kindly to Loriga's feature, which the pre-publicity, poster, and personae of director and star had led them to believe would be blasphemous exploitation. Conversely, a youthful secular audience was not attracted by the casting of Vega against type. Yet the two re-visions of Teresa have both been ill served by their respective reputations. In spite of its brief glimpses of Illuminist orgies, *El cuerpo de cristo* was by no means blasphemous or irreverent in its portrait of the Saint, especially when compared to the overtly pornographic re-workings of Catholic iconography (including of Teresa) made in the same period by still photographer J. A. M. Montoya (2008). Indeed the film preserved more closely than the TV series the hagiographic trappings of the biopic and, arguably, addressed Teresa's inner life more directly and seriously.

Conversely, although the TV series was blessed by the Church, it distanced and qualified the mystical experience in a way consistent with its director's sceptical humanism (clearly stated at the time), even as it insisted with wearisome frequency on the authenticity of its reproduction of the Saint's external biography. Moreover Molina's version suggests more strongly than Loriga's that Teresa's condition was perhaps psychological in character. Confronted only by the extended sufferings of the female body (including the anorexia and bulimia that were becoming sadly topical at the time of production) and denied access to the Saint's ecstatic interiority, viewers are perhaps more likely to read Teresa's story within the secular 'disease of the week' template of the female-targeted TV movie. While Ray Loriga's vision is much more flashy, glossy, and accelerated than Molina's static, austere, and leisurely narrative, its MTV aesthetic offers a glimpse at least of a dynamic and ecstatic realm, inaccessible to the lay audience, that is vital to the texture of *Su vida*. Fidelity, then, is not to be reduced to facticity.

The two re-visions (their divergent visual and narrative rhetoric) are also, of course, derived from the distinct characteristics of their respective media. As John Caughie reminds us, cinema commenced as vision without sound, while broadcasting began as sound without vision. Loriga emphasizes the visuality of film, inviting us to dream with Teresa. Molina clings fast to the textuality that is shared by television and her scholarly sources, asking us to meditate on her heroine's travails. In addition, each version is inflected by the periods in which they were made, presenting as they do distinct ecologies of film and television. Molina was supported in her pedagogical approach by a TVE devoted at that time to quality projects intended to reinforce the prestige of an embattled public broadcaster that had only recently emerged from the dictatorship. Loriga, on the other hand, may have been sheltered by a powerful film producer, but he was working within a cinema's industry beset by perpetual crisis. Official figures for 2006–07, the year in which his film was produced, show that the most assiduous filmgoers were now 15–19 years old, the same age group as those who volunteer the most hostile attitudes towards Spanish cinema (SGAE 78). In spite of Loriga's attempt to connect with these contemporary viewers through the casting of Paz Vega, the youthful and Hollywood-friendly audience was unlikely to be a prime demographic for *Teresa*.

We have seen that for Custen controversies about truth, accuracy, and interpretation are intrinsic to the biopic genre. Indeed they are a major part of its interest for scholars and critics. While Molina's modest self-presentation, parallel to that of Teresa, managed to avoid damaging polemics when her series was broadcast, her series' concentration on Teresa's works was not without consequences. While still disavowing the label 'realizadora', Molina claimed in 2006 that her lengthy career, in film as in television, had aimed to show: 'la libertad de manifestar nuestro punto de vista sobre el mundo a través de nuestra obra, utilizando para ello cualquier oportunidad y cualquier metáfora' ['the freedom to show our point of view on the world through our work, using to that end any opportunity and any metaphor'] (Palacio, 'Interview' 103) Molina clearly saw Teresa's saintliness instrumentally as a 'metaphor' for what she calls women's 'initiative' in the world, including the male-dominated world of television.

Loriga, on the other hand, while overtly echoing Molina's concern for female agency, also attempted to grant his Teresa greater powers of imagination and emotion. These latter qualities are rescued from Teresa's historical detractors and reinvented for a media-saturated modern audience through dazzling, seductive aesthetics. While both directors engage in 'enculturation' or the creation of 'public history' for a national, if not international, audience and both make separate but equal claims to historical truth, it is by no means clear whose re-vision of Teresa can or should be validated as a legitimate carrier of the lessons of history. Hence although the status of the biopic, in both its cinematic and televisual variants, is widely contested, its transitivity (its capacity to breach barriers of genre and of nationality) is comparable to that of a more despised, but equally mutable, format: the TV sitcom, which we shall examine in the next chapter.

Works cited

CUSTEN, GEORGE F. *Bio/pics: How Hollywood Constructed Public History* (Newark: Rutgers University Press, 1992)

HIGSON, ANDREW. *English Heritage, English Cinema* (Oxford: Oxford University Press, 2003)

LLORENTE, ÁNGEL. *Arte e ideología en el franquismo* (Madrid: Visor, 1995)

PALACIO, MANUEL. *Historia de la televisión en España* (Barcelona: Gedisa, 2001)

———ed. *Las cosas que hemos visto* (Madrid: RTVE, 2006)

———Interview with Josefa Molina, *Las cosas*, 103

PRESTON, PAUL. *Franco: A Biography* (New York: Fontana, 1995)

QUÍLEZ ESTEVE, LAIA. 'Teresa de Jesús.' Palacio, *Las cosas*, 102–03

SGAE. *Hábitos de consumo cultural* (Madrid: SGAE, 2000)

Web sources all accessed 2 August 2010:

Base de datos, <http://www.mcu.es/bbddpeliculas/cargarFiltro.do?layout=bbddpeliculas&cache=init>

MONTOYA, J. A. M. <http://www.jam-montoya.es/>

OCAÑA, JAVIER. 'Crítica: una mujer enamorada' [review of *Teresa, el cuerpo de Cristo*], *El País*, 9 March 2007, <http://www.elpais.com/articulo/cine/mujer/enamorada/elpepuculcin/20070309elpepicin_14/Tes>

UMBRAL, FRANCISCO. 'Tribuna: 22 domingo', *El País*, 29 April 1984, <http://www.elpais.com/articulo/ultima/22/domingo/elpepiult/19840429elpepiult_5/Tes>

CHAPTER 8

Hybrid Fictions

Television Comedy between Soap Opera and Pseudo-documentary:
Los Serrano [Tele 5, 2003–08] and
Camera café ['Coffee Cam', Tele 5, 2005–09]

Blended comedies, blended families

In the credit sequence of *Los Serrano*, an enduringly popular comic series from Globomedia and Tele 5, we see pseudo-home video of the two strands of the blended family that is the subject of the show: Belén Rueda's Lucía plays with her two daughters at the Parc Güell and on the Barcelona beach, while Antonio Resines' Diego roughhouses with his three sons at home in suburban Madrid. The colour of the image is degraded and streaked with the (now incongruous) stripes of vintage celluloid. The theme tune, which plays over the credits, sets up the series' premise: 'one [father] plus one [mother] equals [a new family of] seven.' (Fig. 14) It is sung by boyishly handsome Fran Perea, who played eldest son Marcos for five seasons and leveraged this number one hit to establish a pop career in his own name.

In episode 14 of the sketch comedy *Camera café*, also broadcast by Tele 5 but made by little-known independent Magnolia, mousy secretary Mari Carmen (Esperanza Pedreño) discovers a new drink is on offer at the office coffee machine that houses the single camera from whose viewpoint we see the whole show. The drink is called 'Flips'. When she tries it, the effect is immediate: she collapses to the floor and turns a cartwheel. What is more, Mari Carmen is given access to a new, chemically enhanced perspective. Breathlessly, she tells her sceptical colleagues, Julián in purchasing (Carlos Chamarro) and Jesús in sales (Arturo Valls), that she has discovered that there are people on the other side of the coffee machine, people who are watching them.

In their different ways, both scenes suggest that Spanish television comedy has now become hybridized, fusing in complex ways with other genres and media and commenting reflexively on television itself. This article treats these two prize-winning *telecomedias* (the nearest term in Spanish to 'sitcom'), *Los Serrano* (2003–08) and *Camera café* (2005–09), both of which were the top-rated fiction titles in their

FIG. 14. 'One plus one equals seven': the big family of *Los Serrano*

debut years and later attracted faithful weekly audiences in their millions for the better part of a decade.

While Spanish sitcoms have received almost no academic attention, the US version of the genre is well studied. As is well known, sitcom was long thought to be a notoriously stable and static form, existing in a fictional realm apparently immune to the rigours of socio-historical change and even character development. Yet although the form of the classic sitcom (scheduled for a 30 minute slot and shot with a three camera set-up in front of a live studio audience) has indeed proved surprisingly durable, it remains the case that the content of the genre has incorporated changing social issues, particularly in the workplace, since the 1960s.

Moreover, in the 1990s and 2000s the sitcom was clearly hybridized with at least two other genres. Some examples (such as *Friends*) retained the multi-camera set up and studio audience, but exploited 'deep' narrative threads more typical of soap opera. Beyond verbal and visual comedy, they relied on the parasocial pleasures for the audience of a continuing coexistence with fictional characters who, over the course of the seasons, became barely distinguishable from the actor-celebrities who played them. Others (such as *The Office*, in the UK and, later, the US) blended half-hour comedy and pseudo-documentary, with the single camera claiming to act as the mere observer of authentic, unscripted action. In their different ways, and like the Spanish shows, both blurred the line between reality and fiction, drama and comedy.

To anticipate my argument, it is clear that the long-running family dramedy *Los Serrano*, with its highly personal and even melodramatic plotlines, coincides with the former trend; while the newer workplace sketch comedy *Camera café*, with its minimalist shooting style and workplace setting (if not its exaggerated mode of performance) relates to the second trend. In Spain, however, the so-called classic sitcom, whose conventions survived so long elsewhere, is barely known. Dramas and comedies are often lumped together as 'series', and formats that are elsewhere distinct are already habitually blended together. According to one recent study of TV formats, the sitcom genre still remains 'unfinished business' in Spain today (Saló 175).

The Spanish mediascape presented here thus presents a valuable correction to the Anglo-American model, which generally presents itself as universal. But this chapter will also offer a close textual analysis of the two Spanish series, arguing that in their very different ways they problematize the relation between fiction and reality that has until recently been held to be self-evident in the case of TV comedy.

First, however, we must consider the question of hybridity in both its generic and national variants. As mentioned earlier, even those sources that stress the unusual stability of the sitcom form since the early years of television acknowledge its potential for registering social and historical change. In *The Sitcom Reader*, Mary M. Dalton and Laura L. Linder argue that in TV families 'the more things change, the more they stay the same', with 'the basic paradigm remain[ing] intact' from Ozzy and Harriet Nelson to Ozzie and Sharon Osbourne (3). Work and social class is, however, a different story. Workplace comedies, they note, 'proved a rich venue for exploring gender and social change' (10), with even Doris Day's TV character charting the movement of women from the suburban home into the urban workforce as early as the 1960s. Joanne Morreale notes how, in the following decade, 'elements of drama' were added to the sitcom form (152). This new trend had social implications, since novel themes like death and divorce could now be treated. But it also had formal or generic consequences. No longer marooned in the repetitive or circular stasis of series television, sitcoms borrowed from serials, with storylines progressing in linear fashion from one episode to another and characters developing over time. This serial character- and issue-based form, often difficult to combine with gag comedy, had previously been 'the domain of soap opera' (152).

In his major book on the genre Brett Mills cautions that 'hybrid forms like "comedy drama" are notoriously subjective' (25). But he also suggests that there is 'flexibility not only within the industrial structures which produce sitcom, but also within audiences' reading techniques' (25). Evidence of this mutual development of production and consumption is given in Mills's 2004 article in *Screen*, which offers a new and influential name for contemporary sitcom form: 'comedy vérité'. Refuting once more the supposed 'stability' of the genre, with its allegedly conservative focus on the family (63) and 'domestic normality' (64), Mills argues for a distinction between form and content. Comedy was at one time clearly stylized. For example, its use of a three-camera set up instead of a 'variety of camera angles to create [the] complex and full-formed narrative space' of drama [66]) was an essential part of its appeal. As Mills writes: 'the laughter track, the theatrical shooting style and the displayed performance clearly demonstrate sitcom's artificial status and its clear, precise, single-minded aim: to make you laugh' (67).

Now the sitcom's 'new found engagement with alternative modes of representation', such as the observational docu-soap fictionally recreated in the BBC's *The Office*, 'responds to the debate concerning genre hybridity which [...] undermines purist definitions of genres such as the sitcom and the documentary' (70). With comedy no longer 'transparent', its relationship to the audience is transformed and cannot be reduced to 'the satisfaction of watching [a readily recognizable] sitcom': 'Quite the opposite: by using the characteristics of other genres, and removing those traditionally associated with sitcom, the pleasure offered requires at least a working knowledge of other television forms' (77).

In 'Comedy Vérité? The Observational Documentary Meets the Televisual Sitcom' Ethan Thompson has developed and modified Mills's thesis, placing it within the US context. Calling attention to the competing industrial needs for 'both product differentiation and standardization of the production process', he charts the search for an 'alternative to the standard multi-camera and single-camera modes of production' that would 'reinvigorate the sitcom format' in a way 'suited to the tastes of contemporary audiences' (63). Thompson places comedy within what Jason Mittell has called the 'unprecedented trend [in the 1990s] toward narrative complexity in television storytelling that blurs distinctions between episodic and serial narratives, that exhibits a heightened degree of self-consciousness, and that demands a higher intensity of viewer engagement' (cited by Thompson 63). Moreover 'comedy vérité' is not simply 'a subgenre of television comedy' but 'an emerging mode of production that is being adopted for its efficiency, visual complexity, and semiotic clout' (63).

With traditional sitcoms now 'struggl[ing] to connect with audiences as they once did', scripted television thus appeals to the 'aesthetic grammar of non-fiction TV' for both a 'documentary look' and 'connotations of legitimacy and prestige' (64). Such ambitious and innovative shows (Thompson's examples are HBO's *Curb Your Enthusiasm* and Fox's *Arrested Development*) also mark a shift in humour from the 'joke' (which is set up or constructed) to the comic event (which is, apparently at least, simply discovered) (67). Although Thompson's two examples are very different in the way they exploit the two clearest signs of the subgenre (hand-held camera and improvised performance), they share an accelerated tempo (no need to pause for an audience response when there is no laugh track [70]) and an increased diegetic complexity ('not just a mode of production but a method of reading as well') (71).

In a moment I will contrast the industrial mediascape of US TV (the drift from network to cable, the quest for both product differentiation and standardization of the production process) with the somewhat different situation in Spain. But first we must consider the hybridization of televisual fiction not in its generic but rather in its national form. In *El drama televisivo: identidad y contenidos sociales* ('Television Drama: Identity and Social Contents'), Milly Buonanno (whose concept of 'travelling fictions' I mentioned already in Chapter 6) gives an account of developments in Italian TV fiction of the 1990s, focusing on the theme of the family. While that specific analysis is in itself invaluable for comparative purposes with Spain, it is also embedded within a general thesis of 'indigenization' that has, in turn, wider implications for television as a medium and for the 'reality status' of its fictional worlds.

In this her first Spanish publication Buonanno begins by acknowledging an intellectual debt to Latin American cultural theorists of transnationalization and hybridity such as Martín Barbero and García Canclini (9); and she goes to lament in Italy (as in Spain) the lack of proper scholarly attention to the popular storytelling of series television, an absence that correlates to TV's lowly place in the 'hierarchies of legitimation' (10). Buonanno sets her new paradigm of indigenization against earlier hypotheses of 'cultural imperialism' and 'Americanization', still widely held by both academic and general audiences in Italy (17). For Buonanno, asymmetrical circumstances (the continued quantitative dominance of US production) are offset by locally situated dynamics of appropriation and transformation of foreign models (21). Buonanno proposes that the academic 'lexicon' should shift from cultural dominance and dependence, ideological control, colonization, imitation, and homogenization to asymmetry, interdependence, appropriation, hybridism, and heterogenization (22).

More broadly still, she writes, indigenization suggests new models of communication, of the definition of the local and the global, and of reciprocity (22). Thus, first, communication should be seen not as active to passive transmission of stable content but rather as a 'ritual': a dialogic and interactive practice exemplified by the communal 'ceremony' (23). Secondly, the local and the global are not 'static polarities' (24) but rather 'recombinable' factors, with native traditions often the result of an earlier (and now repressed) contamination (25). Hence, and finally, 'indigene' (or 'native'), although often used as a synonym for 'other' (26), can be applied equally to ourselves, inevitably formed and 'altered' as we are by contact with external forces (26).

Buonanno goes on to give a more detailed and empirical account of this process in European television, distinguishing once more between three levels: the diffusion of the (American) offer, its consumption and success (in Europe), and its influence and effects (in Europe once more) (27). While the majority of audiovisual product in Europe does indeed remain American, its presence has declined on the major networks in mature markets. Here generalist channels are induced by the 'competitive logic of distinction and differentiation' (noted also in the case of the US networks by Thompson, above) to strengthen their own roles as local producers (28). Likewise foreign product has been exiled from the most profitable and competitive timeslots of prime time and access prime time (29). US shows do indeed have competitive advantages for purchasers: economic convenience, the availability of bundles of programming, and advance testing by an audience more vast and varied than any in Europe (31–32). But even when the shows are imported (rather than their formats remade, as is increasingly common), they are no longer the same but rather 'domesticated' or 'indigenized' by new forms of dubbing, advertising, and scheduling (32–33).

As in the case of its offer, the success of US shows in Europe is exaggerated (34). While the cultural imperialism hypothesis casts American shows as a siren song easily seducing naïve natives, most of the titles aired never become either popular or cult successes abroad (35). Shoddy Italian sitcoms have a larger following than their American models, which the connoisseur Buonanno calls 'simply perfect' (36). While local products benefit from a 'cultural proximity', foreign shows are harmed by a 'cultural discount'. This makes it harder for them to activate those mechanisms of recognition and identification that audiences tend to seek from television fiction (37) and which cause them to reject programmes even from neighbouring European countries. Moreover, the relatively transcultural nature of US programming, which correlates to its uniquely broad domestic target, is now disappearing, as the networks' 'general public' (or family audience) continues to fragment and flees to cable (40).

Finally, the influence and effects of those US programmes that are indeed popular in Europe is exaggerated. Far from being 'docile victims' with 'fragile identities', local audiences adopt and adapt foreign material (41). The undoubted 'trace' left by such shows is not equivalent to 'Americanization'. For viewers do not constitute a tabula rasa but are rather 'situated' in their local cultures (43); or again, they do not decode fixed messages transmitted in imported shows, but rather 'incorporate' unstable meanings into the practice of their everyday lives, altering and changing them in that process (44). We shall see an example of this a little later in research on Spanish responses to classic US sitcom *Friends*.

What, then, is the relation between TV fictions and the real? Are viewers, like Don Quixote at the puppet show (Buonanno's echt Hispanic example), incapable of distinguishing between fantasy and reality? (50) Buonanno argues to the contrary that 'life worlds', internally coherent yet diverse and conflicting, are 'stratified'. And the movement between them is a 'border crossing', which we are normally competent both to realize and to recognize (51). Moreover the specific 'mode of presence' of television (53), so different to that of theatre, film, or literature, makes for more 'fluid and continuous' transitions between the real and the imagined (54). Blurring these boundaries, because of its coterminous consumption in everyday life, television calls into question the dichotomy between fact and fiction (57) in that it suggests, against objectivist positivism, that there are subjective, symbolic, and imaginative components to reality (59).

Series drama thus speaks both to and of us (of our must valued emotional investments [63]); it familiarizes us with the social world (taking us home to a shared, consensual space [65]); and it maintains community (preserving shared meanings and protecting us from cultural shock [66]). Yet these functions do not amount to a 'dominant' vision of the world or to cultural 'homogenization' (66). For any study of a national TV corpus will reveal its heterogeneity and differentiation, fuelled in part by genre: for example, Italian drama and sitcom give radically different accounts of 'family feeling' (67). For all their bias towards communality, consensus, and sharing, then, TV series are not simply 'false', but must rather be 'contextualized within the multiple realities in which we live' (68).

A practical example of this theoretical proposition is to be found in the way in which Italian television of the 1990s did not reflect but rather 'explained' changes in the family to local audiences (125) through a double logic of dispersal and recentralization (95). Thus, on the one hand, series sought to reframe the family on the basis of choice and reciprocity, irrespective of biological connection (96); while, on the other, they promoted a 'new normality' in which the presence of children and of a shared house remained essential to a family life held, nonetheless, to be in crisis.

This tendency appears to suggest a 'strong separation between fiction and reality', as Italy was at the time newly registering the lowest birth rate in the world (113). Moreover, the blended families typical of TV, such as a separated woman and widowed man, are found to be vanishingly small in real life (115). It thus follows that while domestic series, a broadly conservative genre, have indeed addressed historic social changes such as the collapsing birth rate, they have only done so by at once accepting novelty and 'negotiating' it, softening shocks to the audience (124). Change is thus rendered acceptable by combining it with continuity: children and the home remain central to the family, however radically that family is reconfigured (125).

Having examined at some length the questions of generic and national hybridism or transitivity, we can now go on to examine how this double process plays out in a Spanish mediascape that is at once so similar, and so different, to its Italian neighbour.

Televisual territories

In February/March 2006 *Television Business International* ran one of its periodic 'territory guides' to Spain. While it noted that 'of the big five European markets Spain is perhaps undergoing the fastest and most fundamental change' (especially with the advent of new, free to air generalist channels Cuatro and La Sexta [1]), it named the survey 'Spain: A Bright TV Picture' and illustrated it with a publicity shot of the seven Serranos beaming on their ample family sofa.

In spite of the 'fragmentation' of audiences, writes *TBI*, shows such as Tele 5's 'top-rating' *telecomedia* (3) still attract millions of viewers. While Tele 5, controlled by Italian group Mediaset, had at this time (briefly) lost the mantle of audience leader to rival generalist broadcaster Antena 3, it remained a 'formidable force in the commercial market' with an unapologetically commercial focus. As the channel's manager of operations, Massimo Musolini, baldly put it, their strategy was to 'make television to sell advertising' by 'broadcast[ing] strong domestic drama and fiction — the most popular programmes in Spain' (4). Tele 5, he says, 'has the unique ability to adapt to viewers' demands and to innovate, with pioneering formats and new programming trends' (6). Coincidentally, Tele 5 also hosted the strongest transnational reality strands: *Big Brother* and *Operación triunfo* (*Pop Idol*). *TBI* points to a specific industrial factor here, unique in Europe: Tele 5 produces 80% of its programming in house (the continental average is just 50%). As state-owned broadcaster TVE flounders in debt, the private web flourishes with national narratives, 'avoiding costly acquisitions' in favour of 'home grown series', such as *Los Serrano* once more (6).

Mario García de Castro, one time head of the Director General's Office at TVE, has given a broader account of what he calls the 'hegemony' or dominance of television fiction in Spain, whose history is based on a double 'renovation' or renewal. Speaking at the University of Navarre in June 2007, he noted the continuing broad based success of such Tele 5 titles as *Camera café* in access prime time (24.5% share) and *Los Serrano* in prime time (25%). García de Castro names as the diverse ancestors of current Spanish fiction: televised theatre in (Francoist) Spain; Latin American *telenovelas*; and US sitcoms and soaps.

The creative and industrial systems required to produce such successful hybrids were developed between 1995–2000, in what he calls 'the first renewal.' This was stimulated industrially by the growth of private television (still relatively new in Spain); the emergence of a new sector of independent producers (such as the powerful Globomedia); the evolution of the European production model towards American standards (such as 26 episodes per season); the development of a new popular and contemporary realism; and the increased knowledge of the audience as a tool for creative and industrial production.

This new policy cycle sought (as we have seen in the case of Tele 5's current management) maximum profitability in a highly competitive market; cost reduction and audience maximization; and the leadership of independent producers. Surprisingly, an unforgiving economic climate led to creative innovation. Primetime national fiction took on new and uniquely Spanish characteristics: series came to be situated generically halfway between comedy and drama; they were intended to have long runs; each episode played for 60 to 70 minutes, not including commercial breaks; and narrative structure was adapted to those commercial breaks with a lengthy four acts (as opposed to the traditional three act structure).

By the end of the 1990s, however, the formula was wearing thin, both creatively and commercially. Formats now seemed exhausted, profit margins decreased, and tastes in humour became more iconoclastic both at home and abroad. García de Castro's examples here are 7 vidas (1999–2006), Tele 5's 'classic' urban sitcom, which came complete with studio audience; and the belated influence of Antena 3's *The Simpsons*, which by 2003 was to reach a 26.7% share, unusually high for an import. The special characteristics of reality television, which peaked in 2000–03, became hybridized with scripted programming in Spain, as elsewhere. Unscripted shows blurred the border between fiction and reality; stressed the everyday nature of dramatic performance; reinforced the sense of the ensemble; relied on local and personal reference points; introduced audience participation; and promoted voyeurism into private life. All of these qualities would prove useful to the second wave of series.

Unexpectedly, then, the challenge posed by reality shows to fictional programming thus led to a second renewal of TV drama, baptized by García de Castro 'the local neorealism.' The new cycle of 2003–06 was characterized by: psychological development in family comedy (such as *Los Serrano*); a reaction against political correctness, derived in part from comic-book sources; and a naturalistic or individualist evolution of characters (the example here is *Camera café*). Heroes are now anti-heroes, and Spanish shows are scheduled to follow on from imports such as *The Simpsons*, once more, which have pioneered such iconoclasm.

Interestingly, in an age of supposed fragmentation, the most popular shows remain family-oriented (TVE's period saga *Cuéntame* is another example). Audiences for such shows are still intergenerational and inter-class, but it is young viewers that lead the consumption choice. The commercial profile of the fiction audience in Spain is: under 45, female, middle and upper class, and urban.

It thus follows that (as in the US) the editorial line of a Spanish broadcaster seeking such a relatively upmarket audience will tend to include shows with increasingly complex narrative and characterization. The demography of the fictional world is also wider than ever, now embracing the family, home, work, and the street, and stressing the psychological evolution of unidealized characters that is expressed through humour. What García de Castro calls 'neo-realism' or 'contemporary *costumbrismo*' is marked by the exploration of social topics in drama and of politically incorrect characters in comedy. Firmly anchored in the present, it incorporates the new moral values of modernity, played out in everyday life and through an ensemble cast, with a point of view that García de Castro describes as a 'double [or perhaps "ambivalent"] moral aspect.' García de Castro thus stresses the cross-fertilization of fiction and non-fiction that we have seen also in US and UK sitcoms, albeit with rather different effects in Spain to those felt in English-speaking countries. But he also notes the uncanny persistence of the family both on and off screen.

Mercedes Medina has led a research group at the Universidad de Navarra that is conducting a major study of the family in three classic Spanish series: *Médico de familia* (Globomedia's first success on Tele 5 in 1995–99), *Cuéntame*, (TVE 1/Ganga, 2001–), and *Los Serrano*. Presenting their interim results in June 2007 (when García de Castro also spoke), Medina's group focused, like him, but in greater detail, on production processes (including script development), economics (including scheduling and commercial exploitation), and narrative (the representation of 'family values' in the series). While their corpus is too restricted to be representative of Spanish TV fiction or comedy as a whole (the Navarra group fail to consider the critical and popular successes that do not feature a traditionally defined family unit), the specific analysis remains valuable.

Medina and her colleagues define 'family series' as those that are broadcast at prime time; target the whole family; place the family unit at the core of the story; tie the family into the main plotlines; and take place mainly in the home. They offer much detailed and original empirical research on such shows. For example, the production agreement for *Los Serrano* (originally called 'Ellos y ellas') reveals that the project was designed for Tele 5 over a two-year development period when once powerful Globomedia was in crisis, having experienced several failures. According to this deal Tele 5, with its so-called 'Fiction Factory', provided the sets (at its large Picasso Studios), technical support (equipment and crew), post-production facilities, and executive production. Independent Globomedia, on the other hand, was responsible for the scripts, the creative team, and the production team. Appendices to the contract between the two organizations included a production timeline, a budget for the first season, and a 'Bible' (containing detailed backstories for the many characters). Vital issues covered in the contract itself included the sharing of different kinds of rights. While Tele 5 gained 70% and Globomedia 30% of income for each episode broadcast, the proportions were reversed for revenue from the (anticipated) sale of the format abroad. Music rights (clearly already intended to be significant) were split 50/50. The ending of this contract, which would much later prove to be a point of controversy, was dependent on audience share falling below a certain point.

In this decision-making process the network was concerned that the series should be in accordance with its editorial line and scheduling strategy for prime time. Tele

5 also retained script and casting approval. The production company was concerned above all with creative issues, such as the development of plot and character.

Production values were relatively high, with a budget of 429K euros per episode (in spite of its starry cast, period rival *Cuéntame* made do with just 342K). With sixteen permanent sets, plus one that was multifunctional, and with 20% of scenes shot in exteriors, *Los Serrano* also strayed far from the classic sitcom or soap's studio-bound limits. And while the show employed four cameras, one crane, and two ENGs (electronic news gathering equipment for exteriors), this was not the traditional multi-camera studio affair but rather a feature film-style production (albeit on Betacam Digital format), with two units shooting three episodes at the same time. (The 'making of' included on the DVD also reveals habitual use of steadycam for location shooting.) Each script was also formally complex, requiring four separate plot lines to fill out the extended 75 minutes. As Thompson showed for US comedy vérité, then, standardization of production processes (rigorously enforced here) was not necessarily the enemy of creative product differentiation.

The production processes of such family series in Spain are, of course, related to the specific demography of their target audience. Medina et al. cite statistics to show that, in spite of a collapse in the birth rate that rivals Italy's, single-person households remain rare in Spain (at around 15% in 2003), while almost 50% of households have three or more members. With an average of 2.9 members, Spanish households are thus half as big again as their German equivalents. Moreover the 16–39-year-olds coveted by advertisers remain by far the largest age group in the country. Unique Spanish time schedules also mean that primetime shows such as *Los Serrano* (which air at the most sought-after slot of 10 p.m.) are amongst the favourite programmes for children aged 4–12 years.

Remarkably faithful to individual series over a number of years, this Spanish family audience is, according to Medina, a valued and willing target for product placement, perceiving domestic brands as a part of the fictional narrative world and as a contribution to localist realism. Surprisingly perhaps, the formats of these Spanish vernacular, neo-contemporary dramas are highly exportable, with *Los Serrano* sold not only to culturally close Latin and Spanish-American countries (Portugal, Italy, and France; Chile and Uruguay), but also to such apparently inhospitable territories as Germany, Turkey, and the Czech Republic.

While the Navarra team conclude that such success is based on the 'adequacy' of the series' content (namely, its acceptable representation of the family), they also confirm García de Castro's view that Spanish televisual form is unique: these are 'merger series', irreducible to traditional formats, that combine aspects typical of sitcom and soap opera and deserve the name 'hybrid.' Moreover this generic hybridity is also national. Successful shows draw on US serials, but exhibit strikingly different narrative rhythms.

One aspect with which Medina et al. are clearly unhappy is the iconoclastic or ambivalent depiction of the family in *Los Serrano*. One of their papers published on the internet ('La cultura') is on audience responses to the show. Posing the question 'What does [*Los Serrano*] communicate?', it reveals a certain anxiety around family values. When asked, 89% of young female respondents claim that the image of the family shown in the series is 'feigned' or 'unrealistic', and 67% reply that it is a model 'not to be imitated'. Only a small minority favour the screen parents' mode of educating their children (which tends to involve threats, bribes, and attempts to ingratiate themselves); and still fewer claim to identify with the young heroine, Eva (Verónica Sánchez, later to appear more decorously as one of *Las 13 rosas*). While most remember the flagrantly vulgar humorous idioms in the show, a majority claim never to have used such colourful expressions. 65% state they are aware that the theme of Catholicism is especially singled out for ridicule, in the person of a stereotypically repressed teacher of religious knowledge. But product placement seems a dubious investment for advertisers: respondents confidently claim to have seen brands that are actually absent from the Serranos' well-stocked kitchen.

Medina and her co-workers are thus left with a paradox. Why is it that a series that is said by its own fans to be 'feigned' or 'unrealistic', whose family values are deficient, and whose influence seems so tenuous can attract such a large and faithful audience? Surely it can only be that the sardonic 'vision of life' it presents (in which neglectful parents aim to be their disrespectful children's best mates) uses comedy to infiltrate young people's minds, making them feel that their own values are 'distant' and 'out of date'.

There may be some practical problems with this approach. Respondents may well venture to offer the opinions they believe researchers wish to hear, especially when the latter come from a conservative Catholic university. Moreover 'Yes/No' answers are a relatively crude guide to viewers' complex interactions with a televisual text. At a more theoretical level, the project illustrates some of the widely held prejudices critiqued by Buonanno above. It reduces televisual communication to the one-way transmission of stable meanings from an active emitter to a passive receiver, seduced by the irresistible siren song of TV fiction.

Ironically, the survey itself provides valuable evidence that points towards a more subtle understanding of communication as ritual: the sharing of communal narratives, dialogues, and even brands that are embedded in the collective everyday life of a nation. Medina notes that while young viewers claim to be uninfluenced by the fictional Eva's (rather revealing) fashion choices, in practice they overwhelmingly share her style of dress. While such relationships may be asymmetrical (the respondents do not themselves have access to a top-rated series to promote their own supposedly authentic preferences in morality or clothing), they do not necessarily imply dominance or ideological control by the mass media. Indeed, the fact that respondents claim both to enjoy and to find fake the family comedy of *Los Serrano* suggests that they are (as Buonanno suggests of Italian audiences) competent to negotiate sceptically the border crossing between the stratified life worlds of reality and fiction.

A further quantitative survey of Spanish viewers' reactions to TV comedy offers a salient contrast, while also providing valuable evidence for another of Buonanno's concerns, the reception of foreign product in a European market. María del Mar Grandío received two and a half thousand responses to her on-line questionnaire on Spanish attitudes to *Friends*, data that was supplemented by two focus groups and ten in-depth interviews (35). Described as the 'perfect' comedy by fans, *Friends* is for

Grandío the 'classic' sitcom, focusing as it does on reaction rather than action and on a frustrated attempt to escape from the everyday (36). Humour thus grows from situation and character rather than relying wholly on verbal funnies and sight gags.

Echoing Buonanno on the relative lack of 'cultural discount' experienced by some US shows, Spanish viewers claim *Friends* is 'universal', 'close to everyday life' (37). But, ironically, the perceived cultural proximity of a US show is the result of a comparison, whether stated or not, with domestic titles (37). While *Friends* can treat even taboo topics with 'elegance' and subtlety, Spanish shows (such as *7 vidas*) are said to be 'vulgar' (44). Unusually in a Spanish context, informants here use 'politically correct' (their description of *Friends*) as a positive term (45), contrasting transnational sensitivity with localist crudity.

Universal, yet close at hand, sexually explicit, yet elegant and refined, *Friends* is also said to be stereotypical, yet subtle in its psychology. Respondents delight in the continuity of character traits (Phoebe remains a ditz, Ross a nerd). But they also take deeper pleasure in narrative and psychological development over the seasons (Rachel begins as a waitress and ends up at Ralph Lauren; the professorial Ross will sometimes act as childishly as Joey [38, 41]). Running verbal gags are enriched by this extended temporal dimension: in a late season Ross tells his baby the story of how he and Rachel were on a 'break' (Spanish 'descanso' [45]) when he was unfaithful to her, reactivating in fans distant memories of a cherished comic situation from long ago. It is this 'extra-textual' (or parasocial) relationship to fictional characters over a full decade that makes the show 'something more than humour' (46) to audiences in Spain, as elsewhere. This is a subjective or emotional element that is, as Buonanno writes, as vital a part of reality as objective factors that are more accessible to positivist verification.

Grandío's article is in a collection on US cult television edited by Concepción Cascajosa Virino under the significant title *La caja lista* ('The Clever Box'). The collection at once confirms and refutes Buonanno's account of the American televisual offer in Europe. For, on the one hand, its very existence and pointed title (TV is often dismissed in Spain as 'la caja tonta' ['the idiot box']) suggests the newly enhanced position of the medium in the hierarchy of legitimation, even in the case of the once despised US product. But, on the other, the collection confirms that such foreign programming, however modified it is by the indigenes who incorporate it into their life worlds, is marginal in European schedules. Unlike its less 'perfect' Spanish rivals, *Friends* was shown on Canal +, a premium cable channel. And Grandío's respondents, although partly protected by the decent obscurity of the internet, are clearly elite educated consumers. Self-described as 'executives', 'architects', or 'doctoral students', they are sufficiently well versed in American culture and language to note that a show like *Seinfeld* is yet more sophisticated than *Friends* (44); or to volunteer that the original English-language *Friends* is even wittier than the dubbed version shown by Canal + (41).

Ironically, then, the imprint of Americanization is here felt not by the proletarian, the passive victim of mass media, but by the educated professional viewer, who actively seeks out a now minority culture of distinction. Yet we have seen that Spanish producers also seek that profitable, quality demographic for their own comedies, even as they connect with the elusive, but persistent, family audience. We can now go on, finally, to explore to what extent the hybrid or transitive fictions of *Los Serrano* and *Camera café* manage to address and negotiate the diverse and competing factors we have seen within genre, nation, and social class.

Family feelings: 'Los Serrano'

> Uno más uno son siete.
> ¿Quién me lo iba a decir
> que era tan fácil
> ser feliz?
>
> [One plus one makes seven./ Who would have thought/
> that it was so easy/ to be happy?] (*Los Serrano*, theme tune)

Daniel Écija has a good claim to be a major auteur of Spanish television. The director of the pioneering series *Médico de familia*, he was also a creator of innovative workplace drama *Periodistas*, and remains an executive producer at Spain's most influential independent Globomedia. An extended interview with him, first published in 2003 (Saló 219–25), the same year that his latest project *Los Serrano* was making its debut, offers a good chance to compare a producer's internal self-image with external and academic accounts from García de Castro and Medina et al.

Écija reveals a keen awareness of hybridity as a competitive advantage for Globomedia and as a generic and national principle of product differentiation. He thus claims that the first reference point for his own series was Steve Bochco and MTM's 'quality TV' of the 1980s, indiscriminately citing drama and comedy titles: *Hill Street Blues*, *LA Law*, *Cheers* (220). While Écija is aware of the use of the term 'dramedy' in the US, he also claims to have 'invented a genre' in Spain, where the unusual length of local shows (65 or 70 minutes as opposed to 44 minutes in the States) made it difficult to sustain 'pure drama' without a strong element of humour. Nonetheless, the Globomedia mode of screenwriting, team-written and guided by script supervisors or 'runners', was imported to Spain for the first time from the US, thus enabling a 'maturity of creative management'.

Écija also looked beyond the US to cultures (unnamed) which were 'relatively similar' to that of Spain (221) for evidence of winning formats. The experience of these European countries suggested that workplace drama could coexist with nuclear family-based narratives. And while he claims that it is a 'lie' that the perennially 'unfinished business' of the classic sitcom ('comedia') will not work in Spain, he insists that a 'Latin' audience has a different 'cultural tradition' to the American. One specific reference point here is Francoist feature film *La gran familia* (1962), cited in the interview as a model for *Médico de familia* (and also name checked on the 'making of' documentary included as an extra to the DVD box set of *Los Serrano*'s first season).

Generic hybridity is thus inseparable from national *mestizaje* (cross-breeding): as in Buonanno, there is no pure native culture but rather a necessary fusion of diverse elements (Francoist film of the 1960s and US quality television of the 1980s). And Écija goes on to make an unusually specific reference to the new crossover between reality and fictional programming. *Big Brother* and *Pop Idol* are based on coexistence, competition, and overcoming setbacks, the same narrative sources as series drama (223). If they are to rival realities in the ratings, then, fictional programmes will now have to become more intense and more realist and to exhibit more innovation and transgression. Spanish producers have also learned that they are no longer dependent on stars: it is the stories that secure viewer loyalty. This is vital for the future, now that budgets are likely to be limited by the fragmenting of the audience (223).

We will see in a moment how Écija's pragmatic vision as executive producer, combining as it does the creative and the managerial, correlates to the textual practice of both *Los Serrano* and *Camera café* (on which he had no input). But first I would like to return to the demography of the elusive family audience. As we have seen, Medina et al. stress the persistence of the nuclear family and the multi-person household in Spain. But sociologist Inés Alberdi's extended monograph on 'the new Spanish family' is more nuanced. Writing as early as 1999, Alberdi's main proposal is that Spanish families are 'longer and narrower' than ever before (81). The collapse in the birth rate has coincided with an extension of life expectancy, with more family members of different generations coexisting: never, she writes, have so few children had so many grandparents. Spain's birth rate rivals Italy's at the bottom of world rankings (they were, respectively, 1.18 and 1.17 in 1995) (90) and, *pace* Medina, the average household size has also fallen rapidly from 3.90 in 1970 to 3.27 in 1991 (93). But the dominance of the nuclear family in Spain remains more complete than in the rest of Europe (96), partly because young people live at home for much longer than their counterparts abroad (97). 'Complex' or 'extended' households are thus very rare (100): divorced women or widows look after their children alone; while divorced men tend to start new families (101).

Although grandparents rarely live with their adult children, Alberdi finds that family ties are stronger and more valued than ever before (106). This is not in spite of the fact that 'hierarchical' structures have broken down to be replaced by more 'democratic' intergenerational relations, but rather because of that welcome change: if children live longer in the parental home it is partly because they enjoy a tolerance and freedom there that would be inconceivable in previous periods (107).

An initial hypothesis would thus be that the premise of *Los Serrano* is a carefully calibrated response to and representation of these contradictory demographic changes. On the one hand, its blended family is (as Buonanno noted for Italy) statistically exceptionally rare, as is its large number of children, which harks back to the 'big families' of the Francoist era. But on the other hand, the coexistence of three generations (of grandmother, uncle, parents, and kids) deeply enmeshed in each other's lives, yet not cohabiting, is indeed typical of modern Spain. As we shall see, much of the series' humour derives from its staging of the breakdown of hierarchical relations in the new familial democracy, a reversal that scholars such as Medina clearly find disquieting. But by framing that revolutionary social change in the context of traditional family values (the primacy of children and of the home), *Los Serrano*, like the Italian shows it so resembles, softens the shock of demographic crisis, even as it is forced to acknowledge the existence of that crisis. *Los Serrano* is thus a prime example of both the neo- or contemporary realism typical of García de Castro's 'second renewal' of Spanish TV drama and the newly 'intense' and 'transgressive' series that Écija claims have learned from reality TV.

Let us take as specimen episodes the first and last of the opening series. This gives us the possibility of addressing that evolution of character and narrative over time that is typical of serial, rather than series, television and yet has so often been grafted onto the most enduring US sitcoms. The official synopses read as follows:

1.1 'Ya se han casao'
(broadcast 24 April 2003; audience 4,286,000, share 26,1%)

Diego y Lucía fueron novios en la adolescencia, pero al alcanzar la mayoría de edad sus vidas tomaron rumbos diferentes. Ella se marchó a Barcelona y allí se casó, tuvo dos hijas y alcanzó un nivel de vida más que aceptable; sin embargo no era feliz y decidió divorciarse. Él no ha salido nunca del barrio, allí se casó y tuvo tres hijos, pero hace cinco años que enviudó y se quedó al cargo de los niños. Cuando los dos vuelven a estar solos, se encuentran en una carretera y deciden formar una familia.

Marcos, Guille y Curro, siguiendo instrucciones de su padre, ejercen de anfitriones con sus nuevas hermanas. Eva y Teté les siguen en su recorrido por la que a partir de ahora será su casa, que nada tiene que ver con la que han dejado en Barcelona, hasta que llegan a su nueva habitación. Las dos jóvenes tendrán que compartir dormitorio y muchas cosas más.

Lucía afronta su primer día en la nueva escuela con bastantes nervios. Le tranquiliza la presencia de Candela, amiga suya desde la infancia, que también es profesora en el centro. De la noche a la mañana se ve convertida en la profesora de Teté y Guille.

Desde que se han casado Lucía y Diego, la actitud de Santiago, el hermano de él, ha sufrido un cambio drástico. Sin ninguna explicación sus visitas al hogar de los Serrano se han ido espaciando y se mantiene bastante al margen de la vida familiar. Todos se dan cuenta de que algo pasa.

[1.1 'Now They've Got Hitched'

Diego and Lucía were involved when they were teenagers, but when they grew up their lives took different turns. She went off to Barcelona, got married, had two daughters, and enjoyed a more than comfortable lifestyle; but she still wasn't happy and decided to get a divorce. He never left his [Madrid] neighbourhood, got married, and had three sons, but lost his wife five years ago and was left in charge of the kids. When the couple are single again they meet on the road and decide to form a family.

Marcos, Guille and Curro, acting on instructions from their father, serve as guides to their new sisters. Eva and Teté follow them on a tour of what will now be their new home (which is nothing like what they left behind in Barcelona), ending with their new bedroom. The two girls will have to share a room and much else besides.

Lucía faces her first day at the new school with a bad case of nerves. She is reassured by the fact that Candela, a childhood friend, is also a teacher at the school. All of a sudden she has become Teté and Guille's teacher.

Since Lucía and Diego got married, the attitude of Santiago, Diego's brother, has undergone a drastic change. Inexplicably he has stopped visiting the Serrano home and he keeps himself at a distance from the life of the family. Everyone realizes that something's up.]

1.13 'La guerra de los Martínez'
(broadcast 15 July 2003; audience 4,889,000, share 36%)

Eva anima a Marcos para que se presente a un concurso de cantautores en la radio, pero como él no se muestra muy animado, decide mandar la maqueta en su nombre. Marcos está entre los finalistas, al igual que Joan Manuel — ex novio de Eva — , quien consigue instalarse en el hogar de los Serrano con la excusa de que no tiene dónde pasar la noche. Joan Manuel reconoce ante Marcos que ha venido para recuperar a Eva, lo que hace que el hijo mayor de Diego se plantee seriamente confesar sus sentimientos ante ella.

Las cosas entre Fiti y Candela cada vez están más complicadas de cara a una posible reconciliación. Ninguno de los dos quiere ser el primero en pedir perdón y, aconsejados por sus amigos, optan por mostrarse duros ante el contrario. Lo cierto es que los dos están destrozados y tanto Santiago como Diego temen que su amigo pueda cometer una locura.

A Teté le gusta uno de los chicos que juega en el equipo de fútbol que entrena su tío. Su interés por entrar a formar parte de la plantilla sorprende a todos, especialmente a Santiago, que se niega en rotundo a que Teté sea uno más de sus jugadores. Carmen, viendo el disgusto de su nieta, emprende una campaña para que Teté pueda ver cumplido su propósito. (formulatv 'Series')

[1.13 'The War of the Martínez'

Eva encourages Marcos to enter a competition of singer songwriters on the radio, but as he doesn't seem keen, she sends in the audition tape herself. Marcos is one of the finalists, along with Joan Manuel, Eva's ex-boyfriend, who manages to worm his way into the Serrano home with the excuse that he has nowhere to stay. Joan Manuel admits to Marcos that he's come to get Eva back, which makes Marcos seriously consider telling her about his own feelings for her.

Things between Fiti and Candela are increasingly complicated as they're thinking about getting back together again. Neither wants to be the first to say sorry and, urged on by their friends, they choose to act tough to each other. The truth is that they're both terribly upset and Santiago and Diego are afraid their friend could do something stupid.

Teté likes one of the boys who plays in the football team trained by her uncle. Everyone is amazed that she wants to join the team, especially Santiago who forbids Teté from playing in the team as if she were just another boy. Seeing how annoyed her granddaughter is, Carmen mounts a campaign for Teté to get what she wants.]

The pre-credit sequence of the first episode of *Los Serrano* shows the wedding of bald, bearded, and beefy Diego (film veteran Antonio Resines) to willowy blonde Lucía (TV star Belén Rueda, familiar from previous Globomedia hits *Médico de familia* and *Periodistas*). This opening gives the show an early chance to show off its authentic exteriors (an impressive church where shooting took place in the gaps between masses) and some unusually edgy camerawork (handheld or steadycam with modish canted angles). Yet, for all this novelty, a wedding is an event that is increasingly rare in real-life Spain; and the sequence is set to a voiceover by youngest child Curro that could hardly be more traditional: 'Today my father's getting married. My father is the most important person in the family.'

When the newly extended family return to their ample, but hardly luxurious, chalet in outer Madrid, there is some old-school physical comedy that seems almost to be crying out for the studio audience and laugh track that are conspicuously absent in the show. Lucía bumps her head when carried over the threshold and is comforted in the kitchen. Meanwhile the boys show the girls around the home, introducing them (introducing us) to this new domestic space. Little Curro is particularly proud of the bedroom, redecorated specially for feminine tastes, claiming it is 'fucking great' ('que te cagas'). Sophisticated Eva, no doubt used to cutting-edge Barcelona design, can barely hide her disdain: 'It's very... florid.'

This battle of the sexes theme is thus also a class struggle over questions of cultural capital. When the girls discover the boys apparently sniffing their lingerie or turn up their noses at greasy churros in favour of healthy muesli, it is not clear whether it is gender or educational level that are at stake here. Likewise the show will at one moment have teenage Eva lecturing her newly married mother on the importance of safe sex and the next have father Diego threaten his smallest son with a foul smelling toilet brush (shit and pee jokes recur with distressing frequency as seven characters share one bathroom). Familial hierarchies are thus broken down, only to be at once erected once more. Tradition and modernity are also built into competing generic modes of humour: coarse Spanish *costumbrismo* coexists with a more cosmopolitan comedy of manners.

Two studio sets extend this conflict outside the turbulent home. Bowing to Spanish social trends, Lucía re-enters the workplace, taking a job as a teacher (after a gap of eleven child-rearing years) in a school where best friend Candela (Nuria González) also attempts to keep the kids under control. Diego, on the other hand, owns the archetypal bar whose staff include his red-faced and foul-mouthed elder brother Santiago (veteran character actor Jesús Bonilla) and his feckless best friend Fito (Antonio Molero). The bar is a 'temple' to the ham that Diego's new vegetarian stepdaughter cannot bring herself to eat.

The workplaces are thus as rigorously gendered as the children's bedrooms. But drama, if not comedy, comes from their mutual contamination. Lucía's school is made yet more uncomfortable (she is mercilessly teased by her pupils) by the presence of a handsome fellow teacher, who is overly solicitous in his attentions; Diego must abandon the bar (and the chance of a 'dream ticket' with his brother to a football derby between Madrid and Barcelona) to attend a first family dinner.

Running gags also stress cultural tensions in the Spain of historic nationalities. One ignorant school kid thinks Teté, proficient in Catalan, must be Polish; Eva has a sly hippy boyfriend back in Barcelona whose songwriting ambitions rival those of her earnest and fresh-faced stepbrother Marcos. When, late in the episode, Eva flees to the local railway station to take a train back to the Catalan capital (another example of realism-enforcing location shooting), stepfather Diego is given a big speech intended to win her back. He says: 'This story isn't just ours [mother and father], it all of yours [the five children]. We may not have many books at home, but we have the best ham in the world.' Refusing at first to return, Eva is, by the close of the episode, back with her new family; and in crowded group shots that include the grandmother and uncle, the whole cast attempt to enjoy a barbecue (although the girls stick to salad). As one character comments, the males and females blend 'like oil and water'.

Often, however, the coarsest conflicts (and most vulgar language) are projected outside the home onto supporting characters. This is the case in the final episode of the season, which is named for the 'war' between the separated best friends of the central couple, waiter Fiti and teacher Candela. Gender dichotomies are still set up strongly here, with little Curro's opening voiceover informing us naively that girls do strange things, like talk to each other and shave their body hair. However comic incongruity at once deflates the child's reasoning. As he tells us 'Men fix things', Diego manages to blow the fuse he is trying to mend (the real skill of the bluffly masculine Diego is cooking).

Throughout the episode some coarsely contrasted comedy comes from this gender divide, as Diego and Lucía coach their separated best friends with conspicuously poor results. Thus both separately advise Fiti and Candela to feign indifference to each other, even as they long to get back together; and farcically confine them to different rooms in the house when each visits independently, seeking support. In a subplot of sexual struggle, young Teté wishes to join the all-boy football team (trained by her uncle Santiago), albeit only to get closer to an attractive schoolmate. With the help of meddling grandmother Carmen (Julia Gutiérrez Caba), the little girl is transformed into a feminist cause célèbre in the local media.

Meanwhile (in the fourth plotline that we remember was required by the production agreement) Marcos is competing for the affections of stepsister Eva with ex-boyfriend Joan Manuel. This is a development set up, as we have seen, in the very first episode. Perhaps the gentlest and most effective character-based comedy here comes when the pair improvise competing love songs in a kind of singer-songwriters' duel. But when Marcos finally confesses his love for Eva to his father, the latter explodes that this is 'incest', calling him 'degenerate' and insisting he hide his feelings at all costs. The stage is thus set for continuing sexual tension that will fuel the show for five seasons before the attractive couple, still implausibly young, will tie the knot in a second Serrano wedding that puts a new spin on 'family feeling'.

Los Serrano thus secured early on one of those precious deep-level plotlines more typical of soap opera than comedy that ensure the fidelity and emotional investment of the audience. And there are striking modulations in tone in this season finale. An overly schematic, even farcical, episode includes nonetheless Marcos's moving confession of (as yet) impossible love and Fiti's convincing suicidal despair at the loss of his family. A newly emphatic textual hybridity accompanies this varied register: in an showy fantasy sequence, Teté imagines herself and her schoolmate as characters in *Grease*; in a rare flashback montage, Marcos thinks back to those many bare-chested and bare-midriffed moments when he came close to kissing Eva; and in a transparent reference to the hugely successful talent contest reality-shows (aired in Spain by Tele 5), the climactic songwriting competition takes place in a real-life radio station offering a panoramic view of the Madrid skyline. Eva looks on, with over-keen interest, from outside the glass walls of the studio (Fig. 15).

I would suggest that it is just this unsettling hybridity, blending genres as it

FIG. 15. Eva (Verónica Sánchez) and Marcos (Fran Perea):
the incestuous step-siblings of *Los Serrano*

does families, that ensured the success of the series in the special circumstances of the Spanish mediascape. Certainly, *Los Serrano* was fully consistent with both the production mentality of its makers and the demography of its consumers. Internet forums confirm that, like the perhaps more sophisticated Spanish lovers of transnational *Friends*, fans of localist *Los Serrano* responded to both the comic and the dramatic elements of the show. But that mediascape is constantly changing, as is revealed by a very different and innovative hybrid or transitive fiction that began to air on the same national channel two years after *Los Serrano, Camera café*.

Working hard for the money: 'Camera café'

En esta ficción, co-producida por Telecinco y Magnolia TV, una cámara instalada en el interior de la máquina de café será testigo de las divertidas miserias del personal de la oficina. Los guiones de *Camera café* — un formato que ha cosechado un enorme éxito en países como Francia e Italia — han sido adaptados al humor español con el fin de recrear roles y situaciones que pueden acontecer cotidianamente en cualquier empresa nacional.

Una máquina de café, una zona de descanso y un ámbito laboral convertido en un 'campo de batalla' por la supervivencia son los elementos fundamentales de *Camera café*, el nuevo proyecto de humor ambientado en las conversaciones que mantienen los trabajadores de una oficina en su tiempo de descanso que Telecinco estrena este domingo 18 de septiembre [2005] a las 21:30 horas y que posteriormente pasará a emitirse de lunes a jueves.

En *Camera café*, las historias cotidianas de la oficina serán recogidas a través del objetivo indiscreto de una cámara instalada en el interior de una máquina de café y presentado a través de distintos sketches de corta duración. (formulatv, Camera café: noticias [18 September 2005])

[In this show, co-produced by Telecinco and Magnolia TV, a camera set up inside a coffee vending machine observes the comic misfortunes of the staff of an office. The scripts for *Camera café*, a format that has enjoyed enormous success in countries like France and Italy, have been adapted to Spanish humour so as to recreate roles and situations that could happen on a daily basis in any Spanish firm.

A coffee vending machine, a leisure area, and a workplace that turns into a 'battle field' where workers fight for survival are the basic features of *Camera café*. This new comedy is based on workers' conversations during their coffee break. It premieres this Sunday 18 September [2005] at 9.30 p.m. and will from then on be aired from Monday to Friday.

In *Camera café*, daily stores of office life are picked up through the prying lens of a camera set up inside a coffee vending machine. The show is made up of short and varied sketches.]

Camera café could hardly be further from *Los Serrano*, marking as it does a radical formal innovation in the supposedly stable form of TV comedy that would appear to make it the *non plus ultra* of stripped-down television. With just one simple set (grey floor, lurid yellow doors, and lift at the far end) and one camera (supposedly located in the coffee machine that is never shown), each sketch of *Camera café* generally consists of four acts of just one minute each, topped and tailed by an equally abbreviated intro and epilogue. There are no cuts but brief moments of static (as if turning off the TV set) between one-take scenes. Trade mark 'cortinillas' or interludes carry the single title credit and a visual gag: a paper coffee cup is alternately filled with noxious concrete, bombarded with billiard balls, or incinerated by raging flames.

Likewise the seventeen characters are played by little-known actors (no stars of the calibre of Resines or Rueda, here). They have precious little backstory and no psychological development. Similarly, the location is unspecified: we never learn what the company buys or sells or where it is situated. One running gag alerts us only to the existence of a neighbouring company in the same office building: a much-envied German multinational, whose business is equally unknown.

Camera café is thus clearly not *Friends*. It offers no warm moments or happy shared memories. Closer in cynical spirit to *Seinfeld*, its characters never hug or learn lessons. But nor, in spite of similarities in the setting, is it *The Office*. If *Camera café* rejects the now exhausted three-camera set up (along, of course, with the studio audience and laugh track), it makes no attempt to mimic the recreation of a complex dramatic space and the aspirations to quality and complexity of 'TV vérité.' For all its reputation for a cringing comedy of embarrassment, the British *Office* still exploited, as much as *Friends* (or *Los Serrano*), the traditional device of long-delayed sexual tension that finally pays off in a successful romantic conclusion. There are no such parasocial pleasures in *Camera café*. In spite of its formal innovations, then, the Spanish show could, ironically, be seen as something of a strategic return to the repetitive or circular stasis of the traditional sitcom, whose aim was simply to make the viewer laugh.

Perhaps better seen as a minimalist parody of the trend to single-camera comedy, *Camera café* draws directly on the most blatantly simple visual technology associated with modern life: close circuit TV or video surveillance. According to Wikipedia, the title evokes in its original French context the Ur-reality show *Candid Camera* (*Caméra cachée*). This voyeuristic mode is a reference point also taken up in the formulatv report cited above, which calls the shows viewpoint 'indiscrete' (Hitchcock's *Rear Window* was known in Spain as *La ventana indiscreta*).

The show's alternative mode of representation thus brings with it a heightened degree of self-consciousness, not to mention an extremely accelerated tempo. And it exploits almost all of those special characteristics of reality television cited by García de Castro: blurring the border between fiction and reality in its everyday plotlines, stressing the everyday nature of dramatic performance in its banal or grotesque characters, reinforcing the sense of the ensemble with an unusually large regular cast, and relying heavily, in spite of its transnational format, on local and personal reference points. This generic hybridism paid off with audiences. The 'undisputed leader' in its timeslot, *Camera café* regularly won a 24% share in its first season, rising to a 27.4% share of the 'commercial target' audience beloved of advertisers (formulatv; 7 September 2006).

In his presentation of the series on its debut (formulatv; 18 September 2005), Alberto Carullo, the director of broadcasting at Tele 5, called attention to the novelty and hybridity of the format, intended as it was to be 'halfway between drama and a comedy show'. This generic border crossing was controversial: while specialist website formulatv lists *Camera café* as a 'programa' (*Los Serrano* is classed as a 'serie'), one indignant fan claims that it is clearly a 'five minute series'. The sketch format also favoured unusual flexibility in scheduling: the show has been stripped at 9.30 pm (access prime time) for between two and five times a week and in slots from 30 to 45 minutes long. The length of each individual skit later proved ideal for YouTube, where micro-narratives from different national versions of the format remain readily available at the time of writing.

At the same press launch, Director Luis Guridi, previously known (under the pseudonym La Cuadrilla) for a small body of distinctively grotesque film comedy, calls attention rather to the national *mestizaje*: drawing on the 'best from each version of the show' he has 'adapted' the format to the Spanish sense of humour, which he calls 'biting, cruel, and black'. The audition process also called for specific qualities: given the speed of the show and the fact that sequences are shot in single takes without edits the actors were required to have theatrical skills. It is certainly the case that much of the humour depends on the distinctive physiognomy of the little-known actors: Carlos Chamarro's nervy purchaser Julián is short and skinny, while Arturo Valls's self-satisfied salesman Jesús is flashy and fleshy (Fig. 16). The cardigan-clad secretary Mari Carmen looks as fragile as her on-off boyfriend, older accountant and mummy's boy Gregorio (award-winning Luis Varela). The exaggerated performance style matches the heightened mise en scene: the fluorescent set (copied exactly from the French original) is matched by the violently clashing colours and patterns of office ties, shirts, and skirts. *Camera café* thus rejects the downbeat naturalism of *The Office* in favour of a neo-realist vernacular that reads in Spain as distinctively local, even as it works within a carbon copy of a foreign format.

Fig. 16. Comedy vérité: Jesús (Arturo Valls, left) and
Julián (Carlos Chamarro) in *Camera café*

Of course, the original here is not American but European. And the appropriation of non-domestic material is clearly based in this case (in Buonanno's terms) on interdependence, not dominance. After all, Tele 5 itself exported titles such as *Los Serrano* to fellow Latin countries. And the show's mode of communication is one of collective ritual rather than one-to-one transmission. After all, what could be more everyday than to gather around a beverage machine?

Camera café strives, nonetheless, to indigenize that universal situation, embedding it in Spanish circumstance and fleetingly engaging with recognizable national narratives and anxieties. Thus in 'Natación' ('Swimming', episode 11) imperfect Spanish bodies are humiliated at the roof-top swimming pool by the athletic Germans of the neighbouring multinational; in 'Invitación a comer' ('Invitation to Lunch', episode 16), Jesús's colleagues are unable to find his new chalet (no doubt similar to that in *Los Serrano*) in a soulless new suburb where all the streets are named for flowers; or in 'Morcillas' ('Blood Pudding', 31), Jesús is harassed by constant gifts of execrable home-made sausage ('The best in the world!') from a colleague's rural aunt. (We saw the same misplaced pride in local gastronomy in *Los Serrano*.)

Often plotlines explore technology, sometimes adding a local flavour. For example, in 'Karaoke' (5) Bernardo borrows his mother's machine for an office party but it plays only *zarzuela* (Spanish operetta). Or again, Jesús attempts to sell antiquated walkmen, made in distant 'Bulvivia' ('El vendedor vendido' ['The Salesman Sold'], 26). Further episodes focus, self-reflexively, on television. The whole ensemble bond over an endless nature series about tortoises ('And they haven't even left Madagascar yet!') ('El documental' ['The Documentary'], 23); a programme on Greenpeace inspires Mari Carmen to 'liberate' the fish in the boss's aquarium ('Los peces' ['The Fish'], 30). Another character's ugly daughter finds a lucrative niche playing the 'before' in commercials for dandruff, acne, etc. ('La madre de la artista' ['The Actress's Mother'], 29).

This reflexivity has provoked viewers to border crossings of their own, attempting to negotiate the technical barrier between real and fictional life worlds. One forum discussion ponders the question of whether the show will ever reveal the eponymous coffee machine. A final poster notes that, of course, the machine does not exist (the actors on set are facing the perfectly normal camera through which we see the show) (formulatv, 'Foros').

As will be clear from my account thus far, *Camera café* is anti-familial. Characters either live alone, single or divorced, or prize the office, however dull or conflictive their labour, as a refuge from family burdens. They also constantly lay plans for adulterous affairs that never come to fruition. Only Bernardo speaks fondly (over-fondly) of his aged mother, who consistently frustrates his potential romance with Mari Carmen. When, in a unique moment of pathos, she shyly confesses her affection for him, he responds that he won't come to work tomorrow 'out of embarrassment', and they agree it would be better to forget all about it ('La sinceridad' ['Truth Telling'], 27).

Unlike in *Los Serrano*, which blends serial comedy and series drama, here there is no hugging, no learning, and no character evolution or plot development. But *Camera café*'s innovations are not simply negative or formal. A standardized production process with a reduced budget led to both creative product differentiation and to new modes of programming and scheduling. This radically new mode of stripped-down humour, which broke all the established and distinctive rules of the Spanish series format, was rewarded with both critical and popular success.

Comedy and reality

In TV terms, neighbouring nations may have less in common than distant continents. In spite of the family resemblance between *Los Serrano* and equivalent Italian comedy-dramas, Buonanno's description of the mediascape to which the latter belong could not be further from Spain: modern, secular audiences in Madrid or Barcelona would hardly welcome the period religious dramas that flourish in Rome. Spanish viewers pondered what far-off Finns made of the exported Serranos, with their all too vernacular language and gastronomy (how did 'Spanish ham' fare in Helsinki?) (Soto); while a Spanish media academic suggested that it was an American series, medical drama *House*, that had contributed most to the tardy 'legitimation of [a] televisual culture' long seen as the symbol of contemporary ills (Ibáñez 213). If the 'smart box' was slowly replacing the 'idiot box', then both transnational universalism and stubborn local particularity continued to cohabit. Cultural proximity joined forces with alleged cultural deficits.

Of course aesthetics and economics are also interlinked here. Stylianos Papatha-nassopoulos has shown how for European television of the digital age 'localization is a strong strategy for survival', adopted by many international brands (161). Back in Spain, Ricardo Vaca Berdayes attributed *Los Serrano*'s success not only to its dominance of the younger demographics (with a share of over 50% for children and youths) but also to its insertion of a record four commercial breaks (205), which would surely try the patience of the audience in the end. Certainly the subsequent success of *Camera café*, with its abbreviated and accelerated format, showed that the uniquely lengthy timeslots in Spain, which required audiences to devote most of the evening to a single show, were not the only way of scheduling innovative and successful television in the country.

When *Los Serrano* came to an end in summer 2008 it was precisely because of this question of scheduling. Tele 5 put the final season up against a new Globomedia product on another network, thus inspiring the production company's angry remonstrations. The broadcaster replied, in turn, that Globomedia had latterly neglected the show, an impression reinforced by frequent complaints of repetition and falling quality by ex-fans on internet forums (formulatv, 'Noticias' 4 June 2008). The loss of popular characters such as the now married Marcos and Eva and Belén Rueda's Lucía, killed in a traffic accident when the actress left to pursue a career in theatre and film (notably *El orfanato*, treated in Chapter 5), also wounded the millions of fans that remained loyal to the show over its five years. Such deep emotions are not to be taken for granted. The likelihood that these investments might, however, survive the show's final season was confirmed when *El País* reported on 20 June 2008 that no fewer than 2,150 clips from the series had been posted on YouTube (Pérez-Lanzac). Tele 5, which was suing the portal, was clearly less enamoured of this treasure-trove than were the fans who had created it.

I have suggested that these two shows, in their very different ways, blurred the boundaries between genres and national traditions, blending fiction and reality (fiction and reality TV) in the process. If they are not as textually complex as Thompson's examples of US comedy vérité, they remain innovative and creative within a Spanish context. And they are clear examples of the creativity of Buonanno's indigenization, borrowing from America and Europe to produce products that are distinctively national in form, content, and narrative rhythm.

They thus also reveal an important corrective to the Anglo-American sitcom models. The blending of comedy and drama in Spain led not to the generically conservative *Friends* but to an innovative weekly format longer and more complex than any in the US; the blending of comedy and documentary led not to the British naturalism of *The Office* but to a minimalist sketch comedy that drew on the voyeurism of *Candid Camera*-style reality while conserving the 'displayed performance' that Mills holds typical of classic sitcom.

While conservative commentators on family values will have found little encouragement in the enduring popularity of either show, more sympathetic observers of family feeling will note how both, again in their very different ways, respond generously and creatively to the threat of social change, embedding it in the consensual rituals of everyday life at home and at work. Although happiness may not be as easy to achieve as *Los Serrano*'s theme tune would have us believe, we could and should not ask for more from the hybrid fictions of modern television comedy. In the next chapter we shall see, once more with the aid of Milly Buonanno, how another despised TV genre, the *telenovela*, also lends its faithful viewers life strategies for mastering time and crossing bridges.

Works cited

ALBERDI, INÉS. *La nueva familia española* (Madrid: Taurus, 1999)

BUONANNO, MILLY. *El drama televisivo: identidad y contenidos sociales* (Barcelona: Gedisa, 2000)

CASCAJOSA VIRINO, CONCEPCIÓN. *La caja lista: televisión norteamericana de culto* (Barcelona: Laertes, 2007)

DALTON, MARY M., and LAURA L. LINDER, eds. *The Sitcom Reader* (Albany: SUNY Press, 2005)

GARCÍA DE CASTRO, MARIO. 'The Hegemony of Fiction Television Today: Hyperrealism and Renewal in Television Series', paper presented at Workshop of Television Fiction at University of Navarre, 8 June 2007

GRANDÍO, MARÍA DEL MAR. '¿A qué se debe el éxito de *Friends* en España?', in Cascajosa Virino, pp. 35–47

IBÁÑEZ, JUAN CARLOS. 'Queremos tanto a *House*: ficción televisiva de calidad y la legitimación del medio televisivo en España', in Cascajosa Virino, pp. 195–213

MEDINA, MERCEDES, et al. 'Managerial and Family Values of Spanish TV Series', research project presented at Workshop of Television Fiction at University of Navarre, 8 June 2007

MILLS, BRETT. 'Comedy Vérité: Contemporary Sitcom Form', *Screen*, 45.1 (Spring 2004), 63–78

—— *Television Sitcom* (London: BFI, 2005)

MORREALE, JOANNE. *Critiquing the Sitcom* (Syracuse: Syracuse University Press, 2003)

PAPATHANASSOPOULOS, STYLIANOS. *European Television in the Digital Age* (Cambridge: Polity, 2002)

PÉREZ LANZAC, C., 'Tele 5 demanda a YouTube por ofrecer sus contenidos', *El País*, 20 June 2008, p. 76

SALÓ, GLORIA. *¿Qué es eso del formato?* (Barcelona: Gedisa, 2003)

'Territory Guide to Spain', *Television Business International*, February/March 2006

THOMPSON, ETHAN. 'Comedy vérité: the Observational Documentary Meets the Televisual Sitcom', *The Velvet Light Trap*, 59 (Fall 2008), 63–72

VACA BERDAYES, RICARDO. *El ojo digital* (Madrid: Fundación Ex Libris, 2007)

Web sources all consulted 29 July 2010:

FORMULATV. '*Camera café*: programas', <http://www.formulatv.com/programas/27/camera-cafe/>

—— '*Camera café*: noticias', '<http://www.formulatv.1,20050918,1483,1.html

—— 'Foros', <http://www.formulatv.com/programas/27/camera-cafe/foros/>

—— 'Los Serrano: series', <http://www.formulatv.com/series/10/los-serrano/>

—— 'Los Serrano: noticias', <http://www.formulatv.com/series/10/los-serrano/noticias/>

MEDINA, MERCEDES, et al. 'La cultura de las series de televisión: ¿qué comunican *Los Serrano*?', <http://www.unav.es/fcom/noticias/docsnot/culturatv.pdf>

SOTO, ADRIÁN. 'Jamón español en Helsinki.' *El País*, 10 February 2008, <http://www.elpais.com/articulo/Pantallas/Jamon/espanol/Helsinki/elpepirtv/20080210elpepirtv_4/Tes/>

WIKIPEDIA. 'Caméra Café', <http://en.wikipedia.org/wiki/Caméra_Café>

❖

CHAPTER 9

Travelling Narratives and Transitional Life Strategies

Yo soy Bea ('I Am Bea', Tele 5, 2006–08) and *Ugly Betty* (ABC, 2006–10)

From threat to resource

In the credit sequence of *Yo soy Bea*, the Spanish daytime serial based on the Colombian *Yo soy Betty la fea* (which premiered on 10 July 2006), the timid mousy heroine (thick eyebrows and glasses, disfiguring braces on her teeth), walks nervously into the campus-like office complex of fictional fashion magazine *Bulevar 21*. Her working-class father and plain childhood friend are left behind at the gate, worriedly watching as she begins a new life, at once glamorous and perilous.

In the pilot episode of *Ugly Betty* (28 September 2006) the US primetime series also based on the Colombian *telenovela*, the Latina heroine (plumper and feistier than Bea, but still boasting prominent eyebrows, glasses and braces) tries to gain access to the offices of 'Meade Publications' for the interview she had arranged sight unseen. The sequence is shot in the gloriously ornate lobby of the Woolworth Building in Manhattan, which features an extended marble staircase, down which Betty will be marched by an officious underling. We cut to her modest family home in Queens (also an authentic location in the pilot), where Betty's young nephew Justin is watching with visible scepticism a flagrantly melodramatic *telenovela* on TV.

Both scenes suggest in a similar way that the show to follow will be a travelling narrative: the protagonist will undertake a journey that is at once geographic, social, and metaphoric. But they also hint that this unique example of a transnational *telenovela* (shown in some seventy countries around the world [Rogers]) will offer its faithful viewers local life strategies, teaching them how to negotiate the metamorphosis that is the key feature of the story. Outside the US at least, where the series structure can have no definitive ending (and indeed *Ugly Betty*'s final episode on 14 April 2010 would prove defiantly open in its plotting), the ugly duckling from the wrong side of town will finally be transformed into a sleek swan and marry her initially feckless and thoughtless, and now hopelessly devoted, boss. In this last chapter, then, I explore the TV genre that seems to be most dynamic in its crossing of borders, both formally (between serial and series) and geographically (between the Americas and Europe).

Where once globalization was widely thought to herald the homogenization or Americanization of culture, it is now more likely to be seen in the way that is suggested by the twin *Betties* above: as inseparable from a renewed intensity of local, regional, or national characteristics. In the case of audiovisual media in general, and of television drama in particular, research has repeatedly suggested (as I have proposed in several chapters of this book) that since the 1990s local audiences in Europe prefer domestic production in prime time, which is widely held to be 'closer' to their own experiences. Foreign programming, whether from the United States or (for Spaniards) Latin America, once widespread in the evening, is now often confined to minority timeslots during the day or late at night, lacking as it does the key attraction of cultural proximity (Buonanno 95).

The Eurofiction Working Group, led by Milly Buonanno and based at the European Audiovisual Observatory, has charted this rise in the fortunes of Spanish television drama, with Spain reaching in 2002 a higher production level and seriality index than the other big European territories (Eurofiction). This suggests that, in spite of the continuing presence of foreign shows in marginal timeslots and on minority channels, Spanish producers have successfully secured the fidelity of domestic audiences to long-lasting local dramas that have found a secure place in national affections and living rooms. The figures for 2006 from Lorenzo Vilches's more recent survey of Spain in the Iberoamerican Television Observatory report confirm the dominance of local fiction in 2006. Mario García de Castro, whom I cited in Chapter 8, has also documented the unique features of the successful 'evolution' of Spanish TV fiction since the 1990s, such as their increasing engagement with social issues, complexity of narrative, and address to a sought-after commercial target audience. (I return in more detail to the analyses of Buonanno, Vilches, and García de Castro a little later.)

This chapter treats an apparent anomaly in this scenario: *Yo soy Bea* (Tele 5, 2006–08) is, as mentioned earlier, the hugely successful Spanish adaptation of the Colombian *telenovela Betty la fea*. As Vilches notes (181), this is the only show in its genre and timeslot to figure amongst the top ten Spanish productions of its opening year and the only one to be adapted from a foreign format. As a control to test the cultural specificity of the Spanish *Bea*, the chapter contrasts it with the equally successful US primetime dramedy *Ugly Betty* (ABC, 2006–10).

Perhaps the most extensive and influential typology of *telenovela* is that of Martín Barbero and Sonia Muñoz, which examines production, reception, and textual composition in Colombia, *Betty*'s original home territory. And it would clearly be possible to examine *Bea* (and the US *Betty*) using his methodology. First comes the structure and dynamic of production (30). Transferred to a Spanish context this would include such questions as the marginalization of *telenovela* in Spain since the early 1990s, when it has only rarely leapt the scheduling fence (as in the case of *Bea* specials) into prime time; and the belated decision to make the US version not a daytime soap or sitcom but a bigger budget long-form dramedy. The context of industrial and communicative competition amongst Spanish and US networks also comes under this heading, with Tele 5 successfully confronting the most competitive market in Europe and ABC attempting to win back network viewers lost to cable and connect with a fast-growing Latino demographic.

Secondly, according to Martín Barbero and Muñoz's methodology, the two shows could be said to reveal distinct social uses and ways of seeing. Habits of consumption and family routines are implied by format and timeslot, as are spaces of circulation, such as the home, neighbourhood, and workplace (31–32). Vital here in Spain is the *sobremesa* ('after-lunch') timeslot, which has come to be seen as a 'second prime time' and can even (as in the case of *Bea*) attract larger audiences than in the evening. Qualitative evidence for audience reception is available here both from trade press coverage of the programs and from internet forums, unusually active in the case of *Bea* and *Betty* from the first episode ('Bea' posted an extended and extraordinarily popular blog written in the first person and directly addressed to 'ugly-surfers' or 'feonautas') (yotambiensoybea).

Martín Barbero and Muñoz's final area is cultural competency and collective imaginaries (33). It is clear that, in the case of the *Betty* format, these are implicitly embedded in the very different textual composition of the shows, in spite of their common ancestor in Colombia. Social actors, conflicts, and places; spaces, times, and symbolic oppositions; and forms of narration and media language reveal significant variants between Spain and the US. For example, the dominant ethnic theme of *Betty* is wholly absent in *Bea*, whose overall look is, unsurprisingly, much less glossy than its bigger budget American sister. TV syntax (Martín Barbero and Muñoz 35–36) thus also testifies to the persistence of national cultures, markets and business interests, with the two shows looking very different from each other. An initial hypothesis would be, then, that even within a rare, indeed uniquely, successful transnational format such as *Betty la fea*, European drama continues to be specifically tailored to domestic audiences and is distinct from both Latin American and North American forms.

I will draw intermittently on Martín Barbero and Muñoz's typology in this chapter. But before examining the shows themselves I would like to propose a new approach adequate to the unusual case of *Betty/Bea*. I will do so by way of Milly Buonanno's theoretical proposal of 'travelling narratives' and 'life strategies' (of distinctive modes of space and time) in TV serials and series; García de Castro's historical account of the specific evolution of popular television fiction in Spain; and Lorenzo Vilches's industrial analysis of the complex relations of cultures and markets within a televisual 'Iberoamerica' which, in his unique survey, is taken to embrace Spain and the United States, as well as Latin America.

In *The Age of Television*, her first monograph to be translated into English, Buonanno proposes 'indigenization' as a model for the native reception and transformation of foreign cultural products (mainly from the US) which goes beyond the prejudices of cultural imperialism and dependency. It is a model that acknowledges its debt to Martín Barbero's *mestizaje* (and García Canclini's hybridity). While this argument is already to be found in her earlier Spanish book *El drama televisivo* (which we addressed in the context of comedy the previous chapter), it is here supplemented by new, but complementary, accounts of both the international flows of formats and the serial structures of narratives.

Buonanno's main argument is that such flows should be seen not as a threat but rather as a resource for the host culture (101). Using theories of travel and movement she suggests that the experience of television involves 'two dimensions of mobility that are interconnected and intersect each other: the physical mobility of the individual in real geographical space; and the transfer of cultural material in forms and symbolic meanings that are amalgamated into a narrative through international and intercontinental televisual flows' (102). When 'moving images meet de-territorialized viewers', this can give rise to 'a new, if fleeting, sense of place'. Although it is 'imagined', this impression is 'perhaps no less important for maintaining identity and the sense of ontological security than the sense of the real place, the result of first-hand experience and territorial knowledge' (102). We might add that it seems likely that *telenovela*, familiar in its different forms in Spain for some twenty years, offers just this kind of reterritorializing opportunity.

Television, then, is a 'travel machine [...] a connection between different and distant spaces, constitut[ing] knowledge embodied into our acquired experience' (103); and viewers are not so much 'sedentary couch potatoes' as 'travellers in transit' (103). Or again: 'Media and migrations create the conditions of possibility for the construction of a plurality of imagined worlds [which] become part of the cultural experience of daily life' (103). TV thus presents us with 'encounters with the other at different degrees of proximity' (105), with its 'mediascapes offering [viewers] the resources to create scripts of "imagined lives, their own as well as others living in other places"' (the internal citation is from Arjun Appadurai) (105). Buonanno rejects arguments that this process is simply the construction of a cordon sanitaire, offering shelter and immunity from the other (106). Soap opera is not just media fantasy, but also an exploration of possibilities and imagined alternatives (106). After all, according to Anthony Giddens, 'virtually all human experience is mediated', if only through language (106).

It remains the case that this potential 'bi-locality' of television, which makes it a 'medium of symbolic mobility', cannot simply be celebrated or sentimentalized. It must rather be analysed within that 'geometry of power' through which social groups have unequal relationships with geographical mobility (107). And, while noting Latin America's 'reversal' of one-way flows in the case of *telenovela* exports (113), Buonanno offers an empirical critique of current trade relations, which undercuts her theoretical optimism. The television landscape in Europe offers three unequal areas: the 'cultural proximity' of the home-grown drama that is dominant in prime time; the 'familiarized alterity' of US programmes, that occupy a secondary position in the schedule (we might include Latin American imports in Spain here too); and the 'marginalized alterity' or 'symbolically nullified otherness' of content from third countries (including European neighbours), which is almost invisible (114).

It is thus clear that the pleasure of travelling (metaphorically, as well as literally) is 'never quite devoid of a measure of anxiety and uncertainty', with 'the near and familiar [...] [often] win[ning] out over new discoveries and familiarization with extraneous matters' (115). Buonanno thus concludes that while 'there is no guarantee that travelling narratives coming from anywhere will inspire a thoughtful awareness of cultural difference' (particularly given the continuing presence of both anti-Americanism and anti-Latin Americanism in the European mediascape), inter-culturality remains a hypothesis that is not impossible theoretically and a disposition that is not implausible empirically (116).

How does this spatial account of travelling fictions, which tracks the transformation of the experience of place, relate to the distinctive temporal dimension of TV narratives? Here Buonanno attempts to go beyond the 'liveness' often held to be central to the medium to offer a broader account of 'stopping time', based on Zygmunt Bauman's 'life strategies' (119). To begin with, the elemental structures of temporality (sequence, duration, location, and recurrence) are expressed in a uniquely regular and pervasive form in television fiction (120). Thus fictional episodes are shown in an irreversible sequence, at standardized lengths and times, and at recurrent intervals.

However for Buonanno this general temporal regime exhibits a specific binary typology between the serial and series (121). The first (such as the Latin American *telenovela*) is linear and evolutionary, implying a world that is 'metamorphic'; the second (such as the Spanish series drama) is based rather on autonomous segments that imply 'cyclical temporality', and a world that is 'iterative' (121). While the former is based on the desire for postponement of an end that is (nonetheless) known to be inevitable, the latter is founded more on a 'repetitive return' or 'multiplying device' (124). Both propose 'life strategies' that tend ultimately to deny death: the first prolongs life (almost) indefinitely; the second, according to Bauman, makes 'the whole of life into a game of bridge-crossing [...] so that no bridge seems to loom ominously like the "ultimate" one' (cited Buonanno 128). Deferral and starting again are thus twin 'opposed and complementary' life strategies for a secularized modernity that is intent on 'mastering time' (132). Like the 'travelling narratives' of nomadic or transitive formats, these elemental structures of temporality thus offer viewers an opportunity that is inherent in television fictions that are 'unprecedented in scale and scope': the multiplication of experiences (132).

Series and serials in Spain and Iberoamerica

It is clear that Buonanno's twin distinctions (between imports as threat and resource and between narrative as postponement and repetition) will prove well adapted for the specific analysis of the travelling *Betty* franchise, which remained a serial in Spain but became a series in the US. But first I would like to ask to what extent Buonanno's theoretical account coincides with the history of series drama on Spanish television; and to what extent that history corresponds, in turn, to recent trends in Spain and Iberoamerica.

Writing in 2002, Mario García de Castro offers what is to my knowledge the only dedicated and exhaustive account of TV fiction in Spain since its beginnings in the 1960s (*La ficción televisiva*), in which he attempts to explain the sudden blossoming of local production in the second half of the 1990s with reference to its little-known history. (This account complements his later version of the more recent Spanish TV 'renewal', which I treated in the previous chapter.) Surprisingly, perhaps, the prologue by industry innovator Daniel Écija stresses the role of travelling narratives in this process: the Hill Street police station, he writes, has now been transferred to Madrid and Lou Grant no longer lives in San Francisco (9). A typical series episode in Spain costs 50 million (old) pesetas, while a US feature film may have a budget of 50 million dollars. But Spanish series have evolved as much in the five years from 1995 as US series did in the previous forty years: home made production is now 'industrial' and is founded on the 'closeness' of characters and stories as well as the 'quality' of new professionals in the industry (10).

Interestingly, García de Castro stresses in his introduction rather the indigenous nature of this phenomenon, deriving as it does from a long and dense tradition of 'popular Spanish realism' (16). Yet he also argues (like Buonanno) that series fiction as a genre is uniquely suited to television as a medium, with its stress on seriality, repetition, and interruption (17).

García de Castro's detailed account of this history can be briefly sketched in intervals of a decade. He writes that the pioneer auteurs of the 1960s (such as Jaime de Armiñán) combined *teleteatro* with *telenovela* (adapted from classic novels) under primitive technical conditions: series were shot on theatrical sets; were more dramatic than comic; featured stereotypical characters (long-suffering wives, husbands, and spinsters); were targeted at a female audience; featured local characters, settings, and vernacular; displayed a sentimental tone on domestic themes; combined realist local colour ('costumbrismo') with some social criticism and universal moralizing (on freedom, emigration, solitude...); and used young actors in casts that verged on ensembles (55–56).

The 1970s saw rather the rise of a cinematic mode, influenced by US series that were economically attractive to TVE (60) and by European-style 'classic' miniseries (63). In this decade the prime auteur is Antonio Mercero, whose *Crónicas de un pueblo* (1971–74) (which we treated in Chapter 3) is said to be the first series to introduce a 'new contemporary realism' (68). While the 1980s marked the high point in the popularity of both US primetime soaps and Latin American *telenovela*s in Spain (although both were aired in daytime slots) (96–97) and the continuing production of local miniseries (often literary adaptations) shot on film (90), for García de Castro the main story is once more the 'realist trend' (now reinforced by lightweight video cameras), based on the 'everydayness of the present' (79). Mercero's *Verano azul* ('Blue Summer', 1981–82) thus treated 'current conflicts and new collective identities' in an innovative 'naturalistic language' using authentic locations (84–85).

The 1990s culminated in a 'consolidation' of this local fiction (99). Yet García de Castro also cites media commentator J. M. Contreras on the 'transformation' of Spanish audience tastes over the decade (100). Thus while the top-rated programmes in 1990–2001 were *telenovela*s and game shows (dismissed as 'archaic'), five years later they were new local genres and formats (101). The 'proximity' and 'immediacy' of such shows is, however, hardly self-evident: hybrid or transitive narratives par excellence (like the sitcoms I treated in the previous chapter), they are said by García Castro to incorporate formulae taken from Latin American *telenovela*s as well as US soaps and sitcoms (103). Moreover after 1995, the *annus mirabilis*, Spanish series 'diversify', chasing fragmented audiences (110). Aesthetically this process involves 'multiplying new expressive possibilities' and technically it exploits multi-camera shooting, faster narrative pacing, and quicker cutting (110).

García de Castro gives a detailed account of the new industrial process required to make such series. For example the introduction of the 'multitrama' (many-threaded narrative) required a team of seven or eight screenwriters who could produce the one hundred or more storylines required for a typical season (previously Spanish shows had relied on a plot/subplot structure written by a single creator) (154–58). A further revolution came about in mise en scene. Where once star actors delivered broad performances more suited to the theatre, now ensemble casts of relative unknowns were explicitly directed to give a 'naturalistic' performance style appropriate to newly realist settings (163).

García de Castro gives five case studies of such innovative series (all made by independent Globomedia), ranging from the family-based (*Médico de familia* ['Family Doctor'], 1995–99) to the pure genre piece (*Policías* ['Police Officers'], 2000–01), by way of workplace drama (*Periodistas* ['Journalists'], 1998–2000). He also offers an original and valuable 'human and social geography' of these series, focusing on their varied depiction of home, work, and leisure spaces; on their (politically correct) attitudes towards current social conflicts; and on their demography (which tends, like their commercial target audience, towards educated, middle-class, urban women) (189–243). García de Castro concludes that such shows reveal a new and more 'daring' realism than any seen before in Spain (243).

Now it is important to stress that, contrary to stereotype, much *telenovela* in Latin America has also engaged with social issues and courted controversy. It remains the case, however, that, unlike the primetime series, the *sobremesa* serial is not generally known in Spain for such characteristics. And if we look at Lorenzo Vilches' survey of the TV fiction of 'Iberoamerica' shown in 2006 we can place the historical Spanish experience within a new context that will help us to understand the contemporary phenomenon of the travelling fiction that is *Betty/Bea*.

While Vilches claims that Iberoamerica is the largest single market in the world for TV fiction, he acknowledges that the increasing vogue for the adaptation of formats proves the primacy of the national over the global (18). His first example of this is precisely *Yo soy Bea*, which wins a 30% share but a yet higher 39.6% of the commercial target audience, thus beating primetime imports *CSI* and *House* (19). While García de Castro stressed the singularity of Spain, Vilches calls attention to its similarity to other Spanish-language territories, where there are 'different models of similar programming' (20). Moreover, comparative analysis of fiction programming (based on two specimen weeks) reveals that, of the eight countries studied, Spain airs the greatest amount of non-fiction programming (24) (it is Colombia, source of *Betty*, that broadcasts the most local fiction [26]); and Spain is one of only three countries in which local production is (just) exceeded by foreign shows even in prime time (30).

Contrary to García de Castro's vision of diversification also, Vilches suggest that 2006 saw a trend towards a certain 'standardization of offer in a great diversity of countries' (33), coupled with a distinct lack of enthusiasm for co-production. Overall Spain also imports more hours and more episodes of Latin American fiction than it produces itself (unlike Argentina, Colombia, or Mexico) (35). However, the number of local titles screened in Spain far exceeds the foreign titles (36). This is because Spain is a leader in series, which are shown only once a week, unlike the (overwhelmingly Latin American) serials that are stripped across the week (41). This implies a much greater financial investment per title in Spanish shows and thus higher production values. Moreover individual episodes of Spanish series are more likely to exceed sixty minutes than in any other country (43). Spain is also the leader in fictions starring a 'mixed group' of men and women and much less likely than Argentina, Colombia, or Mexico to feature a heterosexual couple as protagonists (46).

Vilches's conclusion seems somewhat contradictory. *Telenovela*, he writes, remains a lowest common denominator, or 'eternal return', often going back for its themes to a pre-industrial world that Latin America has left far behind (47). Yet the genre is indeed modernizing and hybridizing with history, comedy, and documentary, and often features a capital city as its location (48). The 'primitive' is thus fused with the 'sophisticated' and 'reality' inserted into basic setups that remain farcical or melodramatic, even in Spain and Portugal (48). Meanwhile both Miami and Mexico have tried to promote a 'neutral' mode of production. This quest for universality extends beyond the well-known desire for an uninflected accent to include a neutral creativity (with Manichean dichotomies and conservative morals); neutral territories (with action taking place in unspecified 'city' or 'country' locations); and neutral expression (no local idioms or references) (157–58).

The trend for neutrality would thus seem to be in conflict with the tendency towards local specificity, which for commentators such as García de Castro is the defining characteristic of Spanish televisual realism. We can now see how this tension between the universal and the particular is played out in the unique case of *Yo soy Bea*.

Travelling Betties

In 2001 the Spanish trade press attributed the 'renewal' of interest in *telenovela* by local audiences, hitherto absorbed by reality shows, to just one title: the Colombian *Yo soy Betty, la fea* broadcast on national network Antena 3 (Sánchez Tena 40). By early 2006 (just before the summer launch of *Bea*), however, *Television Business International*'s territory guide to Spain makes almost no reference to the genre. The broadcast scene is said to be 'in a state of flux' with the recent launch of two new terrestrial channels (Cuatro and la Sexta) into an already crowded national marketplace (1).

This changing situation brings opportunities for travelling fictions, however, as the new channels have schedules to fill and are 'thus opening doors' to foreign product. Cuatro, said to be 'aimed at a younger audience', has acquired quality US series both old (*Friends*) and new (*House*) (10). La Sexta, meanwhile, also said to be targeting a 'young urban audience', has Mexico's Televisa (the world's biggest Spanish-language TV group) as its major stockholder (27). *TBI* writes that that 'it has not always been easy to sell shows into Spain' and that previous 'outside involvement [...] has traditionally come from Latin America, which could deliver the passion, emotion, and unique sense of humour that resonates with Spanish audiences' (27). Televisa, however, will have now to 'branch out in programming terms': its traditional output of *telenovela*s is no longer 'relevant' to its target audience for the new channel. While the established generalist channels (Tele 5, Antena 3, and the public TVE1) would still take the lion's share of viewers, the fragmentation and diversification of the audience noted by Vilches took an international turn with the new minority broadcasters.

One year later *TBI*'s territory guide to Latin America covered the 'new fashions' in *telenovela*, writing that 'Helpings of violence and action have been added to staple themes of romance and heartbreak [...] mov[ing] the *novela* away from being a genre mainly watched by housewives' (15). Moreover 'better production values' are the result of increased competition amongst powerful local producers. The latter are 'hoping eventually that they will be able to compete with US series for worldwide dominance' (17). But the evidence for this outcome seems sketchy. The 'local tastes' of, say, Buddhists in Asia reject the violence newly fashionable at home; while US and European audiences continue to resist 'prime time shows stripped across the week' (17).

Once more *Betty* is the unique case on which the optimistic view relies. As a format it has achieved higher ratings than the channel average from Germany to India; and the US version has achieved the same stellar performance at home on ABC as it has abroad on Britain's Channel 4 and throughout Scandinavia (16). The *Betty* franchise has thus (supposedly) 'opened a window to the world for Latin American programming'. However, one executive from Disney-ABC admits that while *Betty* has 'brought a Latin American format into a US network', 'the *telenovela* hasn't really travelled yet.' The 130 daily episodes of the Colombian original were 'compressed' into just 13 weekly programmes in the US (16).

Variety's review of the US dramedy ('*Betty* discovers America') is also ambivalent. Calling attention to the show's hybrid origin ('this adaptation of a popular Spanish [*sic*] *telenovela* — liberally adorned with swatches of *The Devil Wears Prada*'), the reviewer struggles with the tone of the piece, claiming the 'sweet, storybook quality to Betty's underdog status clashes, sometimes awkwardly, with an overly broad comedic tone' (Lowry 68); or again that 'the series [...] oscillates from screwball comedy [...] to florid soap elements' (82). It concludes that 'creatively the episodic trick will be to prevent the show from becoming too silly or repetitive'.

An extended account of *Ugly Betty*'s scripting process in the official publication of the Writers' Guild of America also focuses on generic hybridism (which can lead to incongruity) and the shift from serial to series form (which can lead to repetition). The 'Americanization of the *telenovela*' was carried out by a writing team as diverse as the adaptation's target audience. Creator Silvio Horta defines himself as a first-generation Cuban-American who always preferred 'traditional network fare' to the *telenovela*s on the TV in his Spanish-speaking household (Martínez 18). Other writers had experience working for *telenovela*s at Televisa, for US Anglo or Latino-based sitcoms, and even for medical drama *Grey's Anatomy*. The team admit that *Ugly Betty* 'has travelled an improbable path' (20). The 'dilemma' was that 'by its very nature [*Betty*] did not lend itself to open ended plotlines'. But the 'most popular series in worldwide television history' had special characteristics, given here as the combination of 'drama with humour' and a 'depth' that came from Betty's place as 'the moral centre in an immoral world', an element vital to the Colombian original with its particular stress on the theme of corruption.

The aim of the US writing team was to 'fuse the deep emotional draw of the *telenovela* with the fast-paced glitz of a hit network sitcom' (21). The 'problem' was to 'take a nightly episode concept with a definitive ending and turn it into a once-weekly hourly episodic with open-ended plotting, while attracting the same loyal following that has made *telenovela*s so popular.' To this end five episodes of the original were compressed into one of the US adaptation; and the show was structured 'to satisfy the true *telenovela* aficionado with a thematic ending while tantalizing the soap addict's need to follow an ever-developing plotline.'

To this hybrid end, the team thus combines Latina and Anglo writers (one of the former says 'I *am* Betty'), with gay writers scripting gay characters and comedy and drama specialists even working in separate rooms. 'Silliness' is undercut by 'dark elements' and the 'harsh reality' of Betty's father's arrest by the immigration authorities (22). 'Stand-alone plots' are resolved in a single episode. 'Continuing plots' lend 'added depth' to family life in Queens, as important as working life in Manhattan. For example, in episode nine Betty struggles with a photo shoot; editor in chief Daniel is depressed over his courtship of Sofía (Salma Hayek); Daniel's nemesis Wilhelmina (Vanessa Williams) plots to take over the magazine; and Sofía plots to take Betty away from Daniel. All of these subplots are resolved, while the immigration drama of Betty's father is left open.

Beyond screenwriting, the ambitions of the series are shown in its stylized cinematography and production design, which attempt nonetheless to remain 'grounded in some sense of reality' (Oppenheimer 56). *American Cinematographer* wrote that 'broad comedy' required 'wide-angle lenses' and 'low angles' to 'show off the architecture' in the main office set (Oppenheimer 57). The cool palette of *Mode* magazine in Manhattan ('offset by wild splashes of orange') is contrasted with the 'vibrant, warm colours and well-worn furniture' of the family home in Queens. And the generous spaces of the first set (produced by glass doors and partitions, circular architectural flourishes, and reflective surfaces) are contrasted with Betty's 'small and narrow' home into which only one camera will fit. Although after the pilot the show was shot in a Los Angeles studio, an uncannily convincing sense of varied urban exteriors is produced using digital plates shot on Betty's modest Queens street, while a 140-foot TransLite backdrop of Manhattan wraps around the high-rise office set.

This close attention to localist realism even within stylized exaggeration is significant. Ben Silverman (later to be President of rival network NBC) further claims that *Betty* has revived the political dimension of comedy, pioneered in the US by Norman Lear in the 1970s: 'Through emotion, through character, through comedy, conversations about race, about class, about differences and distinctions within our everyday life, *Ugly Betty* tangibly connects with real life' (Martínez 23). It is perhaps no accident, then, that a show with such ambitions to present encounters with the other (Latina or gay) should be a travelling fiction that engages both a new and fleeting sense of place and a new mode of temporality, halfway between the evolution or metamorphosis of the serial and the repetition or iteration of the series. We can now move on to see how Spanish producers offered their own, newly indigenized, life strategies to devoted fans of *Yo soy Bea*.

'Yo soy Bea': production, reception, text

Specialist website formulatv.com gives a detailed account of *Bea*'s production process over two years (formulatv). As the series came to its end with the climactic wedding episode, script coordinator Covadonga Espeso spoke on 21 June 2008 of the collective process that required seven writers each for plot and dialogue. Espeso claims that is it was only through 'team spirit' that they could 'stretch' 180 Colombian episodes into more than 460 in Spain. Espeso insists that, unlike the original, their version was taken from 'reality', from the everyday life of Spanish women, and their Bea (unlike Colombia's Betty) was a 'normal' girl you might meet in the street. Nonetheless she admits that it was a 'crazy' job to extend the story as they did (at Tele 5's orders) and to sustain the show's top ratings in its timeslot. The challenge was to keep inventing situations without falling into 'absurdity'.

At the press conference held as shooting had begun on the series two years earlier (19 May 2006), Tele 5's head of broadcasting Alberto Carullo had stressed the process of indigenization. While the story is, he says, 'universal' and 'timeless', the aim of the adaptation was to make Spanish audiences feel the plot, language, dialogue, and situations were 'their own'. Creative director Mariana Cortés stated, along the same lines, that, while remaining 'faithful' to the original, the new version would 'distance' itself from Colombian 'caricature'. More specifically the protagonist's 'family structure' had to change to make it 'believable' to Spanish audiences: the innovation here is that Bea has no mother or siblings and has cared for her widowed father alone for two years. While Bea will be physically 'transformed' she will become 'attractive but not spectacular'; and the theme of 'personal evolution' and 'increasing self-confidence' is equally important.

In spite of this 'modernization' of characters and plotlines (said to include 'suspense' and 'high comedy'), Tele 5 claims that *Bea* remains a genre piece, fulfilling no fewer than nine characteristics typical of *telenovela*: sentimentalism; a happy ending for the central couple; easy-to-follow stories; simple dialogue; female-centred narrative; family complications; high drama and suspense; everydayness and local colour; and easily recognized archetypical characters. These general points are combined with the specific attractions of the *Betty* format, which are said to be: originality; suspense, due to the belated 'transformation' of the star, whose real appearance is kept under wraps; the memorability of the characters; and the moralizing 'message' that brings together two timeless fairytales: the Ugly Duckling and Cinderella.

It was not immediately clear that Tele 5 and independent producer Grundy (later attacked by unions for the 'abusive practices' of overwork and unfair dismissals [2 March 2008]) could achieve this balancing act of memory and modernity. By 10 August 2006 Tele 5 was already trumpeting *Bea*'s success, however, and seeking to associate it with *Ugly Betty*'s imminent bow in the US. This attempt at international triangulation was supported by local stunt casting. On 9 November 2006 it was announced that, in a special prime time outing to mark the hundredth episode, Jesús Vázquez, popular gay host of Tele 5's game and reality shows, would guest star in the undemanding role of the ex-boyfriend of *Bulevar 21*'s art director, the queeny Richard.

Future specials tied the show in to viewers' calendars and extended the franchise: one plot timed for Valentine's Day coincided with a look-alike contest on a talk show (13 February 2007). When a local singing star visited the set the next month (13 March 2007), Bea's internet chat room registered a record 5,480 unique visitors and 57,330 hits. For the two-hundredth episode, in which the unreliable Álvaro somewhat prematurely proposed marriage to Bea, Tele 5 announced (6 May 2007) that every episode of the show had been number one in its timeslot, with over three million viewers and a 32.4% share. While the three-hundredth episode was less happy (Bea is briefly dispatched to prison), it gave Tele 5 a chance to parade more statistics to the press: the production had so far required 10,872 pages of script, six thousand scenes, 142 actors, 3,500 costume changes, and 123 locations (28 September 2007).

In the last year of production, writers continued to add major new characters and foreshadowed the final marriage with a gay wedding episode, also timed for Valentine's Day (14 February 2008). The climactic transformation or makeover episode was scheduled for a primetime Sunday, when it attracted a huge eight million viewers (6 June 2008). It was followed by a unique personal appearance by the cast when Bea's hen night took place by the iconic Puerta de Alcalá in the centre of Madrid (9 June 2008). After the primetime wedding episode (19 June 2008), Bea's internet alter ego took the time to thank faithful fans in a final blog posting which mentioned many of them individually by name (Bea forum, 'Hasta siempre').

Not all viewers were so enamoured of the ending. Some complained on the show's forum that the wedding was wrapped up too quickly and implausibly: Bea quite literally stepped into the shoes of a new character, the pretty blonde Be [*sic*], who walked out of her own dream wedding and thus allowed the central couple to take her place. Others even claimed that a humorous dance performed by the newlyweds was stolen from US sitcom *Friends*, a series to which (as we saw in the previous chapter) Spanish fans are especially attached (Bea forum, 'Enigmas'). Hence Tele 5's demand to 'stretch out' *Bea* to twice the length that was originally intended clearly tried the patience of some viewers as much as it did the creativity of the writers and the endurance of the crew. Tele 5 hoped, nonetheless, that *Bulevar 21* could continue with a new and less original protagonist, the conventionally good-looking Be. It was a conservative moral shared by cosmetic brand Nivea, whose sponsorship of the final episode on the channel's own website featured a tagline that could not have been further from the series' original premise: 'Beauty is freedom.'

In spite of its producers' claims to be distinct from the Colombian original, then, *Yo soy Bea* seems at first to attest to Vilches' standardization of offer across the huge region that is Iberoamerica. While *Bea* is ostensibly based in the modern capital Madrid, it often returns to 'eternal' themes more typical of a pre-industrial Spain (typically, Bea goes back to her unseen pueblo for the Christmas vacations).

Although the rather primitive central premise (Ugly Duckling or Cinderella) is thus set within a supposedly sophisticated setting (the fashion magazine workplace), it is no surprise, then, that in the final episode Bea's wedding will require her to give up the chance of a glamorous job in Miami. And in spite of the claims that *Bea* is less caricatured than the Colombian *Betty*, the Spanish version retains a good number of farcical and melodramatic elements (pratfalls and murder mysteries). Finally, while *Bea* is said to be especially adapted to Spanish social circumstances, it allies itself to some extent with the regressive 'neutral' tendency of Miami (once more) and Mexico. The accent is standard Castilian (only Richard, the unsympathetic gay art director, speaks in a Sevillian lisp); and, defying contemporary Spanish demography, there is not one immigrant or person of colour amongst the regular cast.

The office location, often shown in establishing exteriors, is a bland concrete campus shaded by trees that could be anywhere. While *Ugly Betty* is so insistent on the distance between Manhattan and Queens (between glamorous, treacherous work and dull but cherished home), *Bea*'s physical and social geography is sketchy indeed. *Bulevar 21* does not benefit from the handsome urban backdrop glimpsed through the windows of *Mode*, and nor does *Bea* feature aerial shots of Madrid to rival those of the towers of Manhattan that welcome us back from commercial breaks to *Betty*. Where rare authentic locations are used in *Bea* they tend to be anonymous and suburban: a school in comfortable Pozuelo de Alarcón, the Xanadú shopping mall twenty miles from the city centre are cited in the credits. There are few local references in the script and no mention of current affairs or politics.

In similarly traditional fashion, dichotomies remain mainly Manichean (evil Diego will ceaselessly scheme against Álvaro) and morals are still conservative (single motherhood is permitted only to a supporting character, the receptionist Chusa, whose child longs for a father's attention). Wilfully or perversely, *Bea* thus chooses to neglect the potential for metropolitan sophistication that its milieu would appear to offer so readily. Rare film or fashion references are readily accessible to the widest of audiences. When *Bulevar 21* holds a costume party, staff come dressed in Marilyn's floaty white gown from *The Seven Year Itch* or Audrey's little black dress from *Breakfast at Tiffany's*; when Bárbara's shoe suffers an injury in a catfight with Bea she complains 'My Versace is broken!' Far indeed from the giddy heights of haute couture with which the show's milieu is supposedly obsessed, the credits list some thirty everyday local brands that have paid for placement on *Bea*'s crowded sets.

It is not clear, then, that *Bea* (a unique success) is in the tradition of 'popular Spanish realism' that García de Castro believes has been vital to both the history of Spanish TV fiction since broadcasting began and its recent renaissance since the late 1990s. If anything, *Bea* would seem to have most in common with the *teleatro* of the 1960s, with its stagy set, dramatic moments, stereotypical characters, and focus on a very long suffering female who is prone to moralizing (it is Bea who argues, against the tyrannical bosses, that workers deserve the social solidarity of an office party). The sense of the everyday and of the present prized by García de Castro in subsequent Spanish television is much attenuated here by the almost complete lack of reference to social issues explored by auteurs such as Mercero in the 1980s or in the new professional series of the 1990s.

Fig. 17. Bea (Ruth Núñez) arrives at *Bulevar 21*: *Yo soy Bea*

While the rapid rhythm of daily drama still permits occasional exteriors (the entrance to an apartment building in the first week of the first season; the playground to the school in the last), *Bea*'s spaces of home, work, and leisure (the inevitable staff cafeteria) are indistinct and undistinguished. Where the US *Betty*'s lavish workplace set is shot to show up its depth and height through trademark circular features and frequent low angles, *Bea*'s office set is so small that, when the heroine first arrives (Fig. 17), a fashion shoot, complete with bikinied babes, is taking place in what appears to be a corridor or entrance hall (embracing all the girls, Álvaro kisses Bea by mistake and grimaces broadly). It is true that performance style is (as in current Spanish primetime series) relatively naturalistic and Ruth Núñez's timid Bea is genuinely affecting; but this novelty is undercut by the cheesy musical prompts used to underscore comic or dramatic plot points that come straight from the most traditional of *telenovelas*.

Even compared to contemporary Latin American production, reviewed by *TBI* above, *Bea* seems somewhat conservative. An early hint that *Bea* might be dabbling in the new trend to incorporate violent action is quickly disabused. If Álvaro finds the bloody footprints of his missing sister in the shower (cue *Psycho* reference), she will soon turn up live and well and masquerading as a cleaner in the *Bulevar 21* office. But *TBI*'s survey of Spain is perhaps more fruitful than its coverage of Latin America in offering a hypothesis for *Bea*'s success. With the new free to air national channels opting, we remember, for smart US imports to snare young urban audiences, a space opened up for a traditional *telenovela* for a broader demographic. *Bea*'s local characteristics are thus evident but not excessively marked by an old school *costumbrismo* that is perhaps now rendered embarrassing by the newly sophisticated production values of primetime series made both at home and abroad. In a difficult balancing act *Bea* thus reconciled the modern with the old and familiar.

If the daytime *Bea* kept one eye on prime time (Tele 5 scheduled frequent special episodes for evening viewers), then it also carefully situated itself in transit between Latin America and Spain. Spanish viewers were, of course, already fully aware of the Colombian original of the format that had revived the fortunes of *telenovela* in their country just five years before. Yet, was it an accident that the décor for the main *Bulevar 21* set (against which publicity shots of the cast were also taken) features prominent patches of red and yellow, the colours of the Spanish flag? The art design thus hinted at the need to familiarize the potentially troubling alterity of a fiction that had travelled so far even before it had begun. By examining the first and last weeks of *Bea*'s opening season we can explore the way in which global cultural material can become indigenized in this way, no longer a threat but rather a resource for local producers and consumers.

The first season: opening and closing weeks

1.1 '*Yo soy Bea*' ('I am Bea')
(broadcast 10 July 2006; audience 2,172,000; share 23.5%)

Bea es una joven con un currículum perfecto que busca su primer empleo. Tras la muerte de su madre, se ha pasado dos años dedicada en exclusiva al cuidado de su padre, pero ahora necesita salir de casa y trabajar. En su vida laboral tan sólo tiene un pequeño problema: es muy fea, hasta el punto que nadie la contrata.

   Consciente de esta limitación, se presenta a una entrevista para secretaria de presidencia en la revista *Bulevar 21* sin haber enviado antes su foto. Allí tendrá un breve encuentro con Álvaro, el nuevo director de la revista, que ha llegado al puesto con fuertes opositores y con una sombra en su elección: la desaparición de Sandra, una de las accionistas.

[Bea is a young woman with a perfect c.v. who's looking for her first job. After the death of her mother, she's spent two years just looking after her father, but now she needs to get out of the house and work. She just has one little problem in that area: she's very ugly; so ugly in fact that no one will employ her. Well aware of this factor, she shows up for an interview for a job as an executive secretary at the magazine *Bulevar 21* without sending a photo in advance. There she has a brief meeting with Álvaro, the magazine's new editor, who's got the job in the teeth of fierce opposition and with a shadow hanging over him: the disappearance of Sandra, one of the shareholders.]

1.115 'Destino las islas Fidji' ('Bound for Fiji')
(broadcast 22 December 2006; audience 3,447,000; share 34.3%)

Cayetana está dolida porque Álvaro se niega a publicar un reportaje que Carlos planea realizar sobre las playas caribeñas, por lo que castiga a Bea con un trabajo extra que la impedirá disfrutar de la fiesta navideña que van a montar 'los feos'.

   Sandra se entera y se lo comunica al 'batallón', que no tarda en acudir al rescate de la secretaria del director. Finalmente, logran terminar el trabajo a tiempo para que Bea pueda asistir con ellos a la celebración.

   Entretanto, Cayetana y Carlos se marchan de vacaciones a las Islas Fidji ante la impotencia de Álvaro, que en un arrebato de locura pretende convencer a su ex-novia de que se marche con él de vacaciones. Ante la negativa de ésta, el joven se refugia en su despacho, donde ni la treta para frenar los planes de Diego, ni las palabras de consuelo de Bea y Gonzalo logran hacerle olvidar el asunto.

Mientras, Richard acude a ayudar a Bárbara después de que Sonsoles la ha encerrado en un cuarto de baño. Ambos sospechan que la gamberrada ha sido idea de alguna de 'las feas' y planean vengarse alterando el karaoke preparado para la fiesta. (formulatv, 'Series')

[Cayetana is angry that Álvaro is refusing to publish a report that Carlos is planning to write on beaches of the Caribbean and so she punishes Bea by giving her an extra job, which will stop her enjoying the Christmas party that the 'ugly crowd' are planning to put on.

Sandra finds out and tells the 'battalion', who quickly come to the rescue of the editor's secretary. In the end they manage to finish the job in time so Bea can come with them to the party.

Meanwhile Cayetana and Carlos go off on holiday to Fiji against the wishes of Álvaro, who, in a fit of madness, tries to convince his ex-fiancée to go off on holiday with him. When she says no, he takes refuge in his office and neither plotting to stop Diego's plans nor Bea and Gonzalo's attempts to console him can make him forget the incident.

In the meantime Richard comes to the aid of Bárbara who's been locked in the bathroom by Sonsoles. Both have their suspicions that this dirty trick was thought up by one of the 'ugly girls' and so they plan to take their revenge by changing the lyrics of the karaoke number that Bea is planning to sing at the party.]

Plot synopses from the first season of *Yo soy Bea* would not seem to confirm that it is a 'travelling fiction' in any literal sense. The physical mobility of the individual in real geographical space is not prominent. As mentioned earlier, the Spanish Bea (unlike the US Latina Betty) is placed only approximately in a home environment whose concrete relation to an equally abstracted workplace goes unmarked. And the theme of immigration is absent. Yet I would argue that there is a constant, if less evident, transfer of cultural material in the Spanish series, which registers in forms and symbolic meanings that treat transit and encounters with the other at different degrees of proximity.

The first episode thus begins with a montage flashback to Bea's back story shot in suitably washed-out colours. Having discovered her distinctive plainness early on (a disappointment that is alleviated only by a male friend as ugly as she), Bea experiences a childhood reduced to a succession of academic honours: shown from behind, she morphs from a prize-winning infant into a highflying graduate, shaking any number of anonymous hands in the process. After two years caring for her father in the wake of her mother's death (we are given a brief shot of the latter collapsing under the weight of groceries outside the supermarket), she now resolves to declare her independence from him, even if he cannot break away from her. The 'fish out of water' motif (the ugly girl in the world of fashion) will thus offer both character and audience a chance to create scripts for new imagined lives within a recognizably Spanish context that the Latin American *telenovela*, however 'neutralized', cannot offer.

Álvaro (Alejandro Tous), Bea's cute but feckless womanizing boss, also begins the serial with a journey. He has just been chosen general editor of *Bulevar 21* in an election disputed by his rival and nemesis, the sober-suited Diego (Miguel Hermoso Arnao): a female shareholder (his sister Sandra), who might have preferred Diego, failed to appear at the meeting. Another flashback (parallel to Bea's) cues us that Álvaro had seduced Sandra the night before in an effort to win her vote. The corporate plotting (also pervasive in *Ugly Betty*) may seem conventional. But by juxtaposing and implicitly contrasting the two journeys of Bea and Álvaro from the start, the series suggests that it is not merely offering fantasy, but will stage an exploration of possibilities and alternatives in the social world. As in other versions (including the Colombian original), Bea will be the ethical centre of an unethical world in which (as she is told on her first day) 'image is everything'.

Bea is also contrasted comically and dramatically with Bárbara (Norma Ruíz), a blonde air-head of a secretary whom Álvaro hires as a favour to his raven-haired girlfriend Cayetana (Mónica Estarreado), the magazine's editorial director. While Bea graduated the first in her economics class from Madrid's prestigious Complutense University, Bárbara claims to have studied, in what will become a running gag, at the 'International Institute of Ibiza' (when pronounced, as the pretentious Bárbara does, in English-style the initials recreate the comic interjection: '¡ay, ay, ay!'). Bárbara will ally herself with Richard (David Arnaiz), the gay design editor, while Álvaro's confidant is Gonzalo (José Manuel Seda), the stubble-faced and denim-clad advertising director, who can be relied on to encourage his boss's worst instincts. When Gonzalo offers Álvaro a manly hug in the unisex toilets, Richard quips: 'Next time you have a party in here, let me know.' Álvaro is worried that the sperm he left in Sandra may be discovered in her dead body; collapsing work and sex, flirty Gonzalo concurs with new colleague Bárbara that 'first times are so exciting'. This kind of sexy talk is perhaps surprising in an afternoon show favoured by children.

The cause of Álvaro's concern is the mystery element flagged up by Tele 5's executives as a new Spanish contribution to the Colombian original. With Sandra missing, Álvaro is a prime suspect for her murder. Yet this plot strand also serves simply to reinforce the extravagant masochism of Bea, repeatedly humiliated as she is in the first week's episodes. Having been assigned a filthy box room as her office ('I'll have to be a cleaning lady before I become a secretary'), Bea inadvertently throws out the security tapes that might have cleared her boss. Álvaro tells her with cruel formality: 'Go away ["Váyase"]. I don't want to see you.' Álvaro later fails to introduce Bea at a meeting for the whole cast where his father announces his retirement; and excludes her from the glamorous launch of the summer issue, where (according to Bárbara) her homely appearance will 'frighten the guests'. Typically, of course, Bea saves the day, but only by further humiliating herself in the process. When the incompetent Álvaro forgets his speech she rushes into the meeting, crashing to his feet just as he is announcing his engagement to raven-haired temptress Cayetana.

The first week's episodes thus prove, as Buonanno noted, that the pleasure of TV travel is not devoid of anxiety and uncertainty for characters and audience alike.

Bea's new world is distinctly unpleasurable for her, with the dubious exception of her crush on a boss who maltreats her. But by the final week of the first season, when six months and over one hundred episodes have past, a surprising distance has been covered. Newly prominent is receptionist Chusa (one of the 'battalion of ugly girls'), a single mother struggling to care for the little son who is shown in a cute costume at his school play (all of the main characters are childless). In this Christmas week Álvaro now travels to Bea's house bearing a festive hamper, moved as he is by Bea's story of how she misses her mother in the holiday season. Schooled in family feeling by Bea, Álvaro is, in turn, reconciled with his own father, who is hospitalized after a heart attack. Bea also teaches her colleagues social solidarity, arguing that after going through so many troubles together her co-workers need an office party to celebrate their sense of community.

Evil executive Diego remains unchanged, scheming here to buy the company's debt and thus control the magazine himself. But Cayetana, previously Álvaro's scheming fiancée, has by now herself become the loving dupe of a con artist, who has her pay for the exotic vacation in Fiji for which the final episode is named. Elsewhere, however, personal character development is stymied by professional pressures. The briefly sympathetic Álvaro invites Bea to a romantic dinner; but, to her disappointment, his (barely legal) aim is to persuade to become the nominal head of a straw company that will escape Diego's hostile bid.

While the *Betty* franchise is the metaphoric serial premise par excellence (based as it is on the Ugly Duckling or Cinderella motif) and its plot has strong linear and evolutionary motifs, the unusually elongated Spanish version also participates in that cyclical temporality or iterative structure more typical of the series: Álvaro will repeatedly forget what he has learned from Bea and must be constantly reminded that image is not everything until the final, rushed wedding takes place.

In spite of the incorporation of new naturalistic elements and even social issues such as single motherhood, *Bea* regresses in this final week to farcical comedy and Manichean melodrama. Readily misled by the ugly battalion, secretary Bárbara decorates boss Álvaro's apartment with tacky decorations (including an electric menorah and an inflatable tree), which she has been told are the height of fashion in New York lofts. Álvaro's displeasure reveals that he does not agree that 'Kitsch is back!' Later Bárbara is locked in the unisex lavatory only to be freed by gay Richard ('Don't kiss me!'). Cayetana reverts to stereotype by cruelly scheming to keep Bea from the party that she herself had planned by dumping a load of work on her (Bea is saved when her ugly friends help out).

The climactic party in the last episode features a karaoke performance of the show's theme tune by the ugly battalion; and another by Bea herself. Typically, she is set up for embarrassment when the lyrics of her song are changed so as to accuse her boss publicly of womanizing. The effect is unexpected. Fleeing in shame to the lift, Bea is joined by Álvaro, who says he now realizes how selfish he has been. Whispering 'You're so much more that a secretary [...] you're a woman', he tenderly embraces her. It is a 'magic moment' that Bea will celebrate on her blog and relive (with the faithful audience) over the holiday hiatus.

It comes as no surprise that when the next season premieres, Álvaro will have virtually forgotten this first kiss, thus ensuring that the romantic resolution can be deferred for another three hundred episodes. Combining Buonanno's (or Bauman's) twin life strategies of postponement and repetition, *Bea* thus offers two ways of mastering time and multiplying experiences. Moreover by remaking a Latin American original that was already familiar to Spanish audiences in a somewhat less extravagant and more naturalistic mode, *Bea* creates a kind of televisual bi-locality. It is a fleeting or reterritorialized sense of place in which both continents can be imagined simultaneously, yet without threatening the identity and ontological security of the wide target audience of a generalist broadcaster. As the series had added a million viewers and a ten point share since the first episode, there seems little doubt that spectators identified with Tele 5's revised and indigenized vision of *Betty*, exclaiming, with the show's dedicated website, 'I am Bea too' (yotambiensoybea.com).

Crossing bridges

Pobre muchacha cuando llega a la oficina
¡Ay! Que se pone nerviosita 'perdía'
Que los tiburones se la zampan con papitas fritas
Y es que es ella tan inocente y tan enterita.
¡Ay! Pobre niña que has caído del cielo
Y desde el limbo caes y bajas a este mundo de lagartas.

Ya no se puede ir por el mundo derrochando el amor
En esta vida hay que saber capear
A ti te falta veneno y te sobra corazón
Así vas a llegar a Santa 'na' más.

[Poor girl, when she gets to the office / Oh! she goes all nervous / the sharks will eat her up with fried potatoes / and she's so sweet and innocent too. / Oh! Poor little girl, you've fallen from heaven into this hell, this world of lizards. // Now you can't go around being lovey-dovey / In this life you need to know how to fight back. / You've got too little venom and too much heart. / All you're set for now is to become a Saint.]

In a typically canny example of cross-promotion, the theme tune of *Yo soy Bea* is sung by Edurne, a graduate of Tele 5's reality contest *Operación Triunfo*. The rap-style lyrics stress the defining characteristic of Ruth Núñez's performance as the title character: her timidity. She is a little girl with too much heart and too little 'venom', all at sea in a dangerous workplace full of sharks and lizards. Bea's personality could hardly be further from America Ferrera's Betty, who, in spite of identical reversals and humiliations, remains as feisty as she was in the pilot episode.

Likewise Núñez's physical type is less subversive of beauty norms than that of Ferrera, who was, before *Betty*, best known for the feature *Real Women Have Curves* (Patricia Cardoso, 2002). Unlike the rounded Latina, the fragile Núñez is model-thin, already ready for the transformation that will be effected by a strapless gown and perilous heels. Furthermore while *Bea* deals mainly with class and taste (wealthy Cayetana's spaghetti-strapped little black dresses versus Bea's frumpy mid-length skirts and sensible shoes), it does not address the questions of ethnicity that are centre stage in *Betty*, with its richly detailed Mexican-American family and ruthless African-American executive (Vanessa Williams' Wilhelmina), struggling to reconcile glamorous work with a neglectful father and alienated daughter. Moreover the gay theme is much stronger in the US *Betty*, with episodes focusing on the coming out of assistant Marc to his mother and the education of Betty's effeminate young nephew Justin. In spite of his marriage in a late episode to a man who also has to come out to his family, *Bea*'s Richard is an unsympathetic caricature by comparison.

It follows that *Betty*'s humour is much more based on the coded references of camp than is *Bea*'s and its media references are condensed and allusive (e.g. when Justin says he saw 'Prada, like five times', the viewer must know that he is referring not to the fashion label but to a then recent feature film *The Devil Wears Prada* [David Frenkel, 2006]). While *Betty*'s guest stars impersonate fashion figures (Gina Gershon's grotesque parody of Donatella Versace, James Van Der Beek's sleazy version of the boss of American Apparel, lightly disguised here as 'Atlantic Apparel'), *Bea*'s guest stars, pop singers and TV presenters, pretty much play themselves. Surprisingly perhaps, the US show also has a much stronger sense of family than the Spanish, with Betty supported by a loving, if meddlesome, father, sister, and nephew, while Bea is reduced to the widowed father who is here less sympathetic than in the US. In spite of the importance of family to *telenovela*, then, *Bea* responds closely to changes in Spanish demographics, which have made such claustrophobic family structures newly typical.

Most evident is the difference in the role of travel between the two versions. Betty's family speak often of their origins in Mexico and they visit that country when the father is deported. On her first day at *Mode*, the new secretary sports an unlikely Guadalajara poncho (Fig. 18). Salma Hayek, one the show's producers, takes a featured role as a Latina editor and temporary love interest for Daniel (the Spanish Álvaro). A touching scene between Betty and Daniel takes place on an emblematic Brooklyn Bridge, reminiscent of that game of bridge-crossing or transitivity which is for Bauman a symbol of the life strategy of new beginnings and for Buonanno a privileged motif in the ever renewed series television. In *Bea*, on the other hand, journeys are either unseen or unmade (the Christmas vacation in Fiji or the job offer in Miami); and, in a lost opportunity, the serial makes little explicit reference to its continent of origin, in spite of the fact that Latin American immigrants make up a large and growing community in Spain. While one plotline focuses on a proposed merger with a Mexican media company (frustrated by the evil Diego) no regular characters from the continent appear. *Bea*'s narrative universe would thus seem to be disturbingly homogeneous.

Bea's aesthetic also feels flat. The cramped red and yellow sets cannot compete with *Betty*'s sense of space and place, even though so much of the latter is shot on green screen. *Bea*'s occasional vertical wipes are also no match for the frequent and varied iris effects used in *Betty* to link sequences. Moreover *Betty* skilfully weaves together multiple plot strands (Spanish 'multitrama'). This tendency that climaxes in the first season's finale (episode 23) which crosscuts between Betty's foiled romance with an accountant, the car crash of Daniel's sister, the announcement of the forthcoming marriage of Wilhelmina and Daniel's father, Daniel's mother

FIG. 18. Betty (America Ferrera) arrives at *Mode*: *Ugly Betty*

escaping from prison, and the shooting of the boyfriend of Betty's sister, all to the poignant soundtrack of Justin's performance in his school production of *West Side Story*. The long delayed kiss in the lift between Bea and Álvaro offers a more traditional and less complex source of pleasure.

But this is, of course, not to compare like with like. A (mainly) daytime serial stripped across the week could hardly be expected to have the production values of a once-a-week primetime series, which thinks nothing of recreating the Brooklyn Bridge on digital plates. And, as mentioned by García de Castro earlier, Spain does indeed have a history of evening drama on generalist channels that approaches the sophistication of the US series on which the newer minority stations rely for their ratings (the US *Betty* premiered on Cuatro on 10 June 2008).

Unlike *Betty*, which incorporates fragments of spoof *telenovela* into its episodes and posts them on its website (ABC, 'Telenovela') *Bea* does not explicitly acknowledge its debt to Latin America. But I would argue that this is because bi-locality or interculturality are already implicit in *Bea*'s production, reception, and textual composition. Thus the punishing rhythm of shooting and scheduling five times a week associated *Bea* with the *telenovela*s screened in the same timeslot in Spain. The habit of consumption implied by the *sobremesa* timeslot also implied a connection with rival or neighbouring shows in the schedule that originated in Mexico or Miami. As we have seen in the producers' launch of the serial, the Spanish version was inseparable from the Colombian original in the minds of the programme makers. They thus attempted to distance their version from certain social actors (e.g. the Colombian family structure) and certain kinds of textual composition (e.g. the exaggerated performance style), even as they held on to others (the Ugly Duckling motif, the intrusive music cues).

Ugly Betty sought to confuse reality and fiction to some extent, with ABC publishing a book of the series that mimicked the fictional *Mode* (ABC, 'Book'). In what is perhaps its most important innovation, *Bea*, a daily visitor to its fans' homes, went much further, with Tele 5 launching a monthly magazine called (as in the show once more) *Bulevar 21*, with a print run of three hundred thousand (vayatele.

com). Social uses and ways of seeing were also expanded and exploited through the integration of Bea's blog into the show itself and the direct communication with individual spectators. While many may have been disappointed by the final wedding episode, others vowed never to forget Bea and Álvaro with many uploading their own treasured compilations of clips (often set to new music tracks). Some six months after *Bea* ended (14 December 2008) YouTube still hosted thirty thousand clips from the show.

The travelling narrative thus finally became a life strategy, founded on that definitive ending and final metamorphosis that can only be provided by the serial, however long its climax is postponed. The Spanish *Bea* may thus be the ugly sister of the US *Betty*, lacking the latter's glamorous production values, sophisticated dialogue, and complex plotting. But as its title suggests (with the two words 'Betty' and 'fea' fused into the single 'Bea') it constitutes a skilled form of cultural condensation: a carefully indigenized revision of a foreign format reworked as a resource in a way that makes it distinct from both Latin American and North American norms.

Works cited

BUONANNO, MILLY. *The Age of Television: Experiences and Theories* (London: Intellect, 2008)
——— *El drama televisivo: identidad y contenidos sociales* (Barcelona: Gedisa, 1999)
GARCÍA DE CASTRO, MARIO. *La ficción televisiva popular* (Barcelona: Gedisa, 2002)
MICHELIN, GERARDO. 'Telenovelas: desde Latinoamérica con amor', *Cineinforme*, 755 (1 March 2003), 39–48
'Territory Guide to Spain', *Television Business International*, February/March 2006
'Territory Guide to Latin America', *Television Business International*, May 2007
LOWRY, BRIAN. 'Betty Discovers America', *Variety*, 25 September 2006, pp. 68, 82.
MARTÍN BARBERO, J., and SONIA MUÑOZ. *Televisión y melodrama: Géneros y lecturas de la telenovela en Colombia* (Bogotá: Tercer Mundo, 1992)
MARTÍNEZ, JULIO. 'You Are So Beautiful: Ugly Betty and the Americanization of the Telenovela', *Written By* [sic], 11.3 (1 April 2007), pp. 18–23
OPPENHEIMER, JEAN. 'Prime-Time Pros', *American Cinematographer*, 88.3 (1 March 2007), 50–59
ROGERS, JESSICA. 'The Plain Truth about Betty', *Broadcast*, 12 January 2007, p. 14
VILCHES, LORENZO (ed). *Mercados y culturas de la ficción televisiva en Iberoamérica* (Barcelona: Gedisa, 2007)

Web sources

ABC. 'Book', <http://abc.go.com/primetime/uglybetty/index?pn=book#t=0>, [accessed 14 December 2008]
——— 'Telenovela', <http://abc.go.com/primetime/uglybetty/telenovela/sinsoftheheart/index>, [accessed 14 December 2008]
BEA FORUM. 'Enigmas de la boda', 21 June 2008, <http://yosoybea.mforos.com/1162016/7106495-enigmas-de-la-boda/>, [accessed 14 December 2008]
——— 'Hasta siempre feonautas', 24 June 2008, Tele 5, <http://yosoybea.mforos.com/1161970/7114623-hasta-siempre-feonautas-martes-24-de-junio-de-2008/>, [accessed 14 December 2008]

Eurofiction (Milly Buonanno and the European Audiovisual Observatory). 'Television Fiction in Europe', 18 November 2007, <http://www.obs.coe.int/oea_publ/eurofic/>, [accessed 14 December 2008]

Formulatv. 'Yo soy Bea: noticias', <www.formulatv.com/series/108/yo-soy-bea/noticias/3.html>, [accessed 1 September 2008]

—— 'Series', <http://www.formulatv.com/series/108/yo-soy-bea/>, [accessed 1 September 2008]

Vayatele.com. 'Bulevar 21 en los kioskos', 30 June 2007, <http://www.vayatele.com/2007/06/30-bulevar-21-en-los-kioskos>, [accessed 1 September 2008]

Yotambiensoybea [blog and forum]. Tele 5, <http://www.yotambiensoybea.com/lowres.asp>, [accessed 1 September 2008]

CONCLUSION

Literature, Cinema, Television

In 2010 three cultural events took place. The first was the sixty-ninth edition of Madrid's Feria del Libro ('Book Fair'), which was held in the capital's handsome and historic Retiro Park from 28 May to 13 June. Although attendance was slightly down on the previous year due to inclement weather, there were still four hundred exhibitors, three more than the previous year, of whom 118 represented bookshops, 252 publishers, twelve distributors, and twenty-six official bodies (Feria). The total length of their stalls stretched to some twelve kilometres and bibliophile *madrileños* spent over eight million euros. Proof of the international profile of literature in Spain was the presence of the Scandinavian countries as special guests (the previous year it had been the turn of the more familiar France).

Activities associated with the Fair included such popular options as special events for children and author signings (the 1400 writers taking part included Antonio Muñoz Molina, studied in Chapter 3 of this book). Although, as we saw in Chapter 1, Spaniards have low indices of book readership by international standards (and the Fair's reference to the alleged 'Nordic proclivity for literature' had a wistful ring), Spaniards are clearly avid participants in social events centred around reading. And the practice of reading (and writing) was also linked to an appreciation of other media: opening the Fair with Her Majesty, the Queen Sofía was the Minister of Culture, Angeles González Sinde, a successful film director and screenwriter.

In a year without a new feature from Almodóvar (*Los abrazos rotos* ['Broken Embraces'] had premiered in spring 2009) and with the global financial crisis keenly felt in Spain, 2010 was a time of retrenchment for the film industry. My second event is the release on DVD of one of the biggest cinema hits of the previous year, the emblematically titled *Spanish Movie* (screened in Spain with this English-language title). A guilty pleasure for Hispanist film scholars, as it was for domestic audiences (an unexpected hit, it garnered a cinema audience of over one million), *Spanish Movie* features a game cameo from Leslie Nielsen, veteran of the *Airplane!* franchise, in his last film. The aim of this comedy is to mash up parodies of recent local successes. Thus the heroine of Almodóvar's *Volver* (2006) takes refuge in an old dark house, whose inhabitants seem confused as to whether they are playing in Amenábar's *The Others* (2001) or (the subject of my Chapter 5) Bayona's *El orfanato*. The newly louche Faun from Guillermo del Toro's post-Civil War-set *El laberinto del fauno* ('Pan's Labyrinth', 2006) also makes an unexpected and unsettling appearance. Other genres and films referenced will be less familiar to the few foreigners tempted by *Spanish Movie*: the morose middle-aged unemployed workers of social realist drama *Los lunes al sol* ('Mondays in the Sun', 2002) and the dashing hero of period swashbuckler *Alatriste* (2006), adapted from a best selling novel, sweep the horror heroines off their feet. (Both films had been hugely successful at the domestic box office but were barely seen abroad.)

Transparently trashy, then, *Spanish Movie* still offers valuable evidence for what counts as national cinema for local audiences. And it is striking that that filmmaking tradition is broad enough to encompass the auteur, who, as we saw in Chapter 4, has the most readily identifiable and longest lasting brand (Almodóvar) and the most impersonal and widest ranging of genres (horror, social realism, and costume drama). Moreover television has its fingerprints all over this theatrical feature. *Spanish Movie* is produced by Tele 5 (cited in no fewer than five chapters of this book); and it stars supporting players familiar from the channel's sitcoms *Los Serrano* and *Camera café* (treated in Chapter 8). More important perhaps is the presence of two writers and actors (Carlos Areces and Joaquín Reyes) from an unusually innovative TV sketch comedy with the untranslatable title *Muchachada nui* (TVE, 2007–). Their show, which features amateurish animated inserts, is known above all for its wilfully inept impersonations of celebrities, invariably voiced in thickly incongruous La Mancha accents (in one episode Reyes played successively Pedro Almodóvar, Kirk Cameron, Virginia Woolf, and 'a VHS tape' [14 April 2010]). While *Spanish Movie* lacks the idiosyncratic imagination of the TV show and testifies to its young audience's lack of respect for their own national cinema, it also reveals the inseparability of the two media, which are bound together like the hooded boy of *El orfanato* and the equally troubled girl of *El laberinto*, who is shown in *Spanish Movie* unceremoniously seeing off del Toro's magical fairies with a blowtorch.

My third event relates yet more closely to television. The Second Festival of Television and Radio took place from 31 August to 5 September 2010 in the Basque administrative capital of Vitoria-Gasteiz (FesTVal [*sic*]). Building on the success of the first edition in 2009, it showcased 'world premieres of the star series of the generalist channels'. Screened in the festival's glamorous theatre, 'primetime' premieres included high-budget titles like TVE's martial arts actioner *Águila roja* ('Red Eagle': a mild mannered schoolteacher fights evil as a Golden Age superhero) and Antena 3's stylish mystery *El internado* ('The Boarding School': tortured teens confront treacherous Nazis and mysterious monsters). A third premiere, *La princesa de Éboli*, starred Belén Rueda (of *Los Serrano* and *El orfanato*) as the one-eyed royal acquaintance of Saint Teresa, in a miniseries that would be cut down for release as a feature film. And as crowds queued behind velvet ropes to see their favourite small-screen stars on the signature orange carpet, industry mavens from all six national channels took part in public discussions in a palace located in the medieval heart of the city (the previous year had seen a round table by representatives of Globomedia, producers of series as different as *Los Serrano* and *Águila roja*).

In such newly minted events humdrum television takes on all the glamour that cinema, now so mercilessly parodied, once kept so jealously to itself. And the Spanish small screen effortlessly attracts the young audiences that Spanish big screen cannot: in 2009 Vitoria experienced a minor riot when the stars of Antena 3's teen drama *Física o química* ('Physics or Chemistry', 2008–) faced hordes of screaming fans at their own season premiere. Where television was once credited with the modest virtues of domesticity and familiarity, now it threatens, in Spain as elsewhere, to appropriate the unique cultural prestige and popular acclaim of cinema.

What then is the final moral of these Spanish practices? As we have seen, some very varied texts and media treat the same themes of history and memory, authority and society, and genre and transitivity. Moreover, questions of gender, sexuality, and transnationalism also keep recurring. Given the convergence of production processes and media institutions, which registers in such genres as literary adaptations (funded by holding companies that embrace print and cinema) and miniseries (made under the law that obliges TV companies to fund feature films), there should be little surprise if audiences for all cultural products should also be coming together. Questions of reception, addressed in this book mainly through internet forums, are thus inseparable from industrial versions of production, distribution, and exhibition.

The problem for the scholar of such Spanish practices is to combine qualitative and quantitative approaches, attempting to synthesize the teasing-out of textual meanings with the surveying of the cultural field. As scholars, then we may have something to learn from the bridge-crossing of Betty (and Bea). Such cross-discipline fertilization should result in academic studies that may well be unauthorized or irregular, but will certainly be unexpected and unpredictable.

Works cited

Feria del Libro Madrid, <http://www.ferialibromadrid.com/ficha_avanzada. cfm?id=595>, [accessed 5 August 2010]

FesTVal, <http://www.festivaltelevisionyradio.com/>, [accessed 5 September 2010]

INDEX